The Navajo Political Experience

THE SPECTRUM SERIES
Race and Ethnicity in National and Global Politics
Paula D. McClain and Joseph Stewart, Jr., Series Editors

The sociopolitical dynamics of race and ethnicity are apparent everywhere. In the United States, racial politics underlie everything from representation to affirmative action to welfare policymaking. Early in the twenty-first century, Anglos in America will become only a plurality, as Latino and Asian American populations continue to grow. Issues of racial/ethnic conflict and cooperation are prominent across the globe. Diversity, identity, and cultural plurality are watchwords of empowerment as well as of injustice.

This new series offers textbook supplements, readers, and core texts addressing various aspects of race and ethnicity in politics, broadly defined. Meant to be useful in a wide range of courses in all kinds of academic programs, these books will be multidisciplinary as well as multiracial/ethnic in their appeal.

Titles in the Series

The Navajo Political Experience by David E. Wilkins

American Indian Politics and the American Political System by David E. Wilkins

Forthcoming Titles

Asian American Politics: Law, Participation, and Policy edited by
Don T. Nakanishi and James S. Lai

Latino Politics in America: Community, Culture, and Interests by John A. Garcia

Media & Minorities by Stephanie Greco Larson

The Navajo Political Experience

REVISED EDITION

David E. Wilkins

ROWMAN & LITTLEFIELD PUBLISHERS, INC.
Lanham • Boulder • New York • Oxford

ROWMAN & LITTLEFIELD PUBLISHERS, INC.

Published in the United States of America
by Rowman & Littlefield Publishers, Inc.
A Member of the Rowman & Littlefield Publishing Group
4501 Forbes Boulevard, Suite 200, Lanham, Maryland 20706
www.rowmanlittlefield.com

P.O. Box 317, Oxford OX2 9RU, United Kingdom

Copyright © 2003 by Rowman & Littlefield Publishers, Inc.
Originally published in 1999 by Diné College Press.

British Library Cataloguing in Publication Information Available

Library of Congress Cataloging-in-Publication Data Available

ISBN 0-7425-2398-5 (cloth : alk. paper)
ISBN 0-7425-2399-3 (pbk. : alk. paper)

Printed in the United States of America

∞ ™ The paper used in this publication meets the minimum requirements of American
National Standard for Information Sciences—Permanence of Paper for Printed Library
Materials, ANSI/NISO Z39.48-1992.

Contents

PART I
Foundations of Diné Government and Relations
with the United States

PART II
Institutions of Diné Government

PART III
Political Dynamics of Diné Government

APPENDICES

TABLE AND ILLUSTRATIONS

Preface

This book, originally titled *Diné Bibeehaz'aanii: A Handbook of Navajo Government*, first appeared in 1987. It was published by the Navajo Community College Press at Tsaile, Arizona. Subsequently, the Navajo Nation, her people, and her resources experienced a number of compelling, sometimes traumatic events, which prompted a new and much expanded edition to be published in 1999 by the newly named Diné College Press.

This text, now published by Rowman & Littlefield, is a modestly updated, revised version of the 1999 edition, designed to reach a much wider audience. The modest changes include a revised preface, incorporation of the 2000 U.S. Census data, and an updated Timeline of Diné Political History. The balance of the text is essentially the same because not many dramatic developments have occurred since the revised text appeared in 1999.

In the little more than a decade between the book's first release in 1987 and its revision in 1999, however, there were ample changes in Navajo politics and society. Politically, four Navajo chief executives—Peter MacDonald, Albert Hale, Thomas Atcitty, and Kelsey Begaye (the latter three within a four-month period in 1998)—were forced to resign from the highest office in their land for reasons that are explained later in the text. In 1989 MacDonald—who had only recently been reelected to an unprecedented fourth term in 1987—was indicted and convicted of bribery, fraud, ethics violations, and other charges. MacDonald's ouster was particularly devastating for him personally and the Nation because of his longevity and standing in both Navajo and the larger intertribal, national, and international scenes.

His forced removal also, tragically, led to the deaths of two Navajos in a violent confrontation in Window Rock. MacDonald was later convicted and served over half of his fourteen-year sentence in federal prison for his crimes against the Navajo Nation and the United States. The Navajo Nation Council pardoned MacDonald of his tribal offenses in 1995 and President Bill Clinton commuted the remaining years of his sentence in 2001 just before leaving office.

Important structural changes in Navajo government emerged from this political upheaval. These changes, culminating in fundamental amendments to Title Two of the Navajo Nation Code in 1990 that will be explained in chapter 4, opened the door for additional, if largely unsuccessful, efforts to reform the Nation's government—to reduce the size of the Navajo Nation Council and to return greater self-governing power to local chapters are but two examples.

In addition, the Navajo Nation's population and powers have continued to grow and expand, even in the face of diminishing natural and fiscal resources. Along with their reduced resource bases, the Nation is also confronted with jurisdictional reductions brought on by the U.S. Supreme Court. In 2001 the Court handed down two startling rulings that negatively affected the tribal sovereignty of all indigenous nations (*Nevada v. Hicks*) and Navajo jurisdictional power in particular (*Atkinson Trading Company v. Shirley*).

Economically, the Navajo Nation Council took major steps toward gaining a greater degree of self-sufficiency by enacting two important but controversial resolutions in 2001: a 3 percent sales tax and a gaming ordinance that may eventually give the Navajos of To'Hajiilnee Chapter (Canoncito, New Mexico) an opportunity to establish the first gaming operations run by Navajo people.

Nationally, while indigenous peoples continued to battle the federal government and especially the Department of the Interior over the mismanagement and improprieties regarding their individual and collective trust funds in the late 1990s, the Navajo Nation was directly involved in a specific lawsuit. *Navajo Nation v. United States* centered on an inequitable coal mining lease the Nation had signed in 1964 with Peabody Coal whereby the tribe received royalties of less than 2 percent for its coal.

The Nation had filed suit against the Interior Department in 1993, alleging that then–Interior Secretary Donald Hodel had breached his trust duties owed the Nation under federal law, treaties, and regulations, by meeting privately with Peabody Coal officials and not acting in the best interests of the Indian trust beneficiaries. A federal court of claims ruled in 2000 that while Hodel's actions were a violation of the government's fiduciary duties to the Navajos, federal law did not require the government to provide compensation to the tribe despite the obvious trust violations. Importantly, a federal court of appeals reversed and remanded this decision in 2001, holding that "the existence of a trust relationship between the United States and an Indian or Indian tribe includes as a fundamental incident the right of an injured beneficiary to sue the trustee for damages resulting from a breach of the trust."

Culturally, a deadly outbreak of a "mystery illness," also known as the Hantavirus, and the visitation of two Navajo deities to an elderly Diné woman, forced many Navajos to take stock of their spiritual standing vis-à-vis the Holy People. At the same time, the Navajo codetalkers received ample federal recognition—congressional gold and silver medals from the George W. Bush administration in 2001—and public recognition in the form of John Woo's movie, *Windtalkers,* a well-received 2002 movie about the vital role played by the codetalkers in World War II. Finally, from an environmental perspective, the Navajo-Hopi land dispute and its lesser-known but still extremely disruptive sibling, the Bennett-Freeze land situation, neared some measure of final resolution after several generations of prickly influence on Navajo-Hopi intertribal relations and a depressing influence on Navajos and Hopis living in the affected areas.

These and many other developments prompted me to revise and expand the 1987 text in 1999. The ongoing importance of understanding the Navajo Nation's internal political affairs and their impact on broader national indigenous political developments necessitated the reissuance of this slightly updated text in 2002.

When the book was originally conceived in 1986, I was an instructor in the Navajo and Indian Studies Division of Navajo Community College (now Diné College). During my three-and-a-half years at the college I had the opportunity to teach courses in Navajo history, contemporary Indian affairs, and Navajo tribal government. Besides performing instructional duties, one of my principal goals then and now was to produce curriculum materials. The 1987 text, *Diné Bibeehaz'aanii,* was an example of the kind of work we in the Navajo and Indian Studies program sought to produce: quality curriculum materials that filled an important niche in the literature.

Before settling in the Southwest, I had worked chiefly with southeastern tribes, and had little knowledge of Navajos or other tribes west of the Mississippi. I had heard that the Navajos were the largest tribe, that they inhabited the most expansive reservation, and that politically they were a very sophisticated group. I also understood that Navajos were one of the most "studied" Indian groups in the country; anthropologists, archaeologists, economists, philosophers, historians, geologists, linguists, and other professionals have each taken a turn at analyzing various aspects of Navajo society, culture, and resources.

My arrival on the Navajo Reservation in 1983 confirmed much of this second-hand information. And when I began my search for relevant curriculum materials for my courses, particularly in the area of Navajo government, I discovered that I had stepped into a virtual vacuum. I was surprised to discover that few scholars (or nonscholars) had tackled the subject of Navajo politics and government. I thought this extraordinary given the unique role Navajos occupy in intertribal, state, and federal circles.

Historically, the Navajo Nation has been at the forefront of indigenous political, legal, and social change. Furthermore, on many occasions the federal government has exploited both the Navajo Nation's people and the reservation's natural resources as a "proving ground" for certain Indian policies. Why, I pondered, were so few materials available about Navajo government and politics? Was the Navajo political system that difficult or complex? Or were there other reasons texts on Navajo politics had not been developed?

In my initial research in preparation for the first incarnation of this study, I learned of the existence of a few notable works that treated the Navajo political system. One of the most informative studies of Navajo government was published in 1963 by Mary Shepardson, an anthropologist. Her publication, *Navajo Ways in Government: A Study in Political Process,* was indeed an excellent accounting of government on the reservation. But over thirty-five years had elapsed, and numerous changes had occurred since the book first appeared in print. Shepardson's monograph, moreover, was printed while termination[1] was the federal government's official policy, and she prematurely and wrongly predicted the decline of Navajo self-government by asserting, "I believe that the Treaty of 1868 will not indefinitely protect an illusory sovereignty."[2]

Navajo Political Process, published in 1970 by Aubrey W. Williams, was another valuable work on Navajo political structures. Williams's findings were, however, based on data gathered between 1961 and 1963. A more recent study dealing with some aspects of Navajo government is Peter Iverson's *The Navajo Nation,* first published in 1981 and reprinted in 1983. Iverson is an outstanding historian whose book discusses Navajo political, social, and economic developments, with an emphasis on the period from the 1950s to the late 1970s. While Iverson's work was a welcome contribution, his focus was not on detailing or analyzing Navajo political dynamics or governmental systems, either historical or contemporary.

Since *Diné Bibeehaz'aanii* was first published, several broader works have been produced on tribal governments, providing much-needed information on these increasingly sophisticated governmental operations. The first of these studies, *Indian Tribes as Sovereign Governments: A Sourcebook on Federal-Tribal History, Law, and Policy,* was published in 1988 by the American Indian Lawyer Training Program. It is a brief introduction to the complicated field of federal Indian law and policy.

Sharon O'Brien, a political scientist, published *American Indian Tribal Governments* in 1989. It was the first comprehensive comparative work focusing on federal Indian policy and provided a solid description of tribal governments. O'Brien included a fairly detailed institutional description of five tribes, though the Navajo Nation was not one of her case studies. A third book—authored by James Lopach, Margery Brown, and Richard Clow and titled *Tribal Government Today: Politics on Montana Indian Reservations* (1990, revised in 1998)—is a comparative study examining tribal governments in Big Sky Country. *Modern American Indian Tribal Governments and Politics,* by Howard Meredith (1993), is a concise volume designed to increase understanding about the political processes and governmental structures of contemporary tribal councils.

The author published a text, *American Indian Politics and the American*

Political System (2002), which is the first general study of indigenous politics. It not only emphasizes the distinctive political and legal status of Indian and Alaskan Native peoples but also provides details about tribal governments, economic development, political participation, interest groups, and the media. Last, John M. Meyer edited a reader, *American Indians and U.S. Politics: A Companion Reader* (2002), that pulls together essays focused on indigenous political traditions, federalism, citizenship, civil liberties, and campaigns and elections.

Clearly, and at long last, there is an increasing—though still limited—amount of attention being paid to the governing capabilities, structures, and processes of tribal nations as governing bodies. However, there is still a paucity of first-rate literature on the Navajo Nation's political system, though some very good works have been produced in the last decade. In 1987 Sam and Janet Bingham issued a revised edition of their book, *Navajo Chapters* (Navajo Community College Press), which closely examines the history, function, and role of the chapter (local) system of government in Navajo politics.

Peter Iverson has continued his interest in the Navajo Nation by publishing a short history of the tribe as part of the Chelsea House Publishers series, *Indians of North America*. It is called simply *The Navajos,* and was published in 1990. Peter MacDonald (with Ted Schwarz), the former chairman of the Navajo Nation, had his biography published in 1993. Titled *The Last Warrior: Peter MacDonald and the Navajo Nation,* it is MacDonald's "own story" and details his rise and fall as leader of the largest reservation-based indigenous nation. It includes a fair amount of information related to the political affairs of the tribe from MacDonald's perspective.

Three more books have been published that deal with land-related issues, which of necessity include valuable information about Navajo politics. Two of the works examine the Navajo-Hopi land dispute in detail, though from a decidedly Navajo perspective: Emily Benedek, *The Wind Won't Know Me: A History of the Navajo-Hopi Land Dispute* (1992); and David M. Brugge, *The Navajo-Hopi Land Dispute: An American Tragedy* (1994). The third study is *If You Poison Us: Uranium and Native Americans* (1994) by Peter H. Eichstaedt, who recounts the depressing tale of how Navajo uranium miners were used and abused by big business and the federal government in the U.S. pursuit of nuclear dominance during the Cold War.

The Navajo Nation's Office of Navajo Government Development published a short booklet in 1997 titled *Navajo Nation Government,* which is a useful compilation of information on the basic origins and contemporary structure of Navajo government. Finally, Maureen Trudelle Schwarz published *Navajo Lifeways: Contemporary Issues, Ancient Knowledge* in 2001. While Schwarz is an anthropologist, this book includes several essays that focus on substantive policy topics like the effects of uranium mining on Navajos and other land-rights problems.

Despite the presence of these important works, a need still exists to provide the interested reader with a broad historical and contemporary account of the dynamic nature of Navajo national government and politics, and to describe the relationship between the Navajo political system and the larger society. The revised 1999 text only loosely retained the structure of the original volume and added a considerable amount of new material on the Navajo political experience. It includes description and analysis of the impressive political changes that were sparked in 1989 by Peter MacDonald's political corruption scandal—changes that enveloped the Navajo Nation. That scandal turned into a deadly confrontation in July 1989 with the deaths of two Navajos, prompting the tribal council to adopt new laws aimed at preventing such events. Changes include, but are not limited to, the Amendments to Title Two of the Navajo Nation Code, which entailed a substantial restructuring of the executive and legislative branches. These amendments, codified in 1990, split and renamed the position of Chairman into two new positions—the Speaker of the Council and the President of the Navajo Nation. The Navajo Tribal Council, renamed the Navajo Nation Council, gave the Speaker power to preside over Council meetings and to head the legislative branch. The tribal president was given veto power subject to override by a two-thirds vote of the Council. The Council committee system was reduced from 18 to 12, and the Advisory Committee was stripped of its disproportionate powers.

The Council also voted to approve Rules of Order to save time and money and to ensure fairness to Council delegates. In effect, these changes created a system with greater checks and balances and installed, for the first time, a measure of the separation of powers doctrine by dividing and demarcating the legislative, executive, and judicial functions.

Students will find this book a general reference on political theory, structure, and behavior. I have also sought to outline the theoretical underpinnings of traditional and contemporary government, since few people are familiar with these concepts, which view constitutional governments (representative-type) as being influenced by human rationality and as an end-result of rationality; in contrast, traditional forms of government incorporate another view, which is of a God-given right to govern.[3]

This study begins by exploring what constitutes an indigenous nation. It describes the basic functions of government in general and outlines the historical evolution of the distinctive tribal/federal political relationship. It then details the genesis and expansion of Navajo government from prehistory to the present, analyzing the current scope and structure of the three-branch system of Navajo national government.

In the final part the focus turns to some of the key dynamics of Diné government, examining the role of interest groups, the media, and the Diné electoral process. The study closes with a focused treatment of several key public policies that play an important role in Navajo political affairs, and concludes with some discussion on where the Nation is headed in the new millennium. A number of important appendices are included, along with a timeline of significant political/historical events current up to the time of the publication of this, the 2003 updated text edition.

Too many works about tribal nations treat the group under study in isolation and oftentimes as cultural and historical curiosities. It is mistakenly assumed that the activities of surrounding peoples and their institutions have little or no bearing on the tribe under consideration. Such a narrow focus does an injustice to everyone. Political systems are not static, and they certainly do not operate in a vacuum. Thus we will better understand the Navajo Nation's political system when appropriate comparisons are made and the historical dimension is explored.

Designed to enhance understanding of the Navajo political process, this book has been written to allow for comparisons with other tribal nations and other political systems as well. Thus it should be of immediate use in history classes; in courses on tribal, American, and state and local government; and in Indian studies courses as well. In addition, it provides elected and appointed tribal officials with a broader knowledge of their political system. Beyond that, my greatest hope is that the Navajo citizenry will familiarize themselves with the content of this study so that they will be better informed about their rights and responsibilities as tribal, state, and federal citizens.

Vine Deloria, Jr., and Clifford Lytle noted in their excellent study, *The Nations Within,* that "American Indians are unique in the world in that they represent the only aboriginal peoples still practicing a form of self-government in the midst of a wholly new and modern civilization that has been transported to their lands."[4] This statement is more true now with the striking changes unleashed in the wake of the 1989 Window Rock political revolution and the continuing developments in recent years that have seen the Navajo people clamor for greater political, economic, and cultural self-determination, even in the face of internal and external constraints and limited resources that make this a difficult task. The Navajo Nation is indeed practicing a distinctive and increasingly sophisticated brand of self-government—despite the best intentions of the states their lands extend into and the efforts of the federal government to assimilate Navajos into American society.

Acknowledgments

I am deeply indebted to many individuals for their support, constructive criticisms, and encouragement as I prepared this book for the 1999 text edition. Ed McCoombs, public relations expert and special assistant to the Diné College president, deserves special thanks. He had asked me several times over the past few years to revise the 1987 book after it went out of print—and in the wake of the startling political changes in Navajo government that arose in 1989 out of the violent and scandalous controversy involving Peter MacDonald and his supporters, the Tribal Council, the federal government, and the Navajo people. Ed's support was most instrumental in getting the 1999 text completed.

Special thanks are extended to Ronald D. Haven, Esq. (Navajo). Ron, over the years, has kept me apprised of important laws and policies enacted by the Council, and he generously supplied me with additional information as this new project unfolded. Ron also read a significant portion of the manuscript and corrected me on a number of key points. Besides being a good friend, he is an outstanding advisor for the legislative branch of the Navajo Nation. I also appreciate the inestimable help of Marley Shebala, a gifted reporter for *The Navajo Times,* who provided me with updates of recent political developments.

I also want to thank Dr. Clifford M. Lytle, a retired colleague at the University of Arizona. He helped redefine the boundaries of the study and made valuable suggestions on content and format. Thanks also to Prof. Vine Deloria, Jr., emeritus (Standing Rock Sioux). His continuing friendship and unmatched knowledge of Indian issues continue to guide and inspire me.

My gratitude goes to Victoria Healey, administrative assistant in the Department of Political Science, and Claudia Nelson, program coordinator, of the Office of Community Development, both at the University of Arizona. While I was still in Tucson, they were kind enough to allow me to interrupt their busy schedules when I needed their skilled assistance in preparing the tables and appendices in the text. Thanks also to Susie Jim, Diné College Press secretary, who worked with me in preparing the 1999 manuscript for publication.

Dr. Tsianina Lomawaima (Creek), a dear friend in the American Indian Studies program at the University of Arizona, furnished me with important materials on the land dispute(s) and critiqued portions of the manuscript as well. She made numerous constructive recommendations and editorial suggestions that strengthened the manuscript.

Thanks are expressed to Vivian Arviso (Navajo), who provided me with important insights on the Navajo political process. Thanks also to W. Ron Allen (Jamestown S'Klallam), former executive director of the National Congress of American Indians (NCAI). Ron gave me some good information regarding the relationship between the NCAI and the Navajo Nation.

I am deeply grateful to the students of my Navajo Tribal Government classes for inspiring me all those years ago with their frank questions and genuine concerns about the shape, quality, and future of their government. And, of course, I had many Navajo students during my years at the University of Arizona. They, too, shared fresh ideas and insights that helped with this text.

I also appreciate the support of my current colleagues at the University of Minnesota. Dr. Patricia Albers, a dear friend and distinguished American Indian Studies department head, and Helen Kopietz, Anna Bendickson, and Yvonne Kelly, the department's crack administrative team, make my job easier with their skills and smiles.

I am also indebted to a number of current and past Navajo Nation employees, who were generous with their time, thoughts, and information about their respective agencies or offices. Gwen Salt, formerly of the Nation's Washington Office; Trib Chaudhary, of the Navajo Nation Division of Economic Development; Andrea Becenti, Executive Director of the Navajo Nation Bar Association; Richie Nez, of the Navajo Election Administration; Amy Alderman, an attorney with the Navajo Tax Commission; Leonard Benally of Vital Records; and Aaron Clark of the Data Resource Center.

Special thanks to Jennifer Knerr, vice-president and executive editor at Rowman & Littlefield, and Renee Legatt, her outstanding assistant, both of whom believed that this book deserved a wider audience and provided me the opportunity to reissue it.

To my parents, Daniel and Thedis Wilkins (and their parents), who doggedly encouraged me to give my all to whatever endeavor I chose, I thank you. And a special dose of appreciation is extended to my Diné in-laws.

I owe my greatest debt of gratitude, as always, to my wife, Evelyn, and our three children, Sion, Niltooli, and Nazhone. Their boundless love provides me with all the inspiration and support I shall ever need.

Thanks to you all. I alone assume responsibility for the inevitable, though hopefully few, errors contained herein.

David E. Wilkins
University of Minnesota
2002

The **Diné** (Navajo) inhabit a vast land of beauty, grace, and great diversity. It is a sprawling territory, bounded by sacred mountains and great rivers. The Navajo Reservation, first delineated in the 1868 treaty, has nearly quadrupled in size since then through some twenty-five additions. Today the Diné land base is some 25,351 square miles (nearly 18 million acres), encompassing a large portion of northeastern Arizona, a part of northwestern New Mexico, and some 1,900 square miles in southeastern Utah. Interestingly, the Navajo Nation also includes three satellite (geographically separate) Navajo communities—Cañoncito, Alamo, and Ramah, all in western New Mexico—and completely encircles two other tribes, the Hopi Nation and the San Juan Paiute.

The Navajo **Reservation** represents 36 percent of all Indian lands in the continental United States.[5] This tremendous stretch of land, the largest of the 278 Indian reservations in the country, is slightly larger than the state of West Virginia. Nearly 15 million acres of Navajo tribal land are held in **trust**[6] by the federal government.

According to the Navajo Nation's Office of Vital Records, in 2001 there were approximately 253,124 enrolled Navajos in the U.S., nearly 168,000 of them living within Navajo territory. The 2000 U.S. Census, however, counted 269,202 individuals self-identifying as Navajo, with an additional 28,995 individuals claiming to be at least partially Navajo. The combined 2000 Census population of persons claiming to be Navajo is 298,197, the largest population of any tribe. The Cherokee Nation of Oklahoma, has an estimated 229,723 enrolled members, although over 700,000 individuals self-identify as being at least partially Cherokee.

Unlike many reservations which were allotted (subdivided into individual plots) and opened for white homesteaders, **allotment** was never widely implemented on the Navajo Nation and therefore the number of non-Indians and non-Navajo Indians remains quite small. According to the 1990 Census over 90 percent of the Reservation population was Navajo. Although the Navajo population continues to grow rapidly, economic statistics are not nearly as encouraging. While per capita income for Anglo-Americans is $15,252, it is only $6,651 for Navajos. More than 56 percent of Navajos live below the poverty line, while only 15.7 percent of Arizonans are below that depressing threshold. In 1996, the Navajo Nation had a total labor force of 50,857. However, the unemployment rate

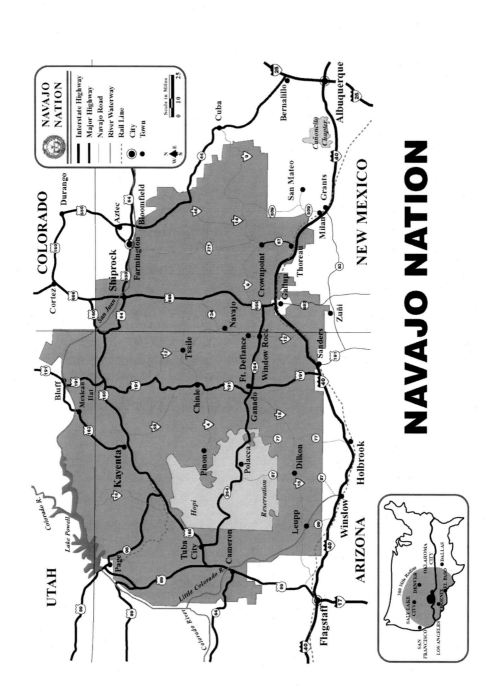

NAVAJO NATION

in that year was 44.61 percent. This figure usually fluctuates between 38 and 50 percent depending on the season. Equally disheartening is the reality that while the total personal income of Navajos was over 1 billion dollars for 1996, less than 300 million dollars were actually spent within the Reservation's borders, a leakage of over 76 percent to off-reservation communities who benefit from the purchasing power of Navajo shoppers.[7]

Politically, Navajos have been fairly active in tribal elections. For example, more than 93,000 Navajos were registered to vote in 1998, although only 42 percent of the registered voters actually participated in the fall presidential primary. This low turnout appears to reflect the disenchantment many Navajos feel with the ethical problems of several of their recent presidents.

Of the five agencies—Western Navajo, Chinle, Ft. Defiance, Shiprock, and Eastern Navajo—Ft. Defiance has the largest number of registered voters: 24,569 as of 1998. There is also evidence that Navajos participate in federal and state/local elections when a candidate's stand on issues of importance to Navajos is evident.[8] Historically, in fact, Navajo voting patterns in tribal elections have been better than the voting percentages of Americans whose turnout in American presidential elections ranks at the bottom of voting rates for twenty-seven countries with competitive elections. In 1992, for example, the turnout rate for the presidential race was only 55 percent. This percentage actually represented a sharp rise from the previous four decades of presidential voting.[9]

The Navajo People's land is laced with a number of historically important and breathtaking sites. Navajo Mountain, Lake Powell and Rainbow Bridge, Monument Valley, and Canyon de Chelly are just a few of the more noted spots. These areas are, of course, prime tourist locales and they attract over one million visitors a year from all over the world. There is, however, a severe shortage of hotels/motels in the Nation, which hinders tourism development.

There is an abundance of other natural resources as well. For example, there are significant stands of coniferous trees at the higher elevations. Minerals, including gold, silver, copper, uranium-vanadium asphalt rock, building stone, clay, gypsum, and lime are plentiful. Coal, oil, and natural gas, which provide the tribe with significant revenue, are also still in ample supply.

The Colorado, Little Colorado, and San Juan Rivers provide precious water for irrigation, livestock, and agricultural purposes. These water resources are critical because the Reservation receives little rainfall and much of the land is agriculturally unproductive, although certain areas produce good crops of corn, beans, alfalfa, potatoes, wheat, and barley.

Finally, more than ninety percent of Navajo land continues to be used for grazing livestock—cattle, goats, and sheep.[10]

Navajo Tribal government and politics is the subject of this book. Government institutions and processes may come into power overnight, but to understand them completely, an historical review must be done. Therefore, a good part of this study is devoted to examining historical developments that shaped Navajo government into its present form.

Historically, Navajo society was welded in part by a highly effective form of **government**. Traditional Navajo governing structures, however, bore virtually no resemblance to the Western European political system. Inroads into Navajo country by other tribes, the Spaniards, Mexicans, and later, Americans, necessitated a gradual altering of the aboriginal form of government which Navajos had employed since the dawn of time.

By the early part of the twentieth century, nearly 400 years of interaction with foreign powers compelled substantial modifications in Navajo institutions and in various aspects of Navajo society and culture. The federal government, in 1923, set into motion a series of events which completely revamped Diné government. In effect, Washington officials "created" a federally recognized political institution, the Navajo Tribal Council, although in its earliest incarnations it was known simply as a Business Council. Vestiges of traditional political structures remained (i.e., headmen or **Naataanii**, the basis of Navajo Chapter government), but the United States wielded the self-ascribed power to grant or withhold both recognition and federal funds from these tribal institutions.[11]

The Navajo Tribal Council, reorganized in 1938 and renamed the Navajo Nation Council in 1989, has been a fixture in Navajo lives for sixty years. It was not until the conclusion of World War II, however, that a majority of Navajo people began to view the tribal council as "their" government. Mary Shepardson summed it up best when she noted that: "The majority of Navajos regard the Tribal Council as capable of meeting important needs of the tribe; increasingly they accept its authority, regard its rules as binding, and view as legitimate its right to use force within the limits permitted by the Federal Government."[12] This statement is more accurate today than ever before and the tumultuous events of 1989 only served to buffer this perception.

There remain, however, some segments of the Navajo citizenry who still challenge the legitimacy of the central government in Window Rock, particularly since the Navajo electorate still has never had the opportunity to express their sovereign will by either participating in a **constitutional convention** or even to vote on the governmental changes wrought by the civil unrest in 1989. We will discuss these important issues in Chapter 5.

The Navajo Nation Council currently consists of eighty-eight delegates. It is led by the Speaker of the Council, who is the presiding officer of the council. The Council's primary function is to **legislate**: that is, it is the law-making branch of a representative **democracy**. Although the Secretary of the Interior continues to wield veto power over certain council decisions, the Navajo political system, with the Title II changes in the executive branch in 1989, has more comparability than ever before to state governments and the federal government.

Many Navajos, however, believe that it is in their best interest to adhere to and enhance what is most distinctive about the Navajo people, especially in the areas of cultural retention, values specific to the Diné, and most importantly, to retain and invigorate the Navajo language. Otherwise, there is a sense that the Nation might face a permanent and irreversible identity crisis. In fact, for some Navajos, this is the lesson of the appearance and destructive force of the hantavirus in 1993 and the reported appearance of two Navajo deities to an elderly woman in 1996, warning the people to revive traditional values and beliefs.

Navajos also understand that sovereignty and self-government imply a necessity and the inclination to negotiate appropriate agreements with surrounding states, other tribes, and the federal government. A good example of this last aspect is the **sovereignty accord** signed in 1992 between President Peterson Zah and the governors of New Mexico, Utah, and Arizona. This policy declared that the interactions of the four sovereigns would "be predicated on a government-to-government relationship" and that all future relations would be "carried forward in a spirit of cooperation, coordination, communication, and good will."[13]

The Navajo Nation operates one of the most complex political systems in Indian Country. The Nation, unlike some other tribal governments, generally approaches the negotiating table with a politically united front, although the events surrounding Peter MacDonald's last days in office threatened that relative political homogeneity for a brief but intense period of time. This is not meant to imply that Navajo citizens are always in agreement with the legislative, executive, or judicial decisions of their policy makers, but rather points out that the intense intratribal conflicts which are presently hampering the Indian self-determination efforts of tribes like the Cherokee of Oklahoma, the Tohono O'Odham of southern Arizona, the Lumbee of North Carolina, and others, are not a major or persistent problem for the Navajos.

Tom Holm, in an excellent article entitled, "Indian Concepts of Authority and the Crisis in Tribal Government," described the internal conflict of the Oglala Lakotas on the Pine Ridge Reservation and of the Creek Nation in Oklahoma. Holm noted that:

(T)ribal factionalism has been along "traditional" versus, "modern" lines and is directly tied to differing concepts of **authority**. Authority in modern tribal government is vested in certain positions within the tribal political system. The people elected to these positions then assume the power of the office.

Authority, therefore, is related to the power of the office within the context of the tribal Constitution. According to many traditional value systems, however, authority is vested in individuals and not necessarily in particular tribal positions. In most tribal societies authority is gained with status and does not imply arbitrary power. Status is accorded to individuals who have excelled in certain skills, practiced generosity, displayed great courage, have knowledge of ceremonial functions, possess spiritual powers, or who have strong analytical abilities or wisdom. Authority is given consistently to the person who has demonstrated over and over again that he or she has the spiritual and physical well being of the rest of the tribe at heart.[14]

In a sense, the political cohesiveness of the Navajo people can be viewed positively. It means that the Navajo Nation Council is the recognized voice of all Navajos, although there are always exceptions (i.e., at present, the Navajos living around Big Mountain may hold a contrary view). But generally, political divisiveness does not threaten the integrity of Navajo National government.

On the other hand, the absence of a politically active traditional government segment implies that a great deal of Navajo tradition has already been displaced. This loss has been more pronounced in the executive and legislative branches. The judicial branch, conversely, has shown a greater willingness to integrate traditional Navajo legal and social values into the already established Western legal system that is generally operative throughout the Reservation.

For instance, in 1982, Navajo judges implemented Peacemaker Courts which utilize traditional Navajo **dispute resolution** techniques to resolve local disputes.[15] These courts will be discussed in Chapter 8. Additionally, the Courts of the Navajo Nation have gone even further and in 1991 adopted a new Code of Judicial Conduct. This code uses many principles of the American Bar Association's Model Code of Judicial Conduct, but it also incorporates a number of uniquely Navajo legal values as well.[16]

The Navajo people have witnessed the executive and legislative branches of their government, and the judicial to a lesser extent, assume the functions, the institutions, the technologies, the **politics**, and in some respects, even the goals of the larger society. Some Navajos feel it is not now possible, or even advisable, to reverse this trend and argue that a revival of traditional Diné structures of governance would disrupt existing internal and external working relationships already in place (i.e., within the tribe, and between the states and federal government). On the other hand, some of the traditional Navajo population and an increasing number of younger Navajos fear that unless immediate steps are taken to re-introduce even more traditional Navajo concepts and structures beyond those already in place in the judicial branch, the qualities that distinguish Navajos from other tribes and racial/ethnic groups may be lost forever.

According to Howard Meredith, most tribes and Alaskan Native villages have at least one of four basic types of political organization:

1. Tribes that have written constitutions approved by the United States Department of the Interior in line with federal statutes, including the Indian Reorganization Act of 1934, the Oklahoma Welfare Act of 1936, and the Alaska Native Act of 1936, which is more restrictive in its application, i.e., the Apache of Oklahoma, the Caddo, the Comanche, the Delaware of Western Oklahoma, the Ft. Sill Apache, the Kiowa.

2. Tribes with governing documents approved by the Department of the Interior outside of any specific federal statutory authority, i.e., the Cherokee Nation, the Navajo Nation.

3. Tribes with traditional, unwritten forms of government based on custom, i.e., the Crow Tribe, the Shoshone on the Wind River, the Onondaga of New York.

4. Interim governments of those tribes recently restored to federal status. In the recent past this would have included the Tunica Tribe of Louisiana.[17]

The evolution of the Navajo political system, which can only loosely be fitted under 2. (Tribes with governing documents ...) for reasons we have noted and will be discussing, is the topic of Parts II and III of this book. In those sections we will analyze the present structure of Navajo government, highlight its strengths and flaws, and analyze the dynamics of Navajo politics.

James Q. Wilson, a noted political scientist, has stated that "judgments about institutions and interests can only be made after one has seen how they behave on a variety of important issues or potential issues."[18] In this regard, Navajo National government, as presently constituted, is still in infancy. Nevertheless, members of the Nation's Council, the judicial system, the **executive branch**, and the growing tribal bureaucracy are part of a very old society with roots dating back hundreds of generations.

Navajo citizens, like citizens of the larger society, tend to assume that the way decisions are made now is the only way decisions can be made. In fact, there are many other ways to operate government based on popular **consensus**. Navajo traditions, history, and beliefs weigh heavily, whether consciously or not, on what is decided by tribal leaders.

While the federal government did indeed create the first business and later tribal councils, the 1850 and 1868 treaties between the Navajos and the United States represent critical sources of Navajo political power. These two ratified agreements acknowledged the sovereign political status of Navajo People. So long as these covenants exist, encircled as they are and suffused by Diné culture and values, the Navajo Nation is entitled to exercise all those powers of self-government not specifically surrendered in those treaties with the United States. And contrary to Mary Shepardson's assertion, the Navajo People and their political officials may expect to continue to enhance the political status they enjoy.

Key Terms

Allotment	Government
Authority	Legislate
Consensus	Naataanii
Constitutional Convention	Politics
Democracy (representative)	Reservation
Diné	Sovereignty Accord
Dispute Resolution	Trust
Executive Branch	

Selected Readings

Deloria, Vine, Jr., and Clifford M. Lytle. *American Indians, American Justice.* (Austin: University of Texas Press, 1983).

Holm, Tom. "Indian Concepts of Authority and the Crisis in Tribal Government." *The Social Science Journal,* vol. 19, no. 3 (July 1982), pp. 59–71.

Reno, Philip. *Navajo Resources and Economic Development.* (Albuquerque: University of New Mexico Press, 1981).

Shepardson, Mary. *Navajo Ways in Government.* American Anthropological Association Memoir, no. 96. (Menasha, Wisconsin: June 1963).

Wilson, James Q. *American Government: Institutions and Politics.* (Lexington, Massachusetts: D.C. Heath and Company, 1980).

Notes

1 Policy designed to end the federal government's financial, legal, and moral responsibilities to tribes and eventually to withdraw its trust protection of reservation lands and resources. Lawmakers believed that termination would speed the integration or assimilation of Indians into American society.

2 See, Mary Shepardson, *Navajo Ways in Government: A Study in Political Process,* American Anthropological Association Memoir, no. 96 (Menasha, Wisconsin, June 1963): 113.

3 See, Tom Holm, "Indian Concepts of Authority and the Crisis in Tribal Governments," *The Social Science Journal,* vol. 19, no. 3 (July 1982).

4 Vine Deloria, Jr., and Clifford M. Lytle, *The Nations Within: The Past and Future of American Indian Sovereignty* (New York: Pantheon Books, 1984). (Reprint ed. Austin, Texas: University of Texas Press, 1998): 2.

5 Most of the statistical data cited below are found in Duane Etsitty, compiler, *NN Fax 93* (Window Rock, Arizona: Division of Economic Development, 1994).

6 Indian trust land is Indian-owned land, title to which is held in trust by the United States. This broadly means that the actual "ownership" of the land is divided between the federal government, which holds the legal title, and the tribe (or individual Indian) which holds the full equitable title. Trust land is not subject to taxation and, in general, neither the federal government nor the Indian tribe or individual owner can sell or otherwise dispose of trust land without the consent of the other party. A major exception to this theory, however, is that the federal government has claimed and acted on a number of occasions to unilaterally "take" Indian land using the controversial and problematic doctrine of "plenary power." Plenary in this instance means absolute or unlimited.

7 Special thanks to Mr. Trib Chaudhury of the Division of Economic Development for these most recent employment and spending figures.

8 See, Jeff J. Corntassel and Richard Witmer, II, "American Indian Tribal Government Support of Office-Seekers: Findings from the 1994 Election," *The Social Science Journal,* vol. 34, no. 4 (1997): 518.

9 Kenneth Janda, Jeffrey M. Berry, and Jerry Goldman, *The Challenge of Democracy: Government in America.* Brief Edition, 3rd ed. (Boston: Houghton Mifflin Company, 1998): 128–129.

10 Philip Reno, *Navajo Resources and Economic Development* (Albuquerque, New Mexico: University of New Mexico Press, 1981): 9.

11 Federal officials created the Tribal Council and funded the establishment of the Navajo Chapters. In the 1930s, when Chapters became centers of opposition to forced livestock reduction, the federal government withdrew its recognition and financial support of those chapters. Many of those units collapsed.

12 Shepardson, *Navajo Ways in Government,* p. 3.

13 Author has copy of this policy accord.

14 Holm, "Indian Concepts of Authority," p. 59–60.

15 See, James W. Zion, *Navajo Peacemaker Court Manual* (Window Rock, Arizona, 1982); Tom Tso, "The Process of Decision Making in Tribal Courts," *Arizona Law Review: Indian Law Symposium,* vol. 31, no. 2 (1989): 225–235; and Robert Yazzie, "Life Comes from it: Navajo Justice Concepts," *New Mexico Law Review: Indian Law Symposium,* vol. 24, no. 2 (Spring 1994): 175–190.

16 See, Tom Tso, "Moral Principles, Traditions, and Fairness in the Navajo Nation Code of Judicial Conduct," *Judicature,* vol. 76, no. 1 (June–July 1992): 15–21.

17 Meredith, *Modern American Indian Tribal Governments,* p. 51.

18 Wilson, *American Government: Institutions and Politics,* p. 14.

Part I

Foundations of Diné Government and Relations with the United States

---

Chapter 1

A Nation Within a Nation

Outline   Introduction

No Universal Legal Definition

A Navajo Understanding of What Constitutes a Nation

The Cultural Side of Navajo National Identity

The Political Side of Navajo Identity

The Distinctive Tribal-Federal Relationship

Tribal-State Relations

Conclusion

Introduction

On April 15, 1969 the Advisory Committee of the Navajo Tribal Council enacted a resolution directing that "all correspondence, stationary, and letterheads ... of the Navajo Tribe, use the designation 'Navajo Nation' to locate the tribe." The committee members considered this important because, in their words, "It appears essential to the best interest of the Navajo People that a clear statement be made to remind Navajos and non-Navajos alike that both the Navajo People and Navajo lands are, in fact, separate and distinct."

This chapter discusses the legal background of tribal national existence, and the political and cultural factors which determine the separate status of tribes in general, and the Navajos in particular. It also briefly describes the distinctive tribal/federal relationship. First of all, let us consider what constitutes an *Indian tribe*.

No Universal Legal Definition

Generally, the term **tribe** is used in an ethnological and a legal-political sense. It is important to distinguish between them because the legal/political definition has important consequences. For ethnological purposes, a tribe is a group of indigenous people linked by kinship, ancestry, cultural values, and language, and occupies a definite territory. But as a result of European and American inroads into tribal life, the term tribe today may also apply to tribal groups which consist of one or more ethnologically distinct tribes, and who may even speak different languages.

In some cases collectivities of several distinctive tribes have become viewed as one tribe because they share a single reservation. The Fort Belknap Indian community in Montana is an example. It is regarded as one reservation and tribal government by the federal government, but in ethnological terms, the Fort Belknap Reservation is actually composed of the Assiniboine and Gros Ventre tribes. The Colorado River Indian Reservation, located in the extreme western part of Arizona and southeastern California, is another example. This reservation is home to four ethnologically distinct tribes: Mohave, Chemehuevi, Hopi, and even some Navajos.

In 1901 the United States Supreme Court, in *Montoya v. United States,* provided the following ambiguous definition of a tribe: "By a 'tribe' we understand a body of Indians of the same or similar race, united in a community under one leadership or government, and inhabiting a particular though sometimes ill-defined territory." Despite the effort of the Supreme Court to define what constitutes a tribe, there remains no universally accepted definition of the term although the term appears in the Declaration of Independence, the United States Constitution, and in hundreds of treaties, federal and state statutes, and in federal regulations.

The Congress of the United States has exclusive authority in the field of Indian affairs because of the Commerce Clause of the Constitution (Article 1, Section 8, Clause 3). In fact, no legal authority prevents Congress from establishing an explicit universal definition of an Indian tribe, although some specific federal statutes contain definitions of Indian and tribe for the narrow purposes of a particular law. Congress, however, has never chosen to adopt a pervasive definition, preferring, with some exceptions, to leave the interpretation of what characteristics constitute a "tribe" to the courts or federal agencies who must implement the law.

There is wisdom in Congress' reluctance to adopt a single definition of tribal existence. The term tribe then has been used to describe a wide array of socio-political systems. It is better, most people argue, to be flexible and inclusive rather than rigid and exclude those Indian communities who otherwise possess all the cultural and social traits of an Indian national group.

Historically, a tribe was recognized for federal purposes based on whether the group had treaty relations with the United States; whether Congress or the President had acknowledged the group; whether the group had been recognized or dealt with by other tribes; whether the group exercised political authority over its members through a council or other governmental form; or whether the group had been treated as having collective rights in lands or funds.[1]

There are a number of groups not presently recognized by the federal government who are actively pursuing that status because they desire, first of all, to have their sovereign status affirmed. They also wish to establish a government-to-government relationship with the United States. **Federal recognition** affords tribes certain rights and powers of self-government (i.e., sovereign immunity, power to tax, right to exercise civil and criminal jurisdiction, and so on). They become eligible for specific benefits and services like those provided by the Bureau of Indian Affairs (BIA), the Indian Health Service (IHS), the Office of Indian Education, the Indian Housing Authority, and others. Federal recognition also subjects tribes to the same largely unlimited federal powers other recognized tribes are subject to. In short, newly recognized tribes are informed that they are now subject to federal plenary power (defined in this instance as both *exclusive* and *absolute*).[2]

Unrecognized or nonrecognized tribal groups may seek federal recognition through a congressional act or they may petition for administrative recognition through the BIA under regulations first established in 1978. If a petitioning tribe is successful in meeting the criteria established by the federal government, the tribe is formally *acknowledged* as an Indian tribe. **Acknowledgement** is comparable to *recognition*. At present, approximately 156 self-identified groups have submitted or are in the process of submitting petitions for recognition as an Indian tribe.

From 1978, when the formal administrative process began, through 1995, nine groups have been acknowledged and thirteen have been denied recognition. In that period, Congress has legislatively recognized six tribes, and restored several others from terminated status. As of 1997, the federal government recognizes the political existence of 557 tribal entities[3] in the United States.

A Navajo Understanding of What Constitutes a Nation

As noted earlier, the Navajo Tribal Council in 1969 declared that henceforth the polity would be designated as *The Navajo Nation*. The terms nation, tribe, and band were often used interchangeably in Indian treaties and statutes, although they actually have somewhat different meanings. We have already defined tribe. **Nation**, first of all, is a collective of people. But what distinguishes the term nation from ethnic, race, or state, is that they are collectives united by shared cultural features (e.g., stories, values) and the belief in the right to territorial self-determination. Nations, in other words, are "groups of people linked by unifying traits and the desire to control a territory that is thought of as the group's national homeland."[4]

Thus, Navajos who support the sovereignty of their nation can be said to be exercising nationalism when they are in pursuit of a set of rights for the self-defined members of the nation, including territorial autonomy and sovereignty. All nationalisms, including the Navajo Nation, share at least two important features. First, they define the territorial boundaries that the nation controls; and second, they define the membership by boundaries of the population that comprises the nation.

There are many small countries in Europe and other parts of the world which have the status of *nations* even though, in some cases, they have smaller populations than the Navajo Nation and some allow larger nation-states to conduct some of their domestic and foreign affairs.[5] Large tribes like the Navajo Nation resemble these smaller nations in many political and in some cultural aspects of their national life.

Finally, a **band**, according to some scholars, refers to a smaller human collectivity than a nation or tribe. For instance, historically the Navajo band consisted of some ten to forty families who made use of agricultural enterprises or the pastoral economy to maintain themselves. Each such band was independent of others who occupied and tended adjacent territory. There was, moreover, no overarching national organization (the Naachid system will be discussed in Chapter 4) and it was rare for more than two bands to act cooperatively on a consistent basis.[6]

The Cultural Side of Navajo National Identity

Diné—The People—existed as a distinct cultural, national, and racial/ethnic group long before the establishment of the federal government or the surrounding states. For untold generations the basis of unity among Navajo Indians has been a well-defined territory, a common language, a shared heritage of customs and beliefs, and a sense of ideological distinction separating them from all other tribes, nations, and groups. Together, these components bind the Navajos as a *cultural presence*. A list of common elements shared by a cultural entity would include, but not be limited to, race, religion, language, traditions and historical events, and values.

Theories of Race

Until recently, American Indian nations were classified by the scientific community as belonging to the Mongolian racial category primarily because most academics believed that Indians once lived in Asia and migrated over the Bering Strait at some disputable point in the distant past. This theory of Indian origins, however, has always been discounted by Indian origin accounts and now a growing amount of scholarly literature is corroborating the Indian versions of their origins which hold that indigenous groups originated on the continent.[7]

Generally, **race** is one of the most misunderstood, misused, and often dangerous terms of the modern world. It is not applied unemotionally by laypeople or even by social scientists. Rather, it tends to arouse powerful emotions such as hate, fear, anger, loyalty, pride, and prejudice. It has also been used to justify some of the most outrageous injustices and mistreatments of humans by other humans. For example, Navajos were often captured and sold as slaves by Spaniards and Mexicans because it was thought that they were an inferior human species.

The idea of race has a long history, extending far back into ancient times. It is in the modern world, however, that the notion has taken on real significance and fundamentally affected human relations. Unfortunately, the term has never been applied consistently and has meant and continues to mean different things to different people. In popular usage, it has been used to describe a wide variety of human categories, including people of a particular skin color (the Mongoloid "race"), religion (the Jewish "race"), nationality (the British "race"), and even the entire human species (the Human "race"). However, none of these applications is accurate and meaningful from a social scientific perspective. Much of the ongoing confusion surrounding the idea of race comes from the fact that it has both a *biological* and a *social* meaning.[8]

Biologically, the essential meaning of race is a population of humans classified on the basis of hereditary characteristics that distinguish them from other human groups. Race is, in other words, a way of categorizing human physical types. But even this seemingly straightforward definition is complicated and there is much variation in thought and almost no agreement among biologists, geneticists, or physical anthropologists concerning the term's meaning.

But whatever its biological validity, if any, the importance of race for the study of the way groups interact lies in its social meaning. Simply put, people attach significance to the concept of race and consider it a real and important division of humanity. As long as people *believe* that differences in physical traits are important, they will act on the basis of those beliefs.[9] The scientific validity is of little consequence. Rather, it is the belief system of a society that provides its significance. What is most important regarding social classification of races is that the perceived physical differences among groups are assumed to correspond to social or behavioral differences. Thus, African Americans are assumed to look and behave in certain ways and to achieve at certain levels because they are black; Euro-Americans are assumed to look, behave, and achieve in other ways because they are of European descent; and Navajos are perceived to have certain physical traits (i.e., pronounced cheekbones, straight and coarse black hair, reddish-brown skin color, and little body hair), are expected to behave in certain ways, and are thought to achieve at certain levels because they are Navajo.

This is evident, in one direct sense, in the ongoing but problematic use of **blood quantum** as a key determinant in who is recognized as an Indian for tribal and/or federal purposes. As Matt Snipp put it:

> The use of blood quantum to define the modern Indian population poses enormous conceptual and practical problems. Conceptually, the development of modern genetics and environmentalism in the social sciences dispelled the validity of eugenics and undermined the intellectual credibility of blood quantum racial definitions. Over time, eugenics came to be viewed as intellectually veiled racism. Confronted by legal challenges, federal authorities were forced to concede that blood quantum definitions cannot be legally enforced for most purposes. Furthermore, the blood quantum information haphazardly collected in the early rolls is at best unsystematic, if not altogether unreliable.[10]

Nevertheless, many tribes still maintain a blood quantum criterion, typically ranging from one-sixteenth to one-half. The Navajo Nation, for example, utilizes the one-quarter quantum as its standard. Despite the archaic and arbitrary nature of this concept, it appears to be one that tribes are reluctant to part with.

A more appropriate term than race would be viewing the Navajo and other tribal nations as **ethnic groups**. An ethnic group is identified by geographical concentration, kinship patterns, cultural distinctiveness, physical differences, religious affiliation, and common history. The final criterion is self-conscious. That is, ethnic groups are self-conscious populations and see themselves as distinct.[11]

The Role of Religion

Navajo religion has a key role in distinguishing Navajos from other groups. Traditional Navajo religion has experienced profound changes in the course of Navajo history, yet it continues to serve as a vital element in Navajo identity. However, other religions have gained a powerful presence among Navajos. Pavlik estimates that the **Native American Church** is today the most popular religion on the reservation. In part this is because it often blends aspects of traditional Navajo customs and beliefs with the Peyote ritual itself. He estimates that 60 percent of the Navajo population participates in Native American Church services.

Mormonism is another major force on the reservation, attracting some 20 percent of the Diné population into its fold. Christian evangelical sects also have converted a number of Navajo. But even those Navajos who worship in other ways often retain some core loyalty to the traditional Navajo belief system. In fact, "most Navajos are associated with more than one religion" with traditionalism and peyotism being the most common merger.[12]

Language and Identity

Many language specialists assert that, along with territory, the maintenance of Navajo language is one of the strongest adhesives welding Navajo cultural identity. The federal government attempted to crush the language along with other indigenous characteristics in the latter part of the nineteenth and through much of the twentieth centuries, through educational policies (e.g., boarding schools) designed to force the assimilation of Navajos into American society. In fact, by 1950 most Indian languages were no longer being learned by Indian children. As of 1993, approximately 150 Indian languages are still spoken, but many of these are virtually extinct, with less than 50 being spoken widely in tribal communities. The Navajo language survives, although there is genuine concern among Navajo speakers and linguists about its long term viability as fewer and fewer Navajos are speaking the language.

Although it is the most researched language of all aboriginal languages, it has only been in the last twenty years that native speakers have initiated important studies of the language in an effort to keep it alive. Bilingual and bicultural programs like those at Rough Rock, the language courses offered at Diné College, and laws enacted by the Navajo Nation

Council and the U.S. Congress, which in 1990 passed the Native American Languages Act, are aimed at empowering the Navajos and other indigenous speakers to become fluent in both written and spoken Navajo.

Traditions and Historical Experiences

The ancient and historical experiences of the Navajos of the First World to those living as we approach the twenty-first century culminated in a distinct identity. From their intertribal activities before the Europeans' arrival, to wars with the Spaniards and Mexicans, to their confinement by the United States military at Bosque Redondo in New Mexico, through the devastating stock reduction period of the 1930s and 1940s, to the land disputes with the Hopi Nation, today's Navajos recognize that their traditions and shared historical experiences also separate and distinguish them from all other racial/ethnic groups. Within these and many other collective experiences, there is a keen awareness and acceptance of the important role that change as well as continuity plays in the construction and perpetuation of Navajo identity. Unquestionably, the future cannot be predicted; but it is safe to say that the Navajos will still remain a distinct people even as they continue their cultural, religious, economic, and political interactions with other sovereigns.

Indigenous Values

These are the principles or standards on which a people determine what is valuable or important in life. When we speak of common values, essentially we are saying that many Navajo people, in general, view the world through a similar, though certainly not fixed, cultural prism. Values, then, are integrated throughout the entire Diné cultural system, and grow out of the group's past experiences. And while holding some values that are similar to those of other Indian groups, the Navajos also abide by a distinctive, if malleable, value system which is unlike any held by other tribes or groups.

For example, many Navajos acknowledge the importance of at least two major values. First, and most important, is the concept **K'e**, which loosely translates to solidarity, but which actually incorporates "many values that bind the individual to family, clan, Navajos in general, and all people. There are even relations and obligations to mountains, plants, animals, Mother Earth, and all of creation."[13] This value provides each Navajo with a desire to work in harmony with all others in society.

Second, the term **Hozho**, defines a value which is also related to kinship and relations. It has been translated as "there is a place for everything in this universe, and there is harmony when everything is in its place, working well with everything else."[14] These preeminent values overarch more specific principles like clan relations, harmony, traditional leadership, taking care of others, and respecting the sovereignty and integrity of other Navajos, to name but a few.

The Political Side of Navajo Identity

Historically there has been little dispute from non-Indians that tribal citizens constitute separate cultural groupings. In fact, much of federal Indian policy was built on the idea that this cultural differentness had to be erased. Disputes have arisen, however, when tribal nations were treated "differently" in a political and legal sense by the federal government in such areas as treaty rights to hunt and fish, liquor laws, taxation exemptions, Indian preference in employment, and so forth.

With regard to Indian preference (hiring policy which gives qualified Indian applicants preference over qualified non-Indian applicants), for example, the distinctive treatment of Indian people as unique political entities rather than as racial congregations was at issue in *Morton v. Mancari* (1974). The United States Supreme Court reversed a lower court's ruling which had held that Indian preference regulations differentiating Indians from others violated the equal protection principle of the Fifth Amendment at that time. The Court unanimously supported the Bureau of Indian Affairs' Indian preference policy, and reaffirmed the separate legal status of Indian tribes as political bodies. The Court threw out the charge that the Bureau's Indian preference policy was racially discriminatory and instead concluded that:

> Indeed, it is not even a "racial" preference. Rather it is an employment criterion reasonably designed to further the cause of Indian self-government and to make BIA more responsive to the needs of the constituent groups. ... The preference, as applied is granted to Indians not as a discrete racial group but, rather, as members of quasi-sovereign tribal entities whose lives and activities are governed by the BIA in a unique fashion.

As distinct political sovereigns, tribal nations are entitled to exercise all those sovereign powers not specifically taken away by federal government or ceded by the tribe to the United States. Inherent political powers of Indian tribes include the power to tax, determine membership, establish their own government, regulate domestic relations of members, prescribe rules of inheritance, regulate property within the jurisdiction of the tribe, and administer justice. Of this abbreviated list, the most fundamental right of Indian people is that of *self-government*. This right to be self-governing, to be and act sovereign, is arguably the most important distinction between tribal nations and other racial/ethnic groups within the United States. No other racial, cultural, ethnic, or linguistic group in the United States can claim such a separate political status.[15] The Navajo Nation, therefore, is a political force wielding a substantial amount of both inherent and delegated political authority.

Tribal self-government is not new or revolutionary. All tribal nations governed themselves long before Europeans came to the Americas. Felix Cohen reminded us to consider how Indian self-government undermined colonial patterns of feudalism, landlordism, and serfdom, economic monopoly and special privilege, divine right of kings, and religious intolerance. As he noted further:

> It was not only Franklin and Jefferson who went to school with Indian teachers, like the Iroquois statesman Canasatego, to learn the ways of federal union and democracy. It was no less the great political thinkers of Europe, in the years following the discovery of the New World, who undermined ancient dogmas when they saw spread before them on the panorama of the Western Hemisphere new societies in which liberty, equality, and fraternity were more perfectly realized than they were realized in contemporary Europe, societies in which government drew its just powers from the consent of the governed. To Vitoria, Grotius, Locke, Montaigne, Montesquieu, Voltaire, and Rousseau, Indian liberty and self-government provided a new polestar in political thinking.[16]

In fact, there is a good deal of recent literature tracing the influence of indigenous democratic values like checks and balances and federalism on the American founders' attitudes prior to the drafting of the U.S. Constitution.[17] The U.S. Senate has also recently recognized Indian influence on American democracy. In 1987 Senate Concurrent Resolution 76 acknowledged the historical debt which this Republic of the United States of America owes to the Iroquois Confederacy and other Indian nations for their demonstration of enlightened, democratic principles of government and their example of a free association of independent Indian nations.

The history of tribal self-government and sovereignty forms the basis for the exercise of modern governmental powers. A tribe's right to govern its members and territory is derived from its preexisting sovereignty which has, of necessity, been modified because of the tribe's unequal political relationship with the federal government. The United States, of course, by signing treaties with tribes which recognized their political, cultural, and territorial rights, including the Navajo, by definition voluntarily limited its exercise of sovereignty as well. Sovereignty, in other words, is not absolute and no nation, state, or other polity is completely sovereign since every government faces limitations of various kinds, whether military, financial, or political.

The federal Constitution, congressional laws, treaties and agreements, court cases and administrative actions all recognize tribal self-government. We have now discussed the all-important concept of self-government; but what are some of the key components that distinguish tribes from other ethnic and minority groups and as political entities?

A Distinctive People

A political entity must have an identifiable population. A tribal member, which is the equivalent phrase to a political citizen of another nation, is a person who owes allegiance to, and in turn receives protection from, a nation. This membership/citizenship entails a dynamic relationship between a person and his/her nation. Broadly, membership/citizenship involves rules of what a person might do (e.g., vote), must do (e.g., pay taxes), and can refuse to do (swear allegiance). The concept also involves specific benefits—entitlements (e.g., royalty payments based on coal extraction) that a member has right to expect from government. The situation of American Indians is complicated by the fact that members of federally-recognized tribes have citizenship in three polities—their tribal nation, the state they reside in, and the United States. This **triple citizenship** is unique to citizens in the fifty states.

The *Navajo Nation Code* includes membership provisions which describe who may be recognized as a citizen of the Navajo Nation. For example, Navajos living in the eastern checkerboard area of New Mexico and in the satellite communities of Ramah, Alamo and Cañoncito exhibit somewhat different cultural traits derived in part from their distinctive historical and geographical situation (these will be discussed later). And in the case of Cañoncito and Ramah Navajo, these two groups also have a semi-autonomous political existence apart from the rest of the Navajo Nation. These differences, however, do not exclude them from being regarded as members of the Navajo Nation.

The *Navajo Nation Code* declares that the membership of the Navajo Nation consists of the following persons: individuals of Navajo blood whose names appear on the official roll of the Nation maintained by the Bureau of Indian Affairs; any person of one-half Navajo blood who has not previously been enrolled as a member of the Nation; and finally, children born to any enrolled member of the tribe, so long as they are of at least "one-fourth degree Navajo blood."

A Defined Land Base

A political entity must also inhabit and exercise jurisdiction over a specific geographical area. This important facet of sovereignty need not be attached exclusively to large land areas. The Navajo Reservation, as noted earlier, is larger than a host of foreign nations and is larger than ten American states. Even the Hopi Reservation, which is much smaller than surrounding Navajo territory, still constitutes a greater geographical land mass than Cyprus, Luxembourg, Western Samoa and Singapore, all of which are regarded as nations by the international community. There are, of course, many tribal nations in the United States who inhabit much smaller land bases, with some having less than 100 acres. And there are a few tribes who have no land base whatsoever.

The *Navajo Nation Code* describes the territorial limits of the Navajo Reservation. This is based on the treaties, executive orders, land exchanges, judicial rulings, and federal laws that have established, diminished, and more frequently expanded the Nation's land base. These geographical limits are critical because tribal laws govern the activities of the Navajo people and, for some purposes, non-Navajo residents as well, within the boundaries of tribal land. The breadth and continuity of Navajo territory has been a vitally important variable in the Navajo people's generally successful effort to remain politically independent.

Before European intrusion, the Navajo people occupied an immense homeland within the confines of sacred mountains and pristine rivers. The Treaty of 1868 limited Navajos to less than one-quarter of their original territory, but subsequent efforts by tribal leaders, supported by federal legislation, have enabled the Diné to regain much of their original territory. Of course, the issue of land acquisition or reacquisition has not been without difficulty as the conflicts with the surrounding states, the federal government, and the Hopi and San Juan Band of Southern Paiute can attest.

The significance of land, however, cannot be overestimated. In addition to playing a preeminent role in the political preservation of the Navajos culturally, land represents—as it does for all indigenous peoples—the spiritual as well as the economic and political foundation of their existence.

Governing Structures

A political entity must continuously maintain some form of government, or exercise some form of political influence or authority over its members.

The existence of a government is a prominent factor separating a political group from a cultural group. Group members delegate some of their inherent political sovereignty to those organs and agents of government which reflect legal sovereignty for the enactment and enforcement of laws which the people agree to obey. The present Navajo National government, as outlined in the *Navajo Nation Code* is recognized by other governments as the institutional manifestation of the sovereignty of the Navajo people, though as we have shown and will discuss later, the Navajo people themselves have not yet formally acted to create or ratify the current structure of Navajo government.

Traditional Diné government, to be discussed in Chapter 4, was vastly different from today's form of government. In basic respects, it was more representative and, therefore, more effective in handling societal problems when they arose. By the 1890s these traditional governing structures had been stripped of much of their authority by United States Indian agent tactics and Anglo education and missionary efforts. Nevertheless, traditional Diné governmental structures and values quietly continued to serve as an important backdrop for future generations of Navajo leaders.

For instance, the Chapter houses and the first Business (later Tribal) Council, both established in the 1920s, elected leaders who were generally recognized and respected by their home communities. Over the last seventy years many additional changes in the structure of Navajo government have occurred. The Navajo Nation today is politically more unified that in the recent past, even though many controversies persist.

Sovereignty

Sovereignty is a very old idea, once used to describe both the power and arbitrary nature of the deity by Near East peoples. Originally it was a theological term that was borrowed by European political philosophers following the Reformation and was used to characterize the king as head of state. These leaders, at least theoretically, were to personify the *will of the people.* Of course, many kings and queens became tyrants who dominated their people. By the seventeenth and eighteenth centuries sovereignty had come to be viewed as an absolutist concept: As vesting undivided and unlimited power in the Crown by divine right. It was, in other words, "the absolute power of a nation to determine its own course of action with respect to other nations."

In fact, the American political founders, after the Revolution, wanted at all cost to avoid the establishment of such unlimited power and this is why governmental power in the American system of democracy was divided into three branches. This division of authority created an effective system of checks and balances between the branches so that no one branch or any single person could gain absolute power. This also explains the federal system of government in the United States, with sovereignty being split to an extent between the federal and state governments.

The United States, in other words, is a *delegated sovereign* power. It is not, and has never been, an absolute power, just as no other state is an absolute power today. All nations and all states are dependent, to some extent, on other nations whether for trade, protection, or services.

As mentioned above, legal sovereignty is vested in American institutions of governance and the agents who operate those organs. Political sovereignty, by contrast, rests in the American people and it is "the people" who cooperate to create the government. This is evident in the first and most important sentence of the U.S. Constitution:

> We the People of the United States, in order to form a more perfect union, establish justice, insure domestic tranquility, provide for the common defence, promote the general welfare, and secure the blessings of liberty to ourselves and our posterity, do ordain and establish this Constitution for the United States of America.

Thus, from an American perspective, sovereignty entails a distinct people within defined territorial limits. "It connotes," says Wilkinson, "legal competence rather than absolute power" and means "the power of a people to make governmental arrangements to protect and limit personal liberty by social control."[18] In other words, sovereignty is a way of differentiating the creation of a government from a business or voluntary organization.

Tribal Sovereignty

This important concept has certain similarities with the way it is defined in international or domestic law: that is, it has, first of all, a legal dimension. We could define it thus: **Tribal sovereignty** is the relative independence of a tribe combined with the right and power of regulating its internal affairs without undue foreign dictation. Such powers include, but are not limited to, the ability to make laws, to execute and apply them, and to impose and collect taxes. This is expressed in Indian treaty relations with the United States and other nations (which confirms tribal *international status*); in tribal commercial, political, and social relations with the United States and the states (which confirms tribal *domestic status*); and in indigenous relations within their own borders (which confirms tribal *internal status*).

Tribal sovereignty, however, has another more distinctive dimension to it—a cultural/spiritual dimension. We could define this aspect of sovereignty this way: It is the intangible, spiritual, moral, and dynamic cultural force inherent in a given tribal community. This force empowers the tribe toward political, economic, and cultural integrity. It is the phychic glue that links a tribe to its territory, its environment, its neighbors, and entails the people's right to think and act freely and to meet their own needs as they see fit.

The African writer Frantz Fanon put it this way when describing his nation, Algeria, and her efforts to be freed from French colonial domination in the 1950s: "The African peoples were quick to realize that dignity and sovereignty were exact equivalents, and in fact, a free people living in dignity is a sovereign people."[19] This is a definition that seems most compatible with many tribal nations, including the Navajo Nation, in their efforts to be self-determining.

The inherent right of tribal sovereignty, while recognized throughout the colonial period in hundreds of treaties and policies, was first recognized by the U.S. Supreme Court in the seminal 1832 case, *Worcester v. Georgia*. The Court stated in part:

> The Cherokee Nation is a distinct community, occupying its own territory, with boundaries accurately described, in which the laws of Georgia can have no force, and which the citizens of Georgia have no right to enter but with the assent of the Cherokees themselves or in conformity with the treaties and the acts of Congress. The whole intercourse between the United States and this nation is by our Constitution and laws vested in the Government of the United States. ... In the management of their internal concerns the Indians are dependent on no power. They punish offenses under their own law, and in doing so they are responsible to no earthly tribunal. They make war and form treaties of peace.[20]

Some governments have been delegated certain powers. For instance, states "give" certain powers to city and town governments. These local governments must answer to the state and are subject to all state laws. But the United States did not delegate to tribes the right to be self-governing; tribes had this right from the moment their nations came into being, a time steeped in the primordial mist. Congress, at various times, has acted to limit the legal expression of certain tribal powers (e.g., tribes may not exercise criminal jurisdiction over fourteen specified "major" crimes—murder, rape, arson, etc.). It did not, however, create tribal powers so tribal sovereignty is not beholden to the federal and certainly not to state governments for its existence. It depends instead on the will of the tribal community's members.

Sovereignty, when used with reference to Indian tribes, can also be divided into two broad categories—internal and external. When speaking of *internal sovereignty* we are referring to a tribe's ability to make and enforce laws over its members, nonmembers to a lesser extent, and tribal territory. *External sovereignty,* on the other hand, refers to a government's right to deal with issues and government outside territorial boundaries. External sovereignty is evidenced most vividly in the many treaties Navajos signed with other tribes, Spain, Mexico, and the United States. Tribes have been described by the U.S. Supreme Court as only *quasi-sovereign* and *semi-independent,* no longer fully sovereign yet possessing certain attributes of sovereignty. However, no national or international law has ever extinguished the sovereign nature of America's Indian tribes. By this description, no sovereign in today's world, including the United States, is absolutely sovereign.

In Navajo society, the sovereignty issue has unique complications. It is, on the one hand, easy to state that the Navajo people are sovereign. And this they are, but only in a defacto sense. For the Navajo people have never formally acted in either the creation of their existing government or even in the ratification of the current governing structure. In effect, the Navajo Nation government can be said to lack core legitimacy because it lacks the express sanction of the people.

The Title II amendments of 1989 helped to dislodge the inordinate amount of power amassed in the executive branch and more clearly defined and delimited the powers of the legislature and the executive office. In addition, the amendments, in separating these two powers, also created an effective checks and balance system. Yet these changes have never been placed before the Navajo electorate for their approval.

Since the 1980s, the Government Reform Project has sponsored a number of public hearings, given presentations, and conducted several surveys on the subject of tribal government and the message they have received is that the Navajo people want a fully representative government that is responsible and accountable to the People. And while the Nation's governmental personnel are producing changes that are incrementally taking the Nation towards a more representative democracy, until the People themselves have had the opportunity to create or to at least sanction the current structure, it cannot be said that the Nation's government truly belongs to or is beholden to the People. Until such a development occurs, some Navajo will view the national government as an external, almost alien system to their lives—nothing more than a pipeline for material benefits that flow from the capitol to outlying areas when the right individuals are contacted.

What is the nature of governmental power wielded by the organs of the Navajo Nation government? What must be done before the government is deemed fully accountable to the Navajo people? What sovereign powers, if any, do Chapter governments exercise? What is the exact governmental status of townships, like Kayenta? Finally, have the Navajo clans retained any governmental authority or has their inherent power been effectively overridden by the Chapters or tribal delegates? What explicit steps can be taken to strengthen the legitimacy of the Navajo Nation government, the Chapters, the Townships? What needs to be done to inculcate more citizenship values so that Navajos feel that they are the sovereign the government is derived from? These are difficult but timely questions, and they and others will be explored throughout this text.

The Distinctive Tribal-Federal Relationship

Indian tribes are not parties to the United States Constitution or explicitly institutionalized as part of the federal system of governmental power; yet, similar to states, tribes do retain that degree of governmental sovereignty which they have not relinquished to the United States. The Constitution, in fact, mentions Indians three times. In two places Indians are excluded from official population counts for determining congressional representatives (Article I, Section 2, Clause 3) "... excluding Indians not taxed ..." and the Fourteenth Amendment, Section 2, which also refers to "Indians not taxed."

In the third instance, Indians, or rather tribes, are explicitly mentioned in the Commerce Clause (Article I, Section 8, Clause 3) which gives Congress power to "regulate Commerce with foreign nations ... States ... and with the Indian tribes." The Constitution specifies two other important sources of power which have been employed when dealing with tribes: the Treaty-making power and the power to make war and peace.

Tribes, in their relation to the United States, are similar to states in their situation vis-à-vis the federal government. In the Constitution, the states delegated certain powers to the federal government and retained other powers. The Tenth Amendment declares that "the powers not delegated to the United States by the Constitution, nor prohibited by it to the States, are reserved to the States respectively, or to the people." Similarly, Indian tribes, pursuant to treaties and agreements, relinquished certain powers to the federal government while retaining all others.

In 1924 a congressional law enfranchised all tribal members who had not received federal citizenship by then, and recognized that tribal members were also citizens of their own tribal nations. Later, as reluctant states extended the right to vote to Indians, the concept of tribal members as **treble citizens** was born. Tribal members are thus recognized as having three layers of rights and privileges.

Moreover, there are other basic sources of Indian law that confirm the distinctive relationship between tribal nations and the United States. Indian treaties, the trust relationship, and exclusive federal authority over Indian affairs are but three examples of principles which set Indian affairs apart. Each of these sources of authority has received the attention of scholars, policymakers, and others. We will, therefore, touch upon them only briefly.

The Treaty Relationship

A **treaty**, simply stated, is a contract between sovereign nations. Tribal nations entered into many treaty arrangements with other tribes long before the first European settlements. Many of the treaties between tribes and Europeans and early American negotiators followed Indian protocol and symbolism.[21] The process of treaties between tribes and foreign nations dates back to 1607. At least 175 treaties were concluded during the colonial period ending in 1776.

The Constitution authorizes the president, with the consent of two-thirds of the Senate, to enter into treaties on behalf of the United States. Treaties, according to the Constitution, are "the supreme law of the land." This means they are superior to state laws and constitutions and are equal and sometimes superior to congressional statues. The first ratified treaty between an Indian tribe and the United States was the treaty with the Delaware Nation on September 17, 1778. The last official ratified treaty, during the first wave of treaty making, was with the Nez Perce on August 13, 1868.

Until 1871 treaties were the principal method by which the federal government conducted its affairs with tribes. A total of 372 treaties were negotiated and ratified by the U.S. Senate before the process was changed in 1871. There are also an equally large number of treaties that were negotiated with tribes but for various reasons were never ratified by the Senate. The treaty procedure was modified in 1871 largely because the House of Representatives resented being excluded from the treaty-making process. Nevertheless, treaties, now named agreements, began anew in 1872. Congress continued to authorize and fund treaty commissions to visit reservations to seek land cessions and for other purposes. Congress ratified these treaties by incorporating their texts into congressional statutes. These treaty/agreements were made with tribes until 1911. Altogether, 73 agreements were negotiated.

Formal agreements were seldom negotiated from 1911 to 1950. But beginning in 1950 and continuing through the Alaskan Native Claims

TABLE 1
Navajo Treaties and Agreements

Spanish		
Date	*Place*	*Primary Purpose(s)*
1706	Santa Fe	Peace and alliance
1786	Rio Puerco River	Military alliance
May 12, 1805	Jemez Pueblo	Peace, trade, and alliance; exchange of prisoners
Aug. 21, 1819	Jemez Pueblo(?)	Peace, return of Navajo captives
Mexican		
Oct. 29, 1822	Zia Pueblo	Peace, trade, return of all white captives
Feb. 12, 1823	Paguate Pueblo	Peace, return of all white captives
Jan. 20, 1824	Jemez Pueblo	Peace
July 15, 1839	Jemez Pueblo	Peace, trade, and alliance; return of all white captives
May 8, 1841	Santo Domingo Pueblo	Peace, trade, return of all white captives
Mar. 23, 1844	Santo Domingo Pueblo	Peace, trade, return of all white captives
United States		
Nov. 22, 1846	Bear Springs (Ft. Wingate, NM)	Peace, trade, exchange of prisoners
May 20, 1848	Monte Del Cuyatana (Beautiful Mountain)	Peace, trade, return of all Navajo captives
*Sept. 9, 1849	Canyon de Chelly (Arizona)	Peace, trade, return of all Navajo captives
1851	Unknown	Unknown
July 18, 1855	Laguna Negra (Arizona)	Trade; established Navajo Reservation boundaries

TABLE 1 (continued)

United States		
Date	*Place*	*Primary Purpose(s)*
Nov. 20, 1858 (Armistice)	Ft. Defiance, Arizona	Peace
Dec. 25, 1858	Ft. Defiance, Arizona	Peace; established Navajo Reservation boundaries
Feb. 15, 1861	Ft. Fauntleroy, NM	Peace
**June 1, 1868	Ft. Sumner, NM	Peace; established Navajo Reservation boundaries

* Ratified by the Senate, Sept. 8, 1850; proclaimed by the President, September 24, 1850

** Ratified by the Senate, July 25, 1868; proclaimed by the President, August 12, 1868

Sources: J. Lee Correll, comp. *Through White Men's Eyes: A Contribution to Navajo History.* Window Rock, Arizona: Navajo Times Publishing Co., 1976

See also: Bill Acrey. *Navajo History: The Land and The People.* Shiprock, New Mexico: Rio Grande Press. Inc., 1979

Settlement Act of 1971, federal legislation depended on Indian approval, a key ingredient in a treaty relationship. Since 1971 negotiated settlements with tribes have taken the place of formal treaty making. But as Vine Deloria, Jr. has observed: "the settlement act is thus the modern equivalent of the old treaty proceedings."[22] Along with negotiated settlements, compacts are also used today to hammer out political arrangements between sovereigns. The Indian Child Welfare Act of 1978 and the Indian Gaming Regulatory Act of 1988 are two recent examples which authorize the negotiation of compact proceedings.

One of the most important doctrines protecting Indians and their treaty rights is the **reserved-rights doctrine**. In other words, while tribes ceded certain lands and other specific rights to the United States during treaties, anything not expressly ceded by the tribe is presumed to remain—is reserved—to the Indian nation. This doctrine often shields Indians against any implicit erosion of their rights and shatters the myth that the federal government "gave" Indians their lands and other powers. Treaties, in other words, are not the historical curiosities they are sometimes depicted. They have an ongoing symbolic and substantive significance and are still the most important device for creating and maintaining the unique political relationship between tribes and the United States.

The Navajo Nation entered into ten treaties with Spain and Mexico and nine with the United States. Of the nine Navajo/U.S. treaties, only the 1850 and 1868 documents were ratified by the Senate. (See Appendices C and D for copies of these documents.) The Navajo treaties confirm the international standing of the Nation, affirm their national sovereignty and right to self-government, provide a series of specific individual rights (e.g., right to hunt), and guarantee the nation and her members specific property rights as well (e.g., reservation lands).

A clear example of a specific treaty benefit involves education. Article 8 of the 1868 Navajo treaty states:

> In order to insure the civilization of the Indians entering this treaty, the necessity of education is admitted ... and it is hereby made the duty of the agent for said Indians to see that this stipulation is strictly complied with; and the United States agrees that, for every thirty children ... a house shall be provided, and a teacher competent to teach ... shall be furnished. ...

This article, like some others dealing with services or provisions, had a specified time limit. Negotiators for the United States stated that "the provision of this article (8) to continue for not less than ten years." In other words, if the federal government had provided the required number of schools and teachers by 1878 then legally the United States' obligation for this benefit would have terminated. The requisite number of schools and teachers were not constructed or hired, however, and even today this provision has not been fulfilled.

The Supreme Court of the United States has adopted certain rules which theoretically govern the interpretation of Indian treaties. There are three basic canons: (1) uncertainties in treaties must be resolved in the Indians' favor; (2) Indian treaties must be interpreted as the Indians would have understood them; and finally, (3) Indian treaties must be liberally construed in favor of the Indians. These principles form the basis for the Navajo Nation's argument that the federal government must still provide educational services and structures to the people.

And because tribal land and some other assets are "held in trust" for the tribes by the Department of the Interior, the purchases exchange or lease of tribal-trust property has unique aspects. The Secretary of the Interior, in his role as "trustee" occupies a prominent role which is discussed later in the book.

The Trust Relationship

The foundation of the indigenous/federal relationship is one of trust. From a tribal standpoint, the Indians trust that the United States will fulfill the legal and moral obligations entered into during the treaty-making period (obligations generally traded in exchange for tribal land). The federal government, the tribes believe, must honor this **trust relationship** and fulfill its treaty commitments.

Most commentators who write about this term suggest that in modern Indian law the trust relationship, although not constitutionally based and thus not enforceable against Congress, is a source of enforceable rights against the executive branch and has become a major weapon in the arsenal of Indian rights. The issue of enforceability, however, depends on which of the "three kinds of trust" the federal courts may be considering: the general trust, a limited or bare trust, or a full-blown fiduciary relationship.

A general trust is simply an acknowledgment of the historic relationship between tribal groups and the federal government, according to Nell Jessup Newton.[23] This is usually dated back to John Marshall's opinions in the *Cherokee Cases* of the early 1830s: *Cherokee Nation v. Georgia* (1831) and *Worcester v. Georgia* (1832). The general trust is also in evidence in *Seminole v. United States* (1942). In that case the Court said:

> This Court has recognized the distinctive obligation of trust incumbent upon the Government in its dealings with these dependent and sometimes exploited peoples. ... In carrying out its treaty obligations with the Indian tribes, the Government is something more than a mere contracting party. Under a humane and self-imposed policy which has found expression in many acts of Congress, and numerous decisions of this Court, it has charged itself with moral obligations of the highest responsibility and trust. Its conduct, as disclosed in the acts of those who represent it in dealings with the Indians, should therefore be judged by the most exacting fiduciary standards.[24]

The bare or limited variety, on the other hand, deals with a trust established for a narrow and limited purpose. An example of this would be the key provision of the General Allotment Act of 1887 which spelled out the actual allotting process. These subdivided lands, which were to be held in trust for 25 years, created a limited trust. The trust in this definition, is "limited to the original purpose for the statute, which is protecting Indian land from taxation and involuntary alienation because of failure to pay taxes or debts."[25] Finally, there is the so-called fiduciary relationship. This is the most comprehensive type of trust, even though there is usually nothing in a statute, policy document, or judicial opinion authorizing its establishment.

In Anglo-Saxon law there is a special relationship known as a "trust" in which one party agrees to perform certain legal duties for another. The person promising to perform such duties is the "trustee" and the person receiving the benefit of the trust is generally called the "beneficiary." Because the trustee exercises legal responsibilities on behalf of the beneficiary, the trustee is held to the highest legal and ethical standards, similar to the kinds of standards which traditional Diné government vested in the leader of a band or in a medicine man or healer.

The trust relationship between the United States and Indian peoples means simply that the United States must not legally or morally engage in actions which might injure Indian lives, rights, or resources. If the federal government, states, or private parties engage in such activities then the United States may be called into court and held accountable for this behavior.

Congressional Plenary Power in Indian Affairs

The ultimate source of federal power over Indian affairs lies in the United States Constitution. The most important constitutional power is the Commerce Clause. The Treaty Clause, the Property Clause, the War Powers Clause, and several other lesser known clauses are also important. Only Congress, because of the Commerce Clause, has been specifically empowered to deal with Indians; and consequently, both the executive and judicial branches have understood that Congress must take the lead in creating or modifying Indian policy.

Thus, the most important and accurate meaning of congressional **plenary power** is as *exclusive* authority. This is the definition Congress uses most frequently when enacting Indian-specific legislation such the Indian Reorganization Act of 1934 or when it enacts Indian preference laws that withstand reverse discrimination suits (*Morton v. Mancari*, 1974). This is an exclusively legislative power Congress may exercise in keeping with its policy of treating with tribes in a distinctively political manner or to provide a recognition of rights, like the American Indian Religious Freedom Resolution of 1978, that Indians have been deprived of because of their extraconstitutional standing.

Plenary also is an exercise of federal power which may preempt state law. Again, Congress's commerce power is an example, as is the treaty-making process, which precludes state involvement. Constitutional disclaimers that eleven western states had to include in their statehood measures and in their constitutions are evidence of federal **preemption**. Typically, these disclaimers consist of provisions in which the state declares that it will never attempt to tax Indian lands or property without both tribal and federal consent.

Finally, there is plenary meaning unlimited or absolute. This third definition is the most disturbing because it implies that the federal government can act without limitation. This violates the essence of constitutional democracy and the letter and spirit of the treaty relationship. Strangely, there is ample evidence in Indian law and policy of plenary power being applied by the legislative branch and the federal courts in all three ways—exclusive, preemptive, and unlimited/absolute.

When Congress is exercising plenary power as the voice of the federal government in its relations with tribes and is acting with the consent of the tribal people involved, it is exercising legitimate authority. Likewise, when Congress is acting in a plenary way to preempt state intrusion into Indian Country, it is properly exercising its authority. However, when Congress claims that it has complete and unqualified power over tribes, their rights, and resources, it is acting in an unconstitutional capacity and tribes must forcefully remind the government that its behavior violates the fundamental laws of the United States and the tribes.

The U.S. Congress and Indian Affairs

The Congress, under the Commerce Clause, has the principle constitutional responsibility for administering the federal government's affairs with indigenous nations, although the other two branches and the bureaucracy are also charged under the treaty relationship and trust doctrine with helping the nation fulfill its commitments to tribes.

Early on, Congress's primary role was in carrying out the obligations and executing of the powers outlined in the presidentially executed treaties. The second principle of congressional power, discussed earlier, is in the regulation of commerce with Indian tribes. Trade regulation was, of course, a vital power in the early days of the American Republic. And even though tribes do very little actual trading with the federal government today, the Commerce Clause is still the only explicit power granted to the federal government and remains extremely important.

As the lawmaking authority of the federal government, the Congress —divided into the House of Representatives and the Senate—beginning in the mid-1870s, began to introduce laws designed to assimilate individual Indians into the American polity and also introduced measures designed to force Western criminal law onto tribal nations. Laws like the Indian Appropriation rider of 1871 which transformed the treaty relationship; the Major Crimes Act of 1885 which imposed federal jurisdiction over certain criminal acts; and the General Allotment Act of 1887 which individualized Indian lands, were designed to force an American version of civilization onto tribal nations. Federal laws and policies have vacillated since this period, as we shall see in Chapter 3. Nevertheless, the role of Congress is crucial because tribes are keenly aware that it is to the political branches (both the Congress and the President) that they must look for proper enforcement of their vested extraconstitutional treaty-based (as tribes) or constitutionally-defined citizenship-based (as individual Indians) rights.

Congressional Committees

Congressional committees and subcommittees are at the heart of governance in the federal government (and state and tribal governments as well). The House and the Senate and the Navajo Nation government are divided into committees to develop and use expertise in specific areas. **Committees** prepare legislation for action by the respective houses and they also may conduct investigations. Most *standing* committees (permanent committees that specialize in a particular area of legislation) are divided into subcommittees which study legislation, hold hearings, and report their recommendations to the full committees. However, only the full committee can report legislation for action by the entire legislature.

A number of congressional committees—*standing, select* (a temporary committee created for a specific purpose), *joint* (a committee made up of members of both the House and Senate), and *conference* (a temporary committee, created to work out the difference between House and Senate bills) committees—and subcommittees, have operated over the years in matters involving war, trade, treaties, boundaries, and general Indian-White intercourse. At the present time, the two most important committees in Congress are the Senate's Committee on Indian Affairs (a full standing committee) and the House Committee on Natural Resources which has a Subcommittee on Native American Affairs. The Senate Committee on Indian Affairs is the authorizing committee for programs of the Bureau of Indian Affairs, the Indian Health Service, the Administration for Native Americans in the Department of Health and Human Services, and the Office of Indian Education in the Department of Education. Furthermore, the Committee has oversight responsibility for operation of programs in all other federal agencies with programs affecting Indians, including the Indian Housing program of the Department of Housing and Urban Development.

These responsibilities dovetail with matters relating to tribal and individual lands, the federal government's trust responsibilities, Indian education, health, Indian claims, natural resources, and so on. In effect, the Senate Indian committee and House subcommittee are charged with an enormous task: the oversight of Congress's continuing historical, constitutional, and legislative responsibilities for all 500+ tribes.

The U.S. President and Indian Affairs

The American president has been compared to an elective monarch, but very few kings or queens today exercise the same degree of authority as does the president of the United States. He is traditionally accorded the unofficial designation as chief of state. As such, the president is recognized as the symbolic embodiment of the United States and its citizens, and thus is accorded the same honors due a reigning sovereign. The president also performs many of the functions of a prime minister or premier in a parliamentary democracy.

Article II of the Constitution vests the executive power in the president. Thus, the president is, first and foremost, the chief executive of the government. He presides over the cabinet and manages the executive branch. He is also the commander-in-chief of the armed forces. The Constitution also vests the president with the powers to make treaties and to appoint ambassadors, cabinet officers, and judges of federal courts, with the advice and consent of the Senate.

Although the president has no express constitutional responsibility for Indian tribes, he does have the primary role in conducting the nation's foreign affairs. And because Indian nations were considered "foreign" (in a political sense) to the United States during the early years of the Republic, the president's role in treaty making with Indian affairs was very important. The president, either by himself or with instructions from the Congress, "nominates treaty commissioners, supervises the preparation of treaty provisions, and submits the treaty for senatorial advice and consent prior to ratifying the treaty."[26]

The executive branch frequently provides the content of Indian programs and treaty rights, and the office of the president provides the symbolic and moral focus of Indian policy. This symbolic power along with the president's veto power and appointment authority—especially of supreme court justices and other federal judges, and cabinet officers— (like the Secretary of the Interior and the Assistant Secretary of Indian Affairs)—provides the president with a potent array of powers that can work both good and ill toward the sovereign rights of tribes.

The Secretary of the Interior and the Bureau of Indian Affairs

The Interior Department, created in 1849, was originally responsible for the westward migration of the American nation and the control of the distribution of public lands and resources. For much of its history it was a center of controversy over corruption and opportunism as well as the sometimes brutal control of indigenous peoples and the frequent mismanagement of their lands and natural resources.

Interior is home to a number of diverse and sometimes competitive agencies: Bureau of Land Management, Fish and Wildlife Service, Minerals Management Service, Bureau of Reclamation, National Park Service, Bureau of Mines, the U.S. Geological Survey, and, of course, the **Bureau of Indian Affairs**. Theoretically, it is also the nation's principal conservation agency, and it has responsibility for most of the nationally-owned public lands and natural resources, including over 500 million acres of federal land and trust responsibilities for approximately 50 million acres of Indian lands.

From 1786 to 1849 Indian affairs were handled by the War Department. In 1824, the Secretary of War, John C. Calhoun, created a Bureau of Indian Affairs in the War Department and gave its employees the duties of administering appropriations for treaty annuities, approving expense vouchers, managing funds designed to "civilize" Indians, and so forth. In 1832 Congress authorized an Office of Indian Affairs, also housed within the War Department; but the office was transferred to the Department of the Interior in 1849 in an effort to reduce the amount of armed conflict between tribes and the United States.

The bureau has performed a variety of sometimes devastating tasks toward indigenous peoples over its long history: from Indian Removal in the 1830s, to reservation imprisonment in the 1850s–1890s, to land allotment and forced assimilation from 1880s to the 1930s, to termination in the 1940s–1960s, to the present policies of Indian Self-Determination and Indian Self-Governance from the 1970s to the present.

The Bureau is the largest agency in the Interior Department, and employs over 13,000 employees, most of whom are Indian.

Currently, the BIA has a number of organizational goals:

1. to act as the principal agent of the United States in fulfilling the nation-to-nation relationship with tribes;
2. to carry out the responsibilities of the United States as trustee for property and moneys it holds in trust for recognized tribes and individual Indians;
3. to encourage and assist Indian and Alaska Native people to manage their own affairs under the trust relationship with the federal government;
4. to facilitate with maximum involvement of all indigenous people for the full development of their human and natural resource potential;
5. to mobilize all public and private aids to the advancement of recognized indigenous people for use by them; and

6. to promote self-determination by utilizing the skill and capabilities of indigenous people in the direction and management of programs for their benefit.

The bureau is led by the Assistant Secretary of Indian Affairs, formerly the Commissioner of Indian Affairs. This individual carries out the authority and responsibility of the Secretary of the Interior for activities related to Indians and Indian affairs. The Assistant Secretary is responsible for: (a) providing the Secretary with objective advice on Indian matters, (b) identifying and acting on issues affecting Indian policy programs, (c) establishing policy on Indian affairs, (d) acting as liaison between the Department of the Interior and other federal agencies that provide services to Indians, (e) representing the department in congressional trans-actions, and (f) exercising secretarial direction and supervision over the BIA.[27]

The bureau, as of 1993, had twelve regions or "area" offices. The area offices, and the smaller "agency" offices within the areas, have the majority of the bureau's direct contact with the tribe. The Navajo Nation, because of its vast land mass and large population, is the only tribe with its own area office, located in Window Rock, Arizona.

The BIA, despite some improvement in its handling of Indian affairs, still has a checkered record when it comes to fulfilling its primary role as the principal trust agent of the federal government. In fact, the bureau is currently being sued in a class action suit for gross mismanagement of Indian moneys.

The U.S. Supreme Court and Indian Affairs

Section 1 of Article III of the Constitution created "one Supreme Court." In the early years of the American republic, the federal judiciary was considered the weakest of the three branches of government because, according to Alexander Hamilton, it lacked the "strength of the sword or the purse" and had neither the "force nor will, but only judgment." The individual most responsible for changing this perception was Chief Justice John Marshall. In the pivotal case, *Marbury v. Madison* in 1803, the justices of the court held that the Constitution is "the fundamental and paramount law of the nation" and that "an act of the legislature repugnant to the constitution is void."

This decision established the supreme court's power of **judicial review**, that is, the power to declare congressional acts invalid if they violate the Constitution. With judicial review established, the power of the supreme court equalled, some say exceeded, that of the other branches. For with judicial review, the high court held the final word on the meaning of the Constitution. Later decisions expanded and clarified the judicial review power by ruling that the power of the courts encompasses:

1. The power to declare national, state, and local laws invalid if they run contrary to the Constitution
2. The supremacy of federal laws or treaties when they are in conflict with state or local laws
3. The role of the court as the final authority on what the Constitution means

Throughout its history, the Supreme Court (and to a lesser extent the federal courts of appeal and the U.S. district courts) has occupied a seminal role in elaborating on the distinctive status of tribes and the tribal/federal/state relationship. In fact, besides establishing the power of judicial review, the Supreme Court has also established some important doctrines in Indian law that still govern: the premise that *tribes are domestic-dependent nations,* that *Indian treaties are equal in stature to foreign treaties,* that *tribes have a political status higher than that of states,* and that *Indian land title is as "sacred as the fee title of white,"* to name a few.

It has also, by contrast, developed a number of legal doctrines that have been used at times to diminish the sovereign rights of tribes: the *doctrine of discovery,* the *doctrine of plenary power as absolute and unlimited,* the *idea of Indians as wards of the government,* the *political question doctrine* (which denied tribes a legal forum to test their complaints), and the *rule that the supreme court may impliedly abrogate Indian treaty rights.*

The Supreme Court, in short, has and continues to play a key and often contradictory role in recognizing or denying Indians their sovereign status. Moreover, it has sometimes confirmed and at other times taken away Indian property: it has shielded tribes from state governments and then has encouraged states to assume jurisdiction over Indian peoples and their lands.

A central issue in understanding the role of the judiciary in protecting or damaging the rights of Indian nations focuses on who the justices are. At the current time, the Supreme Court is occupied mostly by conservatives (with only a few moderates), who appear intent on wiping out many of the important legal strides tribal nations have made since the 1970s in such areas as hunting and fishing rights, tribal-state relations, criminal and civil jurisdiction, taxation, and sovereign immunity.

Tribal-State Relations

As we have seen, the political relationship between tribal nations and the federal government is outlined in the Commerce Clause of the Constitution. But the equally important relationship between Indian nations and the states is not outlined in the organic documents of the United States, state constitutions, or tribal constitutions or codes. It is generally accepted by all three sovereigns that the primary relationship for most tribes is at the federal level. In fact, one federal court declared in 1959 that tribes have "a status higher than that of states." This is because of the nation- to-nation relationship tribes enjoy with the federal government, rooted in treaties and trust. States, for their part, cannot enter into treaties, only nations may do that.

Moreover, most western states, including Arizona, New Mexico, and Utah, were required in their enabling acts (their statehood measures) and in their constitutions to forever disclaim (to deny) jurisdiction over Indian property and persons and swore they would never attempt to tax Indian lands held in trust for the Indians by the federal government. For example, the Arizona Constitution declares in Article XX, section 4 that:

> The people inhabiting this State do agree and declare that they forever disclaim all right and title to the unappropriated and ungranted lands lying within the boundaries thereof and to all lands lying within said boundaries owned or held by any Indian or Indian tribes, the right or title to which shall have been acquired through or from the United States or any prior sovereignty. ...

Despite the seeming clarity of this constitutional statement, states have tended to act in disregard of these important clauses. The history, therefore, of tribal-state relations has been contentious for a long time. Tribes and states today stand as mutual, if different, sovereigns. In the 34 states where there are federally-recognized tribes, the two sovereigns share contiguous lands, with every reservation or Indian community being surrounded by a state's border. Equally important, the two polities share common citizens. That is, tribal citizens who live within reservations enjoy tribal, state, and federal citizenship status, while non-Indian residents of reservations enjoy state and federal citizenship but are not tribal citizens.

Although sharing a level of citizenship and land masses, the two sovereigns have jealously guarded and been protective of their collective political, economic, and cultural resources. Tribes resent the states' constant attempts to tax and regulate their lands, wages, and industries, and are displeased that many states are still reluctant to concede the reality of tribal sovereignty and recognize tribal competence to handle increasing regulatory, judicial, and administrative duties. States, especially the western states, have always resented the fact that they lack basic jurisdiction over Indian lands and may not tax those territories without congressional and tribal consent.

Despite this intergovernmental tension, in some areas tribes and states have shown a greater willingness to work out mutually agreeable arrangements because of their shared citizenry and lands. Sovereignty accords, like the one discussed earlier between the Navajo Nation and the three governors, water agreements, land settlements, tax sharing, and public safety agreements are examples of positive action that can emerge when tribes and states agree to work together.

Nevertheless, tribal-state relations promise to remain a dynamic field, complicated by the overarching presence of the federal government which, on the one hand, has treaty and trust obligations to tribes, while on the other hand, is constitutionally connected to the states.

Conclusion

Various laws, court decisions, and actions by the executive branch have in some ways significantly modified the tribal-federal relationship. And, of course, the structures and functions of federal, state, and Navajo governments have evolved considerably as well. Despite these internal and external changes, the basic political relationship between these two sovereigns has remained largely intact. Tribal governments continue to function as cultural and political entities, although the treaty-agreement process has evolved to reflect the changes in the governments negotiating the agreements. But relationships like cultures, are constantly growing, and it is up to the Navajo people to remain vigilant in the protection of their rights as a sovereign people.

Key Terms

Acknowledgement	Federal Recognition
Band	Hozho
Blood Quantum	Judicial Review
Bureau of Indian Affairs	K'e
Committees	Nation
Ethnic Group	Native American Church

Plenary Power	Tribal Sovereignty
Preemption	Tribe
Race	Triple (Treble) Citizenship
Reserved-Rights Doctrine	Trust Relationship
Treaty	

Selected Readings

Berkey, Curtis. "Federal Administrative Power and Indian Sovereignty." *American Indian Journal,* Special Issue (1976), pp. 10–13.

Cohen, Felix S. *Handbook of Federal Indian Law.* Washington: Government Printing Office, 1942. An updating of this classic work is Felix S. Cohen's *Handbook of Federal Indian Law.* Charlottesville, Virginia: Michie, Bobbs-Merrill, 1982.

Cohen, Lucy, ed. *The Legal Conscience: Selected Papers of Felix S. Cohen.* New Haven: Yale University Press, 1960.

Deloria, Vine, Jr. "Self-Determination and the Concept of Sovereignty." *Economic Development in American Indian Reservations,* Development Series No. 1, (Albuquerque: University of New Mexico, 1979), pp. 22–28.

Grinde, Donald, Jr., and Bruce E. Johansen. *Exemplar of Liberty: Native America and the Evolution of Democracy* (Los Angeles: American Indian Studies Center, 1993).

Kickingbird, Kirk, Lynn Kickingbird and Charles Chibitty. *Indian Treaties,* Washington: Institute for the Development of Indian 1977.

Lyons, Oren and John Mohawk, eds. *Exiled in the Land of the Free: Democracy, Indian Nations, and the U.S. Constitution.* (Santa Fe, New Mexico: Clear Light Publishers, 1992).

Marger, Martin N. *Race and Ethnic Relations,* 2nd ed. (Belmont, California: Wadsworth Publishing Co., 1991).

Snipp, C. Matthew. *American Indians: First on the Land.* (New York: Russell Sage Foundation, 1991).

Weatherhead, L. R. "'What is an Indian Tribe?'—The Question of Tribal Existence." *American Indian Law Review,* Vol. 8 (1980), pp. 1–47.

Notes

1 Felix S. Cohen, *Handbook of Federal Indian Law.* Reprint ed. (Albuquerque, NM: University of New Mexico Press, 1972): 271.

2   See Jack Utter, *American Indians: Answers to Today's Questions* (Lake Ann, Mich: National Woodlands Publishing Co., 1993): 30–32.

3   The term "tribal entity" includes Indian tribes, bands, villages, communities, Pueblos, and Alaskan Natives.

4   Lowell W. Barrington, "Nation" and "Nationalism:" The Misuse of Key Concepts in Political Science," *Political Science & Politics,* vol. 30, no. 4 (December 1997): 713.

5   Brunei Darussalam, population 369,000 in 1992; Kiribati, population 74,000 in 1992; Liechtenstein, population 28,642 in 1992; Luxembourg, population 392,000 in 1992; the Marshall Islands, population 50,000 in 1992; Monaco, population 29,712 in 1992; Nauru, population 9,460 in 1992; and the Vatican City, population 802 in 1992.

6   Edward Spicer, *The Cycles of Conquest* (Tucson: University of Arizona Press, 1967): 385.

7   See, e.g., Vine Deloria, Jr., *Red Earth, White Lies: Native Americans and the Myth of Scientific Fact* (New York: Scribner, 1995).

8   Martin N. Marger, *Race and Ethnic Relations,* 2nd ed. (Belmont, CA: Wadsworth Publishing Company, 1991): 18–25.

9   Pierre L. van den Berghe, *Race and Racism: A Comparative Perspective* (New York: John Wiley and Sons, Inc., 1967).

10   C. Matt Snipp, *American Indians: First on this Land* (New York: Russell Sage Foundation, 1991): 32.

11   Stephen Cornell and Douglas Hartmann, *Ethnicity and Race: Making Identities in a Changing World* (New York: Pine Forge Press, 1998): 19.

12   Steve Pavlik, "Of Saints and Lamanites: An Analysis of Navajo Mormonism," *Wicazo Sa Review,* vol. 8, no. 1 (Spring 1992): 21–30.

13   Tso, "Moral Principles," p. 17.

14   Ibid.

15   The only exception to this would be the Commonwealth of Puerto Rico and her citizens. Like American Indians, Puerto Ricans were conferred U.S. citizenship by federal law (Indians in 1924; Puerto Ricans in 1917); like American Indian nations, Puerto Rico and her citizens are subject to the plenary power of Congress; like American Indians much of Puerto Rico's inherent sovereign powers have been appropriated by the federal government which exercises jurisdiction over communications, labor relations, postal services, and controls all matters relating to foreign affairs and military defence. There are, of course, some important differences as well. Puerto Ricans residing in the Commonwealth cannot vote for the president of the United States while American Indians may exercise this right. Puerto Rico has a nonvoting Resident Commissioner who sits in the House of Representatives. This person can vote in congressional committees, but cannot cast a final vote on legislative proposals in the House. American Indian tribes have no direct

representation whatsoever in the House or Senate. Finally, it is problematic whether the Puerto Rican Constitution of 1952 has the status of a treaty. Most tribes, as discussed earlier, signed at least one or more treaties with the federal government and the process under a different name is still going on today.

16 "Indian Self-Government," in Lucy Cohen, ed. *The Legal Conscience: Selected Papers of Felix S. Cohen.* (New Haven: Yale University Press, 1960): 305–306.

17 See, e.g., Bruce E. Johansen, *Forgotten Founders: How the American Indian Helped Shape Democracy* (Boston: Harvard Common Press, 1982); and Donald A. Grinde, Jr. and Bruce E. Johansen, *Exemplar of Liberty: Native America and the Evolution of Democracy* (Los Angeles: American Indian Studies Center, 1991).

18 Charles S. Wilkinson, *American Indians, Time, and the Law: Native Societies in a Modern Constitutional Democracy.* (New Haven: Yale University Press, 1987): 54–55.

19 Frantz Fanon, *The Wretched of the Earth.* (New York: Grove Weidenfeld, 1991). Originally published in 1963.

20 31 U.S. (6 Pet.) 515, 561, 581.

21 Francis Jennings, ed., *The History and Culture of Iroquois Diplomacy: An Interdisciplinary Guide to the Treaties of the Six Nations and Their League.* (Syracuse: Syracuse University Press, 1985).

22 Deloria, "Treaties," in Mary B. Davis, *Native America in the Twentieth Century: An Encyclopedia.* (New York: Garland Publishing Co., 1996): 646–647.

23 Nell Jessup Newton, "Rethinking the Trust Doctrine in Federal Indian Law," *American University Law Review,* vol. 98 (1992): 422–440.

24 316 U.S. 286, 296–297 (1942).

25 Newton, "Rethinking the Trust," p. 802.

26 Vine Deloria, Jr., "The Application of the Constitution to American Indians," in Oren Lyons and John Mohawk, eds. *Exiled in the Land of the Free.* (Santa Fe: Clear Light Publishers, 1992): 285.

27 The United States Government Manual, 1991/92 (Washington, DC: Government Printing Office, 1991): 338–360.

Chapter 2

Governmental Structure:
Its Form and Function

Outline   Introduction

What Is Government?

What Are Politics and Political Science?

Why the Need for Government?

Who Has the Power in Government?

Ideology Within American Politics

Three Principal Functions of Government

Types of Governing Structures

What Is Democracy?

Division of Governing Functions

Conclusion

Introduction

Navajo society has always had governing structures. Like the federal government, the form and function of Navajo government has been modified on occasion. Although the federal government and Navajo government are very different, they also share some important features. This chapter explains the basic principles of government, provides working definitions of key concepts, and provides an overview of government structure.

What Is Government?

Government may be defined as the legitimate use of force within specific geographical boundaries to control human behavior. All governments, of necessity, require their citizens to give up some of their freedom as part of being governed. But why do individuals surrender some of their freedom to this control? Generally, we give up some freedom to obtain the benefits that government can provide. Broadly, government serves two major purposes: *maintaining order* (protecting the safety of the group) and *providing public goods* (education, sanitation, welfare). Some governments in recent years, including the United States, have also sporadically pursued a third goal: *promoting equality* (all citizens should have an equal claim on the political and economic rewards of society). Government may also be defined as the set of institutions which makes and enforces decisions. Any group or society that endures for any length of time creates some kind of government, although the form and makeup of government differ from place to place and group to group. A key factor of any government is its authority to make binding decisions for those it governs. The important word here is *authority*. A government's authority is its *power* to make binding decisions, to give commands as to how its decisions will be carried out, to take action to see that the decisions are implemented, and, if necessary, to enforce compliance with its decisions.

What Are Politics and Political Science?

The story of politics and political science is the story of the human species. **Politics** began when the first people, experiencing themselves as different individuals, tried to find a way to get along. In other words, politics is a social process characterized by activity involving rivalry and cooperation in the exercise of power and culminating in the making of decisions for a group.[1] Politics can also mean striving to share power or striving to influence the distribution of power, either among states, tribes, or groups within those two.

Political Science began when the first people, finding it difficult to live with one another, started to consider how they behaved when they acted together and how they might create a more comfortable and peaceful community.[2] In short, political science is the study of the way in which decisions are made for a society and why they are considered binding most of the time by most of the people.

The study of politics, therefore, is full of interesting questions. Who exercises political power and for what purposes? Why do people accept political authority? And what causes individuals and groups to act politically?

Why the Need for Government?

James Madison, one of the authors of *The Federalist Papers,*[3] described in Paper No. 14, some functions of politics and government. He stated:

> We have seen the necessity of the union, as our bulwark against foreign danger; as the conservator of peace among ourselves; as the guardian of commerce, and other common interests; as the only substitute for those military establishments which have subverted the liberties of the old world; and are the proper antidote for the diseases of faction, which have proved fatal to other popular governments, and of which alarming symptoms have been betrayed by our own.[4]

This statement reflects that politics and government have many functions including, but not limited to, maintaining order, resolving conflicts, achieving justice, and protecting people and resources. But each of these can be categorized under one of the three broad values mentioned earlier: order, freedom, and **equality**.

Compare Madison's statement with the rationale behind the existence of the ancient Navajo **Naachid**, which was a periodic tribal assembly of clan leaders—Naataanii—who would periodically meet to discuss issues of importance to Navajo people. Navajo oral informants tell us that the Naachid served political, governmental, and ceremonial purposes. The leaders exchanged views and arrived at decisions about such issues as intertribal relations, planting and harvesting, the choice of hunting areas, and raiding. The Naachid is discussed in more detail in Chapter 4.

Both the Naachid and U.S. Constitution carried out some similar functions. In other words, both American founding fathers and traditional Navajo clan leaders were interested in achieving and maintaining order and stability, and protecting the liberty and freedom of their citizens. The issue of equality, of course, is more problematic. The two nations differed, at least historically, in whether or not equality was a value that should be sought, especially on the issue of economic equality.

Navajos, like most indigenous peoples, believed strongly that redistributing income was a moral mandate and practiced give-aways often. Charity (voluntary giving to the poor) has a strong basis in Western traditions, but this is different from the moral/spiritual charge that tribal nations adhered to. In fact, one of the principal differences between traditional tribal cultures and those of Europeans/Americans centered on the fact that tribal governing structures generally reflected:

Religious values of reciprocity and harmony. The community and an individual's responsibility to the community were more important than the individual and his or her rights within society. A person's rights and privileges never exceeded that person's duties and responsibilities. Power came from the community and flowed upward to the leaders.[5]

Tribal governments, like those of the Naachid, were highly decentralized and democratic and were steeped in the tradition of rule by the people.

The moral equality of human beings, which was a cornerstone of traditional societies regardless of their other differences, meant that individuals were responsible for their own conduct. This primacy of individual conscience necessitated "a very pure form of democracy characterized by its lack of central authority and in which any collective action requires the consent of everyone affected—or at least the consensus of all their families."[6] In traditional tribal society, coercion or force was loathed—consent was the key.

Who Has the Power in Government?

The difference in power between government and its people—"the leaders and the led"—has created some tension in every society. Power may be used to promote the common good but it may also do serious harm. The concentrated power of government is capable of sending children to war, emptying cities of their people (as happened in Cambodia), misusing public resources, or enforcing racial segregation (as in South Africa, until recently). It is not surprising, then, that people in most political systems fear government even as they need it; for individually, the people are generally weak and government is generally stronger.

Here again, there are impressive differences between traditional tribal societies and European and Euro-American governments. Most Western nations rely on representation and majority rule which compromise individual integrity. Majoritarianism, thus, arises from the view that society is little more than a collection of selfish and highly competitive individuals and interest groups. In such a society consensus is virtually impossible to achieve, if it is even sought. Indigenous nations, on the other hand, rested on a sense of universal kinship—across time, space, and species.[7]

While Western peoples presume that political behavior is motivated by selfishness and greed—hence the need to have laws to protect the ruled from the rulers—indigenous peoples saw political leadership as a "burden upon the selfless, an obligation for the most capable, but never a reward for the greedy."[8] In the tribal context, political leaders were not unattached decisionmakers. Rather, they were to be coordinators, peacemakers, teachers, and comedians who were self-effacing, patient, and self-reliant. There was no room in traditional tribal government for individuals who sought power, because there was no power.

In countries striving to be democratic, the friction between the leaders and the led is especially striking. The United States has struggled to create traditions, institutions, and practices that allow for peaceful change. Euro-Americans firmly believe that people should control their own destinies. The democratic process makes the continued tension between political leaders and American citizens a central aspect of American political life. The structure of American government allows people to question and challenge authority. But the cost of this is that American citizens are constantly faced with the contrast between their ideal of peaceful popular control of government and the reality of disparate power.

Ideology Within American Politics

Political **ideology** is a concept used by political scientists to refer to the more or less consistent set of values that historically has been reflected in the political system: economic order, social goals, and moral values of a given society. It is, in other words, "the means by which the basic values held by a party, class, group, or individuals are articulated."[9] The term first arose during the French Revolution to refer to a school of thought, separate from religion, about how a government should be arranged. Today it generally means the philosophic belief of true believers of whatever credence.

The question of how far government should go in keeping order, providing services, or pursuing equality determines where individuals stand on an ideological spectrum. At one end are individuals who believe that government should do everything. At the other extreme are those who believe the government should not exist, or if it must exist, it should have a limited role.

The two dominant political ideologies in the United States are **liberal** and **conservative**. Historically, and to a lesser extent today, small segments of the American population follow libertarianism—political principle of persons who oppose all government action except that which is essential to protect life and property. And a small number of Americans identify themselves as supporters of socialism. **Socialism**, like communism (the doctrine of revolution based on the works of Karl Marx and Friedrich Engels that maintains that human history is a struggle between the exploiting and the exploited classes) centers on the government's role in the economy and is an economic system based on **Marxist** theory.

The scope of government from a socialistic perspective extends to the ownership or control of the basic industries (e.g., transportation, communication) that produce goods and services. Generally, Americans detest the symbol represented by the word socialism, yet they favor limited socialistic measures like Aid to Families with Dependent Children, the Tennessee Valley Authority, and other agencies which provide assistance to people in need.

Liberals

Individuals who consider themselves liberal tend to favor extensive governmental involvement in the economy and the provision of social services. They also take active roles in protecting the rights of women, minorities, the elderly, and the environment.

Conservatives

Individuals who believe that a government is best that governs least and that big government infringes on individual, personal, and economic rights are usually considered to be conservative. They support local and state action over federal action and believe fervently in free enterprise. Of course, these are broad and generalized definitions and surveys reveal that many individuals who refer to themselves as liberal, also hold some conservative views on issues and vice versa. For example, some persons are liberal on social issues (education, abortion, and **civil rights**), but quite conservative on economic issues (wage rates, taxes).

American Indians, according to the few studies available, are not strongly linked to either the Democratic (liberal) or Republican (conservative) party, but tend to lean toward the liberal side. There are certainly important differences between the 560 tribal entities.[10] For example, the Tohono O'Odham (formerly Papago Nation) since the 1950s, have consistently voted Democratic. And tribal nations in the upper midwest (Wisconsin, Minnesota, and North and South Dakota) between 1982 and 1992 also generally voted for Democratic candidates.

Navajos, on the other hand, over the last 40 years or so, "have shifted from Republican to Democratic and, during the Reagan years, slightly back to the Republican" at least in national elections.[11] At the state and local level, however, Navajos retain a strong Democratic preference. For example, a study on Navajo political attitudes and behavior conducted by the National Indian Youth Council in 1984, found that sixty-seven percent (67%)

of the respondents identified themselves as Democrats, eleven percent (11%) as Republican, eleven percent (11%) as Independent, ten percent (10%) had no preference, and one percent (1%) indicated "other" as their party.

Of those listing themselves as Democrats, fifty-one percent (51%) stated they were strong Democrats, compared to only twenty-one percent (21%) who identified themselves as strong Republicans. Better than one-half believed there was "some or a lot of difference" between the Republican and Democratic parties. There was also a similarity of political views between the respondents and their parents' generation.

Three Principal Functions of Government

Nearly all governments perform three distinct functions. Whether performed by one person or three or more branches, a government will normally exercise legislative, executive, and judicial functions.

Legislative

The legislative branch was envisioned by the founders of the American Republic as the most powerful branch of government. Why? Because they thought lawmaking was the most important function of a republican government. Legislators, members of a legislature elected to represent the interests or the voters of a specific constituency, enact laws under Article 1 of the U.S. Constitution. These measures are designed to organize the society and to establish principles for operating government, but may also establish principles of behavior which are applicable in particular situations.

Theoretically, Congress may only exercise **enumerated powers**, which means that Congress can only do what the **Constitution** assigns it to do expressly. Eighteen powers are enumerated in the Constitution. However, the *necessary and proper clause,* or the **elastic clause**, makes it possible for Congress to exercise *implied powers* (insinuated or suggested) that Congress says it must have in order to carry out its enumerated powers.

Legislative functions include the power to:

1. Make laws
2. Confirm executive appointments
3. Override executive veto
4. Impeach justice and judges
5. Create or eliminate courts

Executive

The executive branch is responsible for implementing the legislature's laws, and beyond that its role is more difficult to define than the other two branches. A basic definition of the executive function is "the carrying out of laws," but this task requires a comprehensive organization of institutions. Only a part of the idea of executing law involves direct application and enforcement. The executive branch also sets up and oversees systems which give force and meaning to a government's entire body of law. This involves executive leadership in continuous decision-making within the parameters set by the legislature. Executive power is also seen in the daily operations of administration.

Executive functions include the power to:

1. Veto legislation
2. Recommend legislation
3. Enforce laws
4. Set up and supervise institutions which implement laws
5. Determine policy
6. Grant pardons
7. Nominate judges

Judicial

The judicial branch has power to **review** the actions of the legislature to consider the propriety of these actions, according to law. The judiciary is empowered to:

1. Review and decide legislative acts
2. Review and decide executive actions
3. Determine the meaning of law where there are uncertainties or ambiguities

Types of Governing Structures

No two governments are exactly alike. Yet the following questions are helpful in determining the structure of a particular government:

1. Who and how many have ultimate authority?
2. How are the legislative, executive, and judicial branches related?

3. Are there subunits of government and how do they relate to the central government?

To better understand the distribution of governmental authority, it is useful to imagine all governments on a scale. At one end is an autocratic government—in which one person possesses all the power. At the other end of the spectrum is a pure democratic government. In a true democracy, power is located in all the people. The preceding examples of government are extremes; most contemporary governments fit somewhere between these two.

Many centuries ago, Aristotle classified governments into three broad categories: government by one person (monarchical), government by the few (aristocratic), and government by the many (democratic). This remains a useful classification system. Let's examine some of the variants on these three types.

Autocracy: A kind of government in which one person (autocrat) has supreme power. (Adolph Hitler, the infamous Nazi leader, is the foremost example; Joseph Stalin of the former Soviet Union; and Pol Pot of Cambodia)

Aristocracy: A government where a privileged minority rule, who are usually of inherited wealth and social position.

Theocracy: Literally, "the rule of a state by God." A government in which rulers are seen as deriving their authority directly from God. A theocratic government conducts its affairs according to religious doctrine. (certain Hopi villages and the Pueblo Nations of New Mexico)

Oligarchy: A form of government in which the ruling power belongs to a few persons who gained office by means of wealth, military power, or membership in a single political party. (contemporary China)

Plutocracy: Similar to oligarchy, but this type of government permits only a wealthy few to rule.[12]

Most residents of the United States believe that **democracy** is the only appropriate kind of government. Let us look briefly at what democracy is and how it works.

What Is Democracy?

Democracy is an ancient political term, derived from the Greek word *demokratia,* the root meaning of which is *demos* (people) and *kratos* (rule), or "rule by the people." The question, however, is who constitutes the people? Democracy is also a word used to describe at least three different political systems. In one system the government is said to be democratic if its decisions serve the "true interests" of the people, whether or not its people are directly involved in decision-making. This definition allows various authoritarian regimes, the former Soviet Union, China, Cuba, and other countries, to claim that they "democratic." The second way in which democracy is used describes those governments which closely mirror Aristotle's ideal of the "rule of the many." A government is democratic if all or most of its citizens participate directly (direct democracy) in either holding office or making policy. New England town meetings and Navajo Chapters, in an ideal sense, most closely resemble this ideal.

The third definition of democracy is the principle followed by most democratic nations, including the United States and, increasingly, the Navajo Nation, in part because direct democracy proved impractical. According to Joseph Schumpeter, "the democratic method is that institutional arrangement for arriving at political decisions in which individuals (i.e., leaders) acquire the power to decide by means of a competitive struggle for the people's vote." This method is often referred to as **representative democracy**, or indirect democracy. For representative government (**republicanism**—a government rooted in the consent of the governed) to work, there must be an opportunity for people to select their leadership by ballot. In turn this requires that individuals and parties vie for political office, that communication be free, and that voters be given a choice in determining leadership.

The American political system is based on the idea of balance between the legislative, executive, and judicial branches; between the state and federal governments (and increasingly, tribal governments); between the wants of the majority and the minority; and between the rights of the individual and the best interests of the nation as a whole.[13]

American democracy has a number of key characteristics which enable it to maintain some semblance of balance.

> **Popular Consent:** The idea that a government must draw its powers from the consent of the governed. This was also central to traditional Navajo society and to the drafters of the American Declaration of Independence. A citizen's willingness to vote or actively participate represents his or her consent to be governed.
>
> **Political Equality:** The idea that all votes should be counted and weighed equally.
>
> **Popular Sovereignty:** The right of the majority to govern itself. Political authority fundamentally rests with the people who have the

inherent power to create, modify, or terminate their governments. The notion that all legitimate governments draw their power from the people is found in the Declaration of Independence and the U.S. Constitution. At the current time, this concept is not fully relevant to the Navajo Nation because "the people" were not the creators of the Navajo government and have still not acted in a collective way to legitimate its existence.

Majority Rule: Even though the authority of leaders is limited, they still make decisions based upon certain criteria. In the event of disagreement, the theory of democracy provides that the will of the majority prevail. This provision is not always easy to follow or always desirable. Still, it offers a standard against which the legitimacy of governmental decisions may be judged. Protection of **minority rights** is also important as recognized by the U.S. Bill of Rights.

Individualism: Americans emphasize individual rights and responsibility more than most other nations. Individualism holds that the primary function of government is to enable the individual to achieve his or her highest level of development. The American emphasis on individual responsibility is strengthened by two beliefs: (1) Americans are skeptical of government power and question government's competence; and (2) Americans firmly believe that hard work and persistence pays off.[14]

Personal Liberty: **Liberty** is freedom. Freedom from government interference and freedom to pursue one's interests. Thus, this may be the most important characteristic of all. The Declaration of Independence declared that all individuals (at the time this only meant white propertied males) were entitled to the following unalienable rights: "life, liberty, and the pursuit of happiness." And the Preamble to the Constitution stated that securing "the blessings of liberty to ourselves and our posterity" was one of the primary motivations for the new republic. The protection of liberty is, of course, a key for Navajo government as well.

Checks and Balances: The notion that constitutional devices can prevent any power within a nation from becoming absolute by being balanced against, or checked by, another source of power within that same nation. Thomas Jefferson put it best when he stated that "the powers of government should be so divided and balanced among several bodies of magistracy, as that none could transcend their legal limits, without being effectively checked and restrained by the others." This separation of power, according to James Madison was "essential to the preservation of liberty." The Navajo

Nation finally achieved the legal establishment of checks and balances and separation of powers with the changes in government in the amendments to Title II in 1989. These will be discussed in Chapter 5.

Division of Governing Functions

When we examine the organization of government and performance of basic functions, we are looking at the process of governing, rather than who has authority to govern. A **presidential system** of government has some separation of powers. The chief executive is elected independently of the other branches for a fixed tenure. The executive is not connected to the legislature and does not wield greater power. Instead, each branch acts in a separate sphere. This system also includes certain checks and balances. This means that the three branches are not entirely disconnected. For example, the law sometimes provides for a presidential veto, but lawmakers may override this veto by a majority vote. In other words, each branch has certain ways to restrain the other two.

On the other hand, in a **parliamentary** (cabinet) **system** of government, the executive and the legislative functions are more connected. In this system the voters select the legislature, and these lawmakers then choose the executive (usually called the prime minister). The executive plays a role in drafting and passing legislation, but the executive must govern according to the desires of the legislature. Hence, there is no true separation of powers.

The Navajo Nation government, until the important structural changes in 1989, had elements of both of these systems. The then chairman and vice-chairman of the tribe were part of the Council and participated in lawmaking as in the parliamentary system; and yet, since 1938, those officers had been popularly elected, as in a presidential system. But as we will discuss later, this is no longer the case and today the Navajo Nation government has three fully separate yet connected branches of government with effective checks and balances built into the system.

Subunits of Government

Besides being separated according to function, governing power is often distributed among several bodies. If there is only one source of authority, this is known as a **unitary system**. When local governments exist in a unitary system, they are merely tools of a central government and have no independent powers. There is only one sovereign. France, Israel and South Africa are examples of unitary systems.

In a federal government, on the other hand, ultimate authority is shared among the national and state governments. This sharing of power is what is meant by the term **federalism**, and it characterizes a federal system or federation. The United States, Australia, Mexico, and India are examples of federal systems. The Hopi and many other tribes also follow this system. Although Navajo Chapters exercise some local governing functions, they are largely subordinate to the central government in Window Rock. The Navajo Nation Council's decision in 1998 to adopt the Local Governance Act which "addresses the governmental function of Chapters, improves the governmental structure and provides the opportunity for local Chapters to make decisions over local matters," signifies a significant step toward a more federal system of government. We will discuss this more in Chapter 10.

A third possible system is a **confederation**. In a confederated system, central government is actually subordinate to the local units. This organization is more loosely knit than a federal system. The local units set up an organization to handle matters of common concern without surrendering their autonomy. Examples of this system would be traditional Navajo government, the Iroquois Confederacy (still functioning), and the American colonies during the Articles of Confederation period.

Structure of the Legislature

The two types of legislature are unicameral and bicameral. A **bicameral** system is characterized by two separate houses. Each house is independent and its members are usually selected on a separate basis. The United States and every state (except Nebraska) have bicameral legislatures.

A **unicameral** system, as the name suggests, has only one legislative body. The Navajo Nation Council is a unicameral system. The advantages of a unicameral system include: greater economy and efficiency of operations; elimination of conference committees to hammer out policy differences; and more accurate accountability of elected representatives. But a one-house legislature also has certain disadvantages. For instance, special interests groups are able to concentrate their influence more easily; a single large geographical area could control the body; and finally, hasty legislation may be enacted because only one house makes and reviews the laws.

Conclusion

It is impossible to have a "perfect" government, and "democracy" is an elusive ideal. Technological innovations, industrial development, ethnic conflicts, environmental considerations, and many other factors influence the type of government we have. Whether governmental systems have the resilience and capacity to productively channel the inherent tension between leaders and citizens is an important consideration. A democratic government must prove that it is not **elitist**, that it can act decisively, and, most importantly, that it reflects the will of the people.

Key Terms

Aristocracy	Majority Rule
Autocracy	Marxist
Bicameral Legislature	Minority Rights
Checks and Balances	Naachid
Civil Rights	Oligarchy
Communism	Parliamentary System
Confederation	Personal Liberty
Conservative	Plutocracy
Constitution	Politics
Democracy	Political Equality
Elastic Clause	Political Science
Elitist	Popular Consent
Enumerated Powers	Popular Sovereignty
Equality	Presidential System
Federalism	Representative Democracy
Federalist Papers	Republicanism
Ideology	Socialism
Individualism	Theocracy
Judicial Review	Unicameral Legislature
Liberal	Unitary System
Liberty	

Selected Readings

Barsh, Russel. "The Nature and Spirit of North American Political Systems," *American Indian Quarterly* (Spring 1986): 181–198.

Deloria, Vine, Jr. and Clifford M. Lytle. *American Indians, American Justice.* (Austin: University of Texas Press, 1983).

Fiorina, Morris P. and Paul E. Peterson. *The New American Democracy.* (Boston: Allyn and Bacon, 1998).

Janda, Kenneth, Jeffrey M. Berry, and Jerry Goldman. *The Challenge of Democracy: Government in America.* 2nd ed. (Boston: Houghton Mifflin Company, 1994).

McClain, Paula D. and Joseph Stewart, Jr. *"Can We All Get Along?": Racial and Ethnic Minorities in American Politics.* (Boulder, Colorado: Westview Press, 1995).

O'Connor, Karen, and Larry J. Sabato. *The Essentials of American Government: Continuity and Change.* 3rd ed. (Boston: Allyn and Bacon, 1998).

Shafritz, Jay M. *The Dorsey Dictionary of American Government and Politics.* (Chicago: The Dorsey Press, 1988).

Notes

1 William Bluhm, *Theories of the Political System.* (Englewood Cliffs, New Jersey: Prentice-Hall, 1965): 5.

2 Gregory M. Scott and Stephen M. Garrison, *The Political Science Student Writer's Manual* (Englewood Cliffs, New Jersey: Prentice-Hall, 1995): 4.

3 A series of eighty-five essays written by Alexander Hamilton, James Madison, and John Jay (all using the name "Publius"), which were published in New York newspapers in 1787 to convince New Yorkers to adopt the newly proposed Constitution.

4 Clinton Rossiter, ed. *The Federalist Papers* (New York: New American Library, 1961): 99.

5 O'Brien, *American Indian Tribal Governments*, p. 14–15.

6 Russel Barsh, "The Nature and Spirit of North American Political Systems," *American Indian Quarterly* (Summer 1986): 184–185.

7 Ibid., p. 187.

8 Ibid., p. 191.

9 Karen O'Connor and Larry J. Sabato, *The Essentials of American Government: Continuity & Change,* 3rd ed. (Boston: Allyn & Bacon, 1998): 19.

10 Paula D. McClain and Joseph Stewart, Jr., *"Can We All Get Along?": Racial and Ethnic Minorities in American Politics.* (Boulder, Colorado: Westview Press, 1995): 72–73.

11 Ibid., p. 73.

12 Morris P. Fiorina and Paul E. Peterson, *The New American Democracy* (Boston: Allyn & Bacon, 1998): 13.

13 O'Connor and Sabato, *The Essentials of American Government,* p. 11.

14 Fiorina and Peterson, *The New American Democracy,* p. 119.

Chapter 3

Federal Indian Policy: An Historical Overview

Introduction

The 1990 United States Census, which allows for self-identification, tallied 1.9 million individuals who identified as Indian or Alaskan Native. This figure represents less than 1 percent of the total United States population of nearly 250 million. Indigenous nations constitute a unique branch of the human family and they possess and exhibit a wide variety of cultural expressions, political structures, and economic trajectories.

Indians inhabit every state of the union, though the largest number of American Indians live in four states—Oklahoma, California, Arizona, and New Mexico. Interestingly, only around one-fourth of all Indians live on one of the 278 Indian reservations or other lands described as Indian Country, which includes Alaska, Oklahoma, Pueblos, and California

53

Rancherias. Most reservations, not surprisingly, are concentrated in the western states. American Indians have also become much more urbanized over the years. In fact, by 1990, slightly more than 50 percent of all Indians lived in cities.[1]

Although the Indian population is younger than the United States population (average age of 22 versus 30) Indians have one of the lowest life-expectancy rates of any group in the United States; and the health of Indian people, in general, is worse than the United States population by almost every indicator. Heart disease, accidents frequently involving alcohol, and high suicide and homicide rates point to a population in physical trouble. Furthermore, Indians, with the exception of some Indian gaming tribes, still suffer from one of the highest rates of unemployment and fall below the national average in housing, income, and education. Although conditions for Indians have improved somewhat in recent years and tribes appear to have a renewed commitment to their reservation homelands, the underlying problems of governmental indifference and racial discrimination suggest that dramatic improvements in the near future remain unlikely.

American Indians are governed by a complicated and confusing network of laws and regulations. Indian peoples are subject, in varying degrees, to a myriad of tribal, state, and federal laws. In fact, law permeates tribal existence and no other ethnic or racial group is so heavily regulated. Besides the large number of treaties and agreements, well over 5,000 federal statutes, 2,000 federal court rulings, 523 United States Attorney General opinions, 629 legal texts, 141 tribal constitutions, 112 tribal charters, and innumerable congressional hearings and reports have only added complexity to the texture of Indian law.[2]

This massive amount of law is expanded further by applicable international laws, the federal Constitution, Title 25 of the U.S. Code (which contains all the permanent laws of the federal government applicable to Indian Affairs), Title 25 of the Code of Federal Regulations (which contains all the Bureau of Indian Affairs rules), and numerous opinions of the Solicitor of the Interior Department. The majority of the laws regulating Indian peoples' lives and resources have historical roots; hence, it is impossible to understand American Indians in a contemporary setting without first acquiring some knowledge of this history.

The ensuing historical examination is divided into separate periods of federal Indian **policy** but readers should understand that the chronological policy arrangement of material in this chapter is not meant to imply that Indian policy developments of the 1500s, 1600s, or even the 1800s, have ceased to have a bearing on contemporary tribal peoples and places. In fact, many historical Indian policies still are legally valid today and there is actually much more interplay and interconnectedness from the historical to the contemporary than we normally acknowledge. Nevertheless, I use this framework as a way to quickly get the reader up to speed on the major doctrines, events, and personalities that have influenced and shaped the current state of tribal-federal political affairs.

Indigenous Independence: 1492–Colonial Era

Bartolome de las Casas and Francisco de Vitoria, recognized today as two of the founders of international law, drafted documents in the sixteenth century which acknowledged that indigenous peoples had the right of sovereignty over their lands—by the "right of discovery," **colonial** powers gained only a claim against other contending colonial powers and not against the indigenous groups. In addition, they acknowledged that only tribal consent or military conquest in a "just war" could extinguish the Indians' title to their lands.[3]

This recognition of tribal sovereignty, although not entirely adopted by Europeans, nevertheless, established tribes as legitimate entities capable of dealing with European nations by treaty. In fact, most indigenous nations appear to have welcomed the arrival of the Europeans and allowed them to settle on their lands. Many treaties and agreements were then made between the tribes and various European regimes—Spanish, French, English, Dutch, Swiss—in which European goods were exchanged for Indian friendship and sometimes land. Vicious competition between European nations and between those nations and tribal nations over the control of trade and for land led to great conflicts, like the French and Indian War, which broke out in 1763.[4]

The role of Indian policy as one source of tension leading to the American Revolution was clearly fueled by such British policies as the **Royal Proclamation Line** of 1763. This proclamation prohibited white settlement beyond a certain line drawn through the Adirondack mountains.[5]

Early United States Independence: 1776–1828

With the colonists' defeat of the British, Indian tribes confronted the American settlers and their politicians directly. But the federal government could not afford wars with the tribes and realized that treaty-making was the most humane and economical approach to dealing with the tribes. In 1778, the federal government entered into its first ratified treaty with a tribal nation, the Delaware. Besides treaties, the United States enacted laws, such as the Indian Trade and Intercourse Act of 1790 (amended), designed to regulate traders and settlers and to protect Indian tribes from unscrupulous white businessmen and frontiersmen. Trading was an important aspect of federal Indian policy during this early period because the United States was still economically and militarily vulnerable to Spain and Great Britain and needed tribal support. As evidence of this, the United States built and maintained a number of trading houses from 1796 to 1822. These were designed to woo the Indian traders to the Americans by supplying them with material goods at a fair price for their furs. It was also during this era that Secretary of War, John C. Calhoun, created the Bureau of Indian Affairs (BIA) in the War Department in 1824.

The Supreme Court also got involved in Indian policy by handing down the powerful case, *Johnson v. McIntosh* in 1823. This case defined aboriginal title and in its discussion of the doctrine of discovery held that "discovery" gave title against all other European nations. Discovery also gave to the discoverer the exclusive right to extinguish Indian title either by "purchase or by conquest." Indians were recognized as being the rightful occupants of the land, but this occupancy title was considered inferior to the legal title the United States claimed.

Removal—Relocation—Reservation: 1828–1887

Federal Indian policy changed abruptly in 1828 when Andrew Jackson became president. Under Jackson's administration, **removal** of eastern Indian tribes to the West became reality. Congress, in 1830, enacted the Indian Removal Act which authorized the president to "negotiate" with eastern tribes for their relocation west of the Mississippi River.[6] Between 1832 and 1843 most of the eastern tribes had their lands reduced or were forced to sign removal treaties.

In 1832 Congress authorized the president to appoint a Commissioner of Indian Affairs (CIA) who was to have "the direction and management of all Indian affairs." Two years later, in 1834, Congress enacted two other important laws which formed the basis for future government dealings with tribes. The first act was the last of the series of previously temporary acts regulating "trade and intercourse" with tribes.[7] The second measure called for the organization of the Department of Indian Affairs within the War Department. These statutes are still legally relevant today because they set the tone of the U.S. political relationship with tribes.

In 1849 the control of Indian affairs was shifted from the War Department to the Department of the Interior. This was an impressive change and meant a transfer of Indian affairs from military to civilian control.

The Supreme Court was also active in this era and handed down a series of important rulings which have lingering effects on Indian rights. In the so-called Cherokee Cases, *Cherokee Nation v. Georgia* (1831) and *Worcester v. Georgia* (1832), the court held, respectively, that Indian nations were "domestic-dependent nations," and ruled that state law did not apply to Indian lands because the relationship between tribes and the United States was based on internationally-recognized treaties and that tribal sovereignty could not be subsumed by the states.

The **reservation** concept became the dominant federal policy toward Indian tribes beginning in the 1840s. Many tribes ceded much of their lands in exchange for the United States' guarantee of tribal sovereignty over the tribes' remaining lands; and the federal government, as trustee, promised to protect remaining tribal lands and provide other services and goods as well.

Congress began to enact a number of laws during the 1870s and 1880s in an effort to increase federal control over Indians and to force Indian assimilation into U.S. society. By 1887 more than 200 Indian schools were in operation, with an enrollment of over 14,000 Indian students. BIA agents assumed nearly dictatorial powers in Indian affairs.

With the dramatic decline of tribal military power due to diseases and wars, the United States embarked on additional policies designed to further curtail Indian sovereignty and reduce Indian lands. In a move reflecting the federal government's view of diminished tribal sovereignty, Congress, in 1871, prohibited further treaty-making with Indian tribes although, as we discussed in Chapter 1, treaties under different names (agreements, compacts), continued to be negotiated. Still, Congress' action signified that the United States would more often than not act in a unilateral way when dealing with tribal matters.

The first overt congressional intrusion into internal tribal sovereignty came in 1885, with the enactment of the **Major Crimes Act**.[8] This legislation gave federal courts jurisdiction over seven criminal categories on reservations: murder, manslaughter, rape, assault with intent to kill, arson, burglary, and larceny. Although the language of this act is ambiguous, most federal courts have interpreted it to grant exclusive jurisdiction to federal courts over the listed crimes. The constitutionality of this act was upheld in 1886 in *United States v. Kagama.* That devastating case held that Indians were "wards" of the nation and inaugurated the plenary power doctrine in which Congress was deemed to have unlimited and unreviewable authority over tribal peoples, their rights, and their remaining, although dwindling, natural resources.

Allotment and Assimilation: 1887–1921

By the 1880s, reform movements were spearheaded by religious and philanthropic groups who believed that the solution to the so-called "Indian problem" was to completely and quickly absorb tribal people into American society. The General Allotment Act[9] (also known as the Dawes Act), passed in 1887, authorized individual **allotment** of reservation lands to tribal citizens and granted citizenship to the allottee upon the termination of the trust status of the land. This act and its several amendments would be the primary weapon in the American arsenal of forced **assimilation** until 1934. Considering the period of enactment, it was, one could argue, a relatively humanitarian approach to the oddly named "Indian Problem." The consequences of the allotment policy and its legislative progeny, however, proved that despite its humanitarian aims, it was a policy that literally wiped out the bulk of the land base of many tribes.

The rationale behind this policy was that by insisting that individual Indians learn to farm and become private property holders, instead of following their communal lifestyle, the Indians would more easily be assimilated into Western values. Such an attitude, of course, presumed that Indians wanted to become farmers and more powerfully assumed that a communal, non-Christian lifestyle was inappropriate.

The allotment policy not only violated numerous treaty provisions, but bureau agents regularly refused to issue rations and other guaranteed tribal annuities to Indians who refused to farm their allotments. The effect of the allotment policy (and its amendments) was catastrophic. Indian landholdings were reduced from 138,000,000 acres in 1887 to 48,000,000 acres in 1934 when the forced allotment of Indian lands was terminated by the Indian Reorganization Act.[10]

Ironically, while most Indian reservations were allotted, the Navajo Reservation proper[11] was excluded from the act's provisions, and actually quadrupled in size during the course of the allotment years through a number of presidential executive orders and several congressional acts.[12] Two factors influenced this. First, the Navajos had several BIA agents who convinced Washington officials that to allot the Reservation would be disastrous because much of the reservation was not suitable for farming. And second, Navajos themselves were effective lobbyists who made numerous trips to Washington requesting additions to their land base which would support their pastoral lifestyle and rapidly expanding population.[13]

The rest of this period was characterized by federal efforts to enfranchise Indians (e.g., the Indian Citizenship Act of 1924), provide them with education, and expand the plenary power of Congress and the Interior Department over Indian people and reservation resources.

Reorganization and Limited Tribal Self-Rule: 1921–1945

The first major act of this period was the Snyder Act of 1921[14] which gave the Secretary of the Interior general authority to spend federal money for the "benefit, care, and assistance" of Indians throughout the United States. After the Senate was reorganized in 1921, a new period of Indian policy reform began to brew.

Criticism of federal Indian policy had finally convinced federal officials that a survey of the economic and social status of Indians was necessary. The Institute of Government Research in Washington, D.C. received authorization by the Interior Department to carry out this survey. The findings of the Institute, published in 1928 under the title, *The Problem of Indian Administration,* paved the way for some changes in Indian policy. Along with this report, the Preston-Engle Irrigation Report was also released that year. These reports compelled the Senate, in 1928, to provide for an exhaustive survey of conditions prevalent among Indians that was to be conducted by the Senate Committee on Indian Affairs. This survey continued until 1943 and constitutes a wealth of data on the state of Indian Country and Indian citizens during that period.

These changes jelled in 1933 with the presidential election of Franklin Roosevelt and his appointment of John Collier as CIA. Collier had been active in tribal affairs for over a decade and had a sincere respect for tribal cultures and traditions. This is evident in this quote: "No interference with Indian religious life or expression will hereafter be tolerated. The cultural history of Indians is in all respects to be considered equal to that of any non-Indian group."

On June 18, 1934, Congress enacted the Indian **Reorganization Act** (IRA), also known as the Wheeler-Howard Act.[15] The final version of this bill only vaguely resembled Collier's original forty-page measure; nevertheless, Collier still believed that it would "rehabilitate the Indian's economic life and give him a chance to develop the initiative destroyed by a century of oppression and paternalism."

This act formally prohibited the further allotment of Indian lands to individuals, prevented the transfer of tribal land to entities other than the tribe itself, and authorized the Secretary of the Interior to add lands to reservations or to create new reservations entirely. Tribes were also encouraged to adopt their own constitutions and by-laws, although the adopted constitutions were generally standardized and were based largely on the Anglo-American constitutional system. They also could incorporate by means of charters for the purpose of conducting business. Or they could do both. In addition, the IRA indefinitely extended existing trust periods and restrictions on the sale of Indian lands. It directed the Interior Secretary to issue conservation regulations to prevent erosion, deforestation, and overgrazing on Indian lands; authorized annual appropriations not to exceed 250,000 for education loans; and established affirmative action for Indians who wanted to work in the BIA. Finally, a ten million dollar revolving credit fund was set up that tribes could borrow from for economic development purposes.

Unlike prior laws, tribes had two years in which to vote on whether to accept the act's provisions. Within this two-year period, 181 tribes adopted the act, while 77 tribes, including the Navajo, rejected it. However, the Indian "revitalization" which Collier anticipated was never fully realized. Missionaries, land loss, and educational policies had taken their toll on Indian resources and identity. In addition, the advent of World War II led the federal government to reduce its commitment to genuine Indian economic rehabilitation, and tribal growth once again stagnated.

Congress also enacted the Johnson-O'Malley Act in 1934. This law provided for a measure of federal-state cooperation in Indian affairs, especially in education, by means of federal contracts with state or local governments for the operation of federally-funded Indian programs.

Termination: 1945–1961

World War II had a profound effect on the United States in general and tribes in particular. The House in 1944 adopted a resolution authorizing an investigation of Indian affairs. The results of this study, combined with those of the Senate report which had begun in 1928 and ended in 1943, indicated that the Congress was dissatisfied with the IRA and the BIA. Two years later Congress enacted a major policy, the Indian Claims Commission Act,[16] which set up a special commission before which Indian tribes who felt that their treaties or agreements had not been properly enforced could file claims for money damages against the United States. Some observers believe that one of the commission's primary functions was to settle Indian grievances in preparation for the **termination** sentiment that was growing.

In 1953 Congress adopted House Concurrent Resolution 108, not a law, but merely an expression of congressional desire which declared that it was Congress' intent to free "from Federal supervision and control" specified Indian tribes. This resolution called on the BIA to draw up lists of tribes who were deemed economically self-sufficient enough to do without federal services, and to "terminate" such tribes, not only with respect to federal services, but also with respect to federal recognition of tribal governments and these tribes' immunity from state taxation. Conservative

legislators believed termination was sound because it would not only reduce the federal budget but would also "free" Indians from government
restrictions. Liberals, on the other hand, thought it workable because it
would release Indians from the enormous weight of federal discriminatory
legislation.

The two largest tribes subjected to termination were the Menominee of
Wisconsin and the Klamath of Oregon. Termination proved to be a disaster
for both tribes. Altogether, there were about 109 termination cases affecting over 12,000 Indians between 1945 and 1960.[17]

Congress, seeking to further reduce its treaty and trust responsibilities to Indians, enacted **Public Law 280** in August of 1953.[18] This controversial legislation permitted five states—California, Nebraska, Minnesota
(except Red Lake), Oregon (except Warm Springs), Wisconsin (except
Menominee)—to assume full criminal and some civil jurisdiction over
Indian reservations and communities. In 1958 Alaska was given this power
over aboriginal peoples. This was controversial legislation because tribal
consent was not required and because prior to that time states had very
limited jurisdiction over Indian Country because of the doctrine of congressional exclusive power and tribal sovereignty. The result of Public Law 280
was that tribal authority was significantly diminished. Despite this action,
and somewhat remarkably, treaty-established Indian hunting and fishing
rights survived intact and states still could not tax tribal lands.

Fortunately, the Navajo Nation escaped both the termination policy and
Public Law 280, although under Public Law 280 the State of Arizona did
assume water and air pollution control over all land in the state, including Navajo territory. Regarding termination, federal officials believed the
Navajos were simply not ready for full "emancipation."

Public Law 280, at least initially, was viewed differently by officials,
however. When the Navajo-Hopi Long Range Rehabilitation Act[19] went to
President Truman for his signature in 1949, it contained a provision that
would have given Arizona civil and criminal jurisdiction over the Navajo
Reservation. A Navajo delegation rushed to Washington and convinced the
president that the Navajo Nation opposed this imposition. Truman subsequently vetoed the bill. The act was passed the following year minus the
jurisdictional language.

Tribal Self-Determination and Self-Governance: 1961–Present

By the early 1960s, the termination policy had lost much of its steam because many tribes and Indian and non-Indian organizations had rallied
against it. In fact, there were no more termination statutes enacted after

1964, although the BIA occasionally used the threat of termination to force certain tribes to go along with its policies. It was replaced by no sweeping policies, but there was gradual improvement in areas such as health, education, and tribal eligibility for certain new programs. The New Frontier and Great Society programs of the 1960s allowed Indians greater access to federal funds—not as citizens of distinctive political entities but as a segment of the "the poor" or impoverished in American society.

The first major piece of legislation of this period dealing with Indian matters, and one of the most important Indian laws ever enacted, was the **Indian Civil Rights Act** (ICRA) of 1968.[20] It was passed as part of a package of civil rights legislation (one title in an Omnibus Housing Act) and rushed through Congress in the wake of the assassination of Dr. Martin Luther King, Jr. One of the positive aspects of this act was that it amended Public Law 280 by preventing states from assuming jurisdiction over Indian Country without first obtaining tribal consent.

Most of the civil rights confirmed in the act are similar to the civil rights contained in the first ten amendments to the United States Constitution. In fact, it confers all of the fundamental rights outlined in the U.S. Bill of Rights except five. The ICRA does not prevent tribes from establishing a religion or from discriminating in voting based on race. Also, tribes are not required to convene a jury in civil trials, or in criminal matters, to issue grand jury indictments. And last, tribes are not required to appoint counsel for indigent defendants.

This was a powerful law because it was the first piece of federal legislation to impose specific, though modified, provisions of the U.S. Bill of Rights on the actions of tribal governments in relation to reservation residents. The act dramatically changed the substance and direction of tribal courts by forcing tribes to enforce and protect these modified civil liberties for all residents.

President Nixon, on July 8, 1970, articulated a new Indian policy, "self-Determination without termination," also known simply as Indian self-determination. This policy was legislatively outlined by Congress in the Indian Self-Determination and Education Assistance Act of 1975. The cornerstone of the new policy aimed at supporting the concept of tribal self-sufficiency while reaffirming the trust relationship. The self-determination act authorized the Secretary of the Interior and the Secretary of Health and Human Services to contract with tribal organizations for tribal operations and administration of specified federally-funded programs administered by these agencies.

Tribal **self-determination**, for a handful of tribes, evolved into tribal **self-governance** beginning in 1988.[21] In that year, Congress established the experimental Tribal Self-Governance Demonstration Project which was made permanent in October of 1994 with the passage of the Indian Self-Determination Act Amendments of 1994.[22] This act declared that "it is the policy of this title to permanently establish and implement tribal self-governance which is designed, among other things, to enable the United States to maintain and improve its unique and continuing relationship with, and responsibility to, Indian tribes, ... to ensure the continuation of the trust responsibility of the United States to Indian tribes and Indian individuals, ... [and] to permit an orderly transition from federal domination of programs and services to tribal communities."

The flip side of these beneficial policy directives is that as the United States became more socially and culturally conservative, reflected in the election and reelection of Ronald Reagan in the 1980s and more recently with the Republican takeover of Congress in 1994. Because of this conservative swing, combined with the conservative ideology which now dominates the Supreme Court under Chief Justice William Rehnquist's stewardship, tribal nations have suffered crippling blows to their sovereign powers and treaty rights. The rise of state's rights activism—with states clamoring to gain greater control over tribal resources—has also contributed to these impressive tribal losses. Indian gaming operations, while bringing in badly needed revenue for tribes, have also contributed to the intergovernmental tension among tribes, states, and the United States.

Conclusion

Any attempt to predict the future of federal Indian policy is both impossible and foolhardy. For as we have shown, the historic inconsistencies in federal Indian law and policy remain unpredictable and may be radically altered at any given moment. In the course of indigenous/non-indigenous interactions over the last several centuries, tribal nations have weathered a tremendous array of policies designed to destroy their religions, reduce their land bases, and end or dramatically diminish their sovereign powers. Until the fundamental rights and responsibilities of tribal nations as separate if linked political bodies are clarified (by tribes themselves and then by the states and the federal government) there can be no concrete steps forward in the important areas of economic revitalization, self-determination, and ultimately, sovereignty.

Key Terms

Allotment	Removal
Assimilation	Reorganization
Colonial	Reservation
Indian Civil Rights Act	Royal Proclamation Line
Major Crimes Act	Self-Determination
Policy	Self-Governance
Public Law 280	Termination

Selected Readings

Deloria, Vine, Jr. *The Nations Within: The Past and Future of American Indian Sovereignty.* (New York: Pantheon Books, 1984).

_____. *Behind the Trail of Broken Treaties: An Indian Declaration of Independence.* (New York: Delacorte Press, 1974).

Deloria, Vine, Jr. and Clifford M. Lytle. *American Indians, American Justice.* (Austin: University of Texas Press, 1983).

Otis, D. S. *The Dawes Act and the Allotment of Indian Lands,* Francis P. Prucha, ed. (Norman: University of Oklahoma Press, 1973).

Prucha, Francis Paul. *American Indian Policy in the Formative Years: The Indian Trade and Intercourse Acts, 1790–1834.* (Cambridge: Harvard University Press, 1962).

_____. *The Great Father: The United States Government and the American Indians.* 2 volumes. (Lincoln: University of Nebraska Press, 1984).

United States Commission of Civil Rights. *Indian Tribes: A Continuing Quest for Survival.* (Washington: Government Printing Office, 1981).

Notes

[1] Russell Thornton, "Population," in Mary B. Davis, ed. *Native America in the Twentieth Century: An Encyclopedia* (New York: Garland Publishing, 1996): 463.

[2] Deloria and Lytle, *American Indians, American Justice,* p. 10.

3 See Robert A. Williams, Jr. *The American Indian in Western Legal Thought* (New York: Oxford University Press, 1990) for a good accounting of the origins of Western legal thought as it evolved from 1500 to 1800.

4 See, e.g., Wilbur R. Jacobs, *Dispossessing the American Indian: Indians and Whites on the Colonial Frontier* (Norman: University of Oklahoma Press, 1985).

5 Ibid.

6 See Grant Foreman, *Indian Removal: The Emigration of the Five Civilized Tribes of Indians* (Norman: University of Oklahoma Press, 1932).

7 4 Stat. 729.

8 23 Stat. 385.

9 24 Stat. 388.

10 See Lawrence Kelly, *The Assault on Assimilation: John Collier and the Origins of Indian Policy Reform* (Albuquerque, New Mexico: University of New Mexico Press, 1983), for a good treatment of the key personalities and events leading to the IRA.

11 Some individual Navajos, mostly residing in the eastern checkerboard area of New Mexico, took advantage of a provision of the law which entitled any Indian who voluntarily established residence apart from their tribe to secure an allotment. Altogether some 762,749 acres are held as individual Navajo allotments.

12 Iverson, The Navajo Nation, pgs. 16–17.

13 J. Lee Correll and Alfred Dehiya, comps., *Anatomy of the Navajo Indian Reservation: How it Grew* (Window Rock, Arizona: Navajo Times Publishing Co., 1972).

14 42 Stat. 208.

15 48 Stat. 984.

16 60 Stat. 1049.

17 See, e.g., Donald Fixico, *Termination and Relocation: Federal Indian Policy, 1945–1960* (Albuquerque, New Mexico: University of New Mexico Press, 1986); and Larry W. Burt, Tribalism in Crisis: *Federal Indian Policy, 1953–1961* (Albuquerque, New Mexico: University of New Mexico, 1982). For a case study see Nicholas C. Peroff, *Menominee Drums: Tribal Termination and Restoration, 1954–1974* (Norman: University of Oklahoma Press, 1982).

18 67 Stat. 588.

19 A comprehensive measure which provided over 88 million dollars over ten years for such items as irrigation construction, industrial development, road construction, communications, health, education, etc.

20 82 Stat. 79, Title IV.

21 Originally, there were less than ten tribes who lobbied for tribal self-governance. As of 1996, more than 30 tribes have formal contracts with the federal government which provide them with a far greater measure of flexibility in what they can do with their funding than under the original self-determination contracts.

22 108 Stat. 4250.

Chapter 4

Navajo National Government: An Historical Overview

Introduction

As noted in the preceding chapters, government is essential for the maintenance of a stable society and there are a variety of governments in existence throughout the world. When Europeans first settled the North American continent, they brought their own political ideologies, values, biases, and notions of what constituted a "civilized" society. Most European states during the medieval period were led by monarchies and they functioned under a feudalistic system of political organization, where common men and women rendered service to overlords and received protection and land in return.

Spain and Great Britain often tried to impress upon tribal nations the merits of their governmental forms and many Indian leaders were dubbed "King," "General," or "Captain." This ethnocentric effort to appoint Indians to certain preconceived posts and to bestow titles upon them at times was used to foster factionalism among tribal people. At other times, it was simply the result of European ignorance regarding the strength, versatility, and merit of preexisting tribal political institutions.

Despite the attitudes and biases held by Europeans and later Euro-Americans, tribal nations, and for our purposes, the Navajo people, exercised governmental functions which maintained a stable and relatively homogenous society. Traditional Navajo government, as noted earlier, was quite different from feudalistic European states. It was a highly effective though not politically centralized form of government.

This chapter summarizes the history of Navajo governing institutions from the earliest recollections available to the twenty-first century. Pre-Spanish accounts of Navajo government are particularly relevant to the study of contemporary tribal government since, upon closer examination, it will become evident that many Navajos and some segments of Navajo National government still base at least some of their ideas and actions on traditional and historic forms of political mechanics, which are significantly different from those political systems operating in other tribes, in the states, and in the federal government.

Diné Traditional Government

From a Western European political perspective, the Navajo Nation was nonexistent as a representative political body until the 1920s. The Navajo people were, of course, cohesive in that they had a common linguistic and cultural heritage, lived within a well-defined territory, and referred to themselves as Diné. But their political organization, in general, did not extend beyond local bands which were led by headmen, or **Naataanii**. We will soon discuss a political/ceremonial/economic gathering known as the **Naachid** which did, in fact, wield a more regionalized sphere of influence, but it is important to remember that even this body had no coercive powers and apparently never represented *all* Navajos. To put it another way, before the arrival of the Americans in the nineteenth century, the Navajo people did without a tribal-wide representative government that resembled the governments of the United States or Western European countries.

The Naataanii (Headmen and Headwomen of Traditional Society)

The Navajo Origin Story contains the first specific reference to individuals regarded as leaders by Diné. These first **Naataanii** were selected by the *Diyin Diné'* (Holy People) to provide discipline to the people of the Third World. According to the story and contemporary oral accounts, as interpreted by Richard Van Valkenburgh, "[The] function of these leaders ... was directed toward the correction of behavior, the maintenance of certain moral injunctions, such as the prohibition of incest and adultery, as well as the enforcement of economic laws." The Naataanii also served as intermediaries between the Diné and the Diyin Diné'. When the Spanish arrived in the late 1500s, the fundamental political entity in Navajo society was the **natural community.** This collective unit of government was basically economic in nature, geographically determined, and distinct from other local units. Population figures for these communities vary, but the most informed accounts estimate that a natural community contained from ten to forty families. Each of these settlements was directed by a Naataanii, who received advice and counsel from **hastói** and **hataali.**[1] Internal matters, intertribal affairs, hunting, and food gathering were issues regularly addressed by this deliberative body of leaders.

The People recognized, as did other indigenous nations like the Cherokee and the Creek, the importance of having separate War and Peace leaders for the successful functioning of tribal harmony. Seldom did one person fill both offices. To attain the position of a War Naataanii, an individual needed extensive knowledge of one or more of the War Ways. Anyone who had acquired this ritual knowledge was eligible to serve as a War leader. These were ceremonies designed to bring about successful raids or counter-raids against outside forces. The Navajo attitude towards War leaders, according to Hill, was equivocal. That is to say, while these individuals were respected as great fighters, they were also frequently criticized. It was believed by some Navajo that War leaders were largely responsible for the defeat and imprisonment of Navajo at Bosque Redondo in the 1860s.[2]

A Peace Naataanii, by contrast, was chosen or elected if the person had knowledge of the Blessingway Ceremony, and only if he or she had excellent moral character, great oratorical abilities, and charisma. Also, the individual had to possess the ability to serve in both the sacred and day-to-day aspects of Navajo life and culture.

According to Hill, the Navajo community members met to select these Naataanii. He noted that:

> In this the women had as much voice as the men. Usually the choice was nearly unanimous. If two men appeared to have nearly equal capabilities, they might be asked to make speeches in order to determine

the selection. Once a decision had been reached the man was notified and the induction ritual performed.[3]

In effect, the selection of a Naataanii followed a democratic process involving the adult population of a natural community. What follows is one account of the election process:

> The selection of a new headman for the group generally followed a set pattern. Following the death of the previous headman, the people waited from one to three months before they gathered to select a new man. Here the different spokesmen talked to the assembled group about who they thought should be the new Naat'áani. Voting took place by having the candidates stand and letting the people walk over and stand behind the man of their choice. If one man did not clearly win the general agreement by the group, the candidates were given an opportunity to display their persuasive speaking ability. Following this another vote was taken. This continued until one man was agreed on by the group. If the group could not reach an agreement, the selection was put off until another assembly was called, usually within the next six months. During this time people discussed the candidates until the next meeting.[4]

Once selected, Naataanii were put through an initiation ceremony during which the leader's lips were coated with corn pollen taken from the four sacred mountains. This action was meant to enable the leader to give powerful speeches. At such an occasion songs were sung and sacred tobacco, also brought from the sacred peaks, was smoked by distinguished individuals.[5]

The Peace Naataanii was not a hereditary position. However, once in office, the individual usually remained for life. These persons, before their death, were expected to step down and identify a successor, although the community could decide not to accept the recommendation. There is evidence that women were occasionally selected for this important position. The Peace leader oversaw the economic development of the community, arbitrated family disputes, dealt with witchcraft issues, and served as the diplomatic representative between their natural outfit and other local communities, tribes, and later, with the Spanish, Mexican, and American governments. Neither a Peace nor War Naataanii, it is important to remember, had coercive powers, and his or her effectiveness depended almost entirely upon the quality of personal character.

The Naachid

Based largely on oral accounts, there is strong evidence to support the existence of a periodic tribal assembly. This regional gathering of Peace and

War leaders was called a **Naachid**, literally meaning "to gesture with the hand." The most detailed written account of a Naachid (the last one was reportedly held in the 1850s or 1860s) comes from the writings of Richard Van Valkenburgh. He noted that the assembly was called "at two and four year intervals, and, should a tribal emergency arise, could be called in an odd year." Twenty-four leaders—twelve War and twelve Peace (some sources claim that there were six of each)—would meet in a specially constructed hogan. Valkenburgh noted that at a prescribed time during the assembly, a four-day dance was conducted. After the dance, a succession of meetings and dances was held throughout the winter, with the assembly adjourning after the spring planting.

The Naachid was held for several purposes. Ceremonially, it was conducted to ensure an abundance of water and soil fertility. It also served at times as a war council or a peace council. For example, it was reported in December 1840 that "Navajos held a Naachid ceremony west of Canyon de Chelly for the purpose of making peace with the Mexicans. On this date, José Andrés Sandoval, Justice at Jemez, reported to the governor: 'At nightfall of this day [December 14] a Navajo known as Anceluno presented himself in this pueblo [Jemez] soliciting peace in the name of his nation. ...' "[6]

During peaceful years, the Peace Naataanii chaired the assembly. However, when war or other outside threats arose, the War Naataanii had the proceedings. Women played an active role in the Naachid, and could speak openly to the gathered delegates if they had participated in raids or had achieved prominent status through some other means. The decisions of the Naachid were not binding on the assembled Navajos (and certainly not on any outfits not present) and those who disagreed with the gathering's decisions were not compelled to obey and suffered no reprisals.

Throughout the millennia when the Naachid was active, it played a number of vital roles. When war began, many Navajo could gather quickly. Although natural community leaders exercised considerable regional influence, a political regrouping occurred when the Naachid convened. Speakers at the assembly were not chosen by formal votes; instead the general assembly's informal approval and acknowledgment were required. Some accounts stress that the Naachid's primary role was ceremonial in nature and that it functioned politically only when outside threats compelled the assembled Navajo to act as a political unit.

Diné Government: 1700–1846

Despite Spanish intrusion into Navajo country by the early 1600s and continuing through the early 1800s, traditional Navajo governing structures remained intact. Although the Navajo population had gradually shifted west, largely because of Spanish, Ute, and Comanche incursions, the natural communities, the Naataanii, and the Naachid continued to serve as the basic Navajo political units. There is evidence that during the Spanish period five loose Navajo political subdivisions coalesced. These were located at Mount Taylor, Cebolleta, Chuska, Bear Springs, and Canyon de Chelly.

The Spanish, meanwhile, continued to carefully "select" those Navajo leaders who would best serve them as political and military allies. For example, the Navajo headman, Don Carlos, was chosen and anointed by the Spanish as the "Navajo General" of the entire nation. But when he proved to be ineffective, according to the Spanish officials, he was removed from office and replaced by Antonio el Pinto. The Spanish governor, de la Concha, wrote this glowing, if questionable, description of el Pinto and described his alleged authority over all Navajos:

> ... [A]n Indian of extraordinary talent, and one whom the whole nation respects and obeys in the manner which is customary to civilized nations with an authorized commander. These qualities are rare in a class of people who are led along the path of reason by only profit or fear and this is recognized by his own people, which causes them to venerate him.[7]

There were other occasions when the Spanish attempted to "designate" Navajo individuals and declare them the head of all the Nation. In fact, Spanish diplomatic and military efforts to firm up their position in New Mexico by exploiting one group of Navajos against others led to a long lasting schism between the Navajo in the early part of the nineteenth century which lasts to this day.

The separation began in 1818 when a Navajo headman, Joaquin, visited the Spaniards in the Pueblo. Joaquin told the Spanish officials that despite his efforts to maintain peace, other Navajos were preparing for war because they were angry at Spanish encroachments on their lands. Joaquin, frustrated at what he considered the more militant attitude of western Navajo, had physically relocated his own people closer to the Spanish settlements and went as far as severing connections with the rest of the Diné people. This action placed Joaquin's small band into the role of "being traitors to the main Navajo tribe and subservient to the government at Santa Fe. From this time forward, Joaquin's small group would be referred to as the Diné Ana'i or Enemy Navajos."[8]

Schemes to fabricate a central Navajo political figurehead were also employed at various times by the Mexican and United States governments. The anointed "Navajo Generals," however, never represented more than a handful of Navajo families despite the contentions or grandiose terms applied to them by the Spanish, Mexican, or United States governments.

Diné Governmental Change During the Early American Period: 1846–1921

When the United States replaced the Mexican government as the dominant foreign influence in the Southwest in 1846, it was immediately faced with the task of trying to establish peaceful relations with the independent and powerful Navajos, the various bands of Apaches, and many other tribes. This herculean task was complicated by the decentralized Navajo political structure and by enslavement of a large number of Navajo women and children being held in captivity by New Mexicans.

The U.S. military and governmental officials, despite some seventy years of experience in dealing with tribal nations, naively believed that a treaty signed by a few Navajo headman would bind the entire nation. Thus, the American government, like the two preceding nations, equated Navajo political and social structures with those of the federal and European political systems.

Between 1846 and 1868, the Navajo signed nine separate treaties with the United States. The first took place in the fall of 1846 when the U.S. Army and over 500 hundred Navajos led by fourteen headmen, signed a treaty of peace at Ojo del Oso (Ft. Wingate, NM). Navajo raids continued, however, reflecting the decentralized political reality of Navajo tribal existence. This treaty, like those of 1848, 1851, 1855, two in 1858, and 1861, was not ratified by the U.S. Senate. As noted above, only the 1849 and 1868 treaties (see Appendices C and D) were ratified and, because of their ongoing importance, will be discussed in detail. The early non-ratified treaties usually included provisions regarding the establishment of peace, the regulation of commerce, the exchange of prisoners, and the return of stolen property. The later ones focused more on peace and clarification of Navajo territorial boundaries.

Let us digress and discuss in detail the essentials of the two ratified Navajo treaties. We will then return to our overview of Diné government.

Treaty of 1849 (also known as Washington's Treaty)

On September 9, 1849, the Navajo entered what would become the first of two ratified treaties with the United States. Negotiations were conducted in Canyon de Chelly, also known as the "Valley of Cheille." The United States negotiators were Brevet Lieutenant John M. Washington and James S. Calhoun, the Indian agent of Santa Fe. Mariano Martinez signed as "Head Chief," along with Chapitone, his second chief. These were two minor Navajo headmen apparently handpicked by Antonio Sandoval, one of the interpreters, because in the wake of the killing of Narbona (a leading headman), Zarcillos Largos, a good friend, and Manuelito, Narbona's son-in-law, refused to participate. Once again, the United States negotiators displayed their ignorance or arrogance for existing Navajo political structure by referring to Martinez and Chapitone as the leaders of the *entire* Navajo Nation.

This treaty contained eleven articles. Article 1 effectively established a trust relationship between the Diné and the United States, with the Navajo signatories agreeing to be "lawfully placed under the exclusive jurisdiction and protection of the Government of the said United States and that they are now, and will forever remain, under the aforesaid jurisdiction and protection." Article 2 called for an end to hostilities and declared that "perpetual peace and friendship shall exist ... ." The third article brought the Navajos within the scope of preexisting federal Indian policy and declared, more amazingly, that "the territory of the Navajos is hereby annexed to New Mexico." Annexation, of course, literally meant that New Mexico now claimed full and complete jurisdiction and sovereignty over Navajo lands in that territory. No doubt this was one of the reasons the more prominent Navajo leaders refused to participate in these treaty deliberations, sensing that it was, in fact, a legal land grab by the New Mexico Territory and by extension the federal government.

Articles four through seven dealt with the Navajos agreeing to turn over certain criminals to the United States (Article 4), return stolen property taken from New Mexicans (Article 5), protection of Navajos by federal authorities (Article 6), and with the Navajos agreeing to provide to Americans "free and safe passage" through their recently annexed territory. Article 8 contained an important provision from an American perspective in that it gave the United States the right to build trading houses, and more importantly, the right to establish Army forts and agencies anywhere in Navajo country. The United States also got what it wanted in Article 9 by securing the right to create "territorial boundaries" for Navajos and authorized itself to pass any laws it deemed "conducive to the prosperity and happiness of said Indians." Article 10 was the gift-giving provision with the United States agreeing, provided the Navajos complied with all previous stipulations, to provide presents, donations, and assorted implements to the nation.

The final article declared that the treaty would be effective from the moment it was signed although it was subject to any amendments that the United States, not the Navajos, might want to make. Finally, and more positively, the treaty explicitly incorporated one of the basic canons of Indian treaty interpretation. This canon holds that the treaty would "receive a liberal construction [interpretation] at all times and in all places ... ." Immediately thereafter is language to the effect that the Navajo signers would not be held responsible "for the conduct of others." This last statement, it could be argued, is a recognition that Martinez and Chapitone were not, in fact, the actual leaders of the rest of the Nation. The treaty was ratified exactly one year later, on September 9, 1850 by the U.S. Senate. It was then proclaimed by the president a few weeks later.

From a Navajo perspective the content of the treaty was problematic from the first. The fact that no legitimate Navajo leaders participated; the fact that no provision was made for the New Mexicans to return Navajo captives; and the fact that the U.S. government could, through New Mexico, claim to have annexed all Navajo land in that territory despite the lack of full tribal consent: all pointed to a document that would not bring the desired peace. Despite all these problems, this treaty has never been abrogated and many of its provisions have legal merit today.

Treaty of 1868

This treaty was one of many the U.S. Indian Peace Commissioners signed with a number of western tribes in 1867 and 1868. These documents were important because they were the last of the first and most significant wave of Indian treaties which terminated in 1871. They also reflected, as is evident by the name of the United States negotiators, the "Indian Peace Commission," the government's efforts to reform Indian policy by detailing the causes of the seemingly endless conflict between Indians and Americans. These treaties also reflect the government's powerful desire to assimilate and civilize Indians. For example, nearly all these treaties had provisions for arable land for farming, construction of warehouses and mechanic shops, a "land-book" to keep track of individual Indian allotments, compulsory education of Indian children, the provision of seeds and other agricultural tools and products, etc.[9]

The Navajo Treaty was signed at Fort Sumner on June 1, 1868, by General William T. Sherman and Samuel F. Tappan, the Indian Peace Commissioners, and by a large and influential group of imprisoned Navajo leaders, including Barboncito, Armijo, Delgado, Manuelito, Largo, Ganado Mucho, and many others. The commissioners were well aware of how tragic the Bosque Redondo enterprise had been and saw that it would be impossible to relocate Navajos to Indian Territory in present-day Oklahoma, which some officials had pushed for.

The Navajo, for their part, had consistently sought to convince the U.S. Army of their desire to return to their natural homelands and had engaged in ceremonies to that effect. The mutual appeal of establishing and maintaining peace led to the 1868 treaty which provided what the Navajo wanted most—return to their homelands, however diminished—and what the United States sought—impressing upon the Navajo the magnanimity of the federal government.

In the preamble (the introduction) to the treaty, recognizing the signers of the treaty, it is stated that the "Navajo nation or tribe of Indians," was represented by their headmen and chiefs "duly authorized and empowered to act for the whole people of said nation or tribe." This is one of the earliest and most accurate statements acknowledging the collective nature of Navajo sovereignty because a majority of the Navajo Nation had been imprisoned at Fort Sumner. It appears that there was little dispute about Diné leadership at this point. It is also true, however, that not all Navajos were imprisoned at the fort since some bands, particularly in the West, had escaped the Long Walk. There is some question, therefore, about whether this treaty bound unimprisoned Navajos to its conditions.

The treaty contains thirteen articles. Article 1 established peace between the Navajo and the United States. It also contained a clause giving the federal government jurisdiction over crimes committed by non-Navajos. Jurisdiction over crimes by Navajos against other Navajos remained with the Navajo Nation. Reservation establishment for Navajo with allowance for other "friendly tribes or individual Indians" the United States might wish to settle there (Article 2). Importantly, the reservation was largely to be the exclusive domain of the Navajos except for a few specific individuals like soldiers, officers, agents, or other government personnel who were there to enforce federal law.

Article 3 was one of the "civilization" provisions. It authorized the United States to build blacksmith and carpenter shops, schoolhouses, chapels, warehouses, and other buildings. The Navajos Indian agent was authorized under Article 4. Article 5 contained another key assimilation provision. The government believed that agriculture and individual allotments of land were essential to the assimilation of Indians. Article 5 declared that any Navajo interested in farming (again, the United States operated on the inaccurate presumption that Navajos were not already adept at farming) could select tracts of 160 or 80 acres, depending on their age. Each selection was to be recorded in a "Land Book."

Article 6 focused explicitly on the importance of formal Western education of Navajo youth. Navajo heads of households were required "to compel their children" between the ages of six and sixteen to attend school. The government pledged a schoolhouse and staff for every 30 children. This provision was "to continue for not less than ten years."

Article 7 was related to Article 5 in that once individuals had selected their plots of land the government agreed to provide, for three years, seeds and tools to put the land to productive use. Article 8 was a "commodities" provision. Every September 1, for ten years from the date of the treaty, the government promised to provide goods like clothing and other raw materials, plus ten dollars for each Navajo farmer.

Article 9 contained an important right and a number of concessions. First, Navajos, in exchange for their ceded lands, retained "the right to hunt on any unoccupied lands contiguous to their reservation, so long as the large game may range thereon in such numbers as to justify the chase." Navajos also had to agree that they would not oppose railroad construction; would not attack Anglo travellers; would not capture any women or children; would not kill or scalp any white men; would not oppose the building of wagon roads, mail stations, or other utilities (Navajos were to be reimbursed for damaged or lost lands); and finally that they would not interfere with the construction of any military forts.

Article 10 was an important provision regarding any future land transactions. It was agreed that there would be no cession of any part of the Nation's communal lands without the express consent of "at least three-fourths of all the adult male Indians occupying or interested in the same," nor could such a cession occur of individual Indian land provided under Article 5.

The Navajo agreed under Article 11 to proceed to the newly established reservation at the expense of the federal government, with transportation being provided for the "sick and feeble." Article 12 outlined the cost of removal provisions (total of $150,000). The government estimated that the actual removal itself would cost $50,000. It also provided for the purchase of 15,000 sheep and goats, 500 cattle, and a million pounds of corn.

Article 13 entailed a promise by the Navajo signatories that they would make the reservation their home while retaining the right to hunt on adjoining public lands. It was made clear that Navajos who left the reservation would "forfeit all the rights, privileges, and annuities" provided under the treaty. Navajos were also expected, under the provisions of this treaty, to act as lobbyists on behalf of the federal government, by trying to entice other "nomadic" Indians or warring tribes of the "benefits" of reservation life. The treaty was ratified by the Senate July 25, 1868 and was proclaimed by President Andrew Johnson on August 12, 1868.

Importance of the Treaties

As described in Chapter 1, treaties are vitally important in their recognition and protection of Indian sovereign, individual, and property rights. Although both the 1849 and 1868 treaties are solidly entrenched in the law as binding legal covenants, it is the 1868 treaty which has been cited most often in cases of importance to the Navajo Nation. For example, in *Williams v. Lee* (1959), the Supreme Court read Article 2 of the 1868 treaty to mean that "the understanding that the internal affairs of the Indians remained exclusively within the jurisdiction of whatever tribal government existed." The Court held further that the 1871 law ending one phase of Indian treaties did not affect the government's obligations in ratified treaties and "thus the 1868 treaty with the Navajos survived this act." Finally, the Court stated that: "The cases of this Court have consistently guarded the authority of Indian government's over their reservations. Congress recognized this authority in the Navajos in the Treaty of 1868, and has done so ever since."

Six years later, in *Warren Trading Post Company v. Arizona State Tax Commission,* the Court unanimously upheld the vitality of the 1868 treaty. In this case the state was attempting to tax the gross proceeds of the Warren Trading Post, which conducted business on the reservation. The Court denied that Arizona had this right on the basis that the federal government had already preempted the field, leaving state laws no room to enter. The Court relied on the 1868 treaty because that document had created the reservation as a "permanent home" for the Navajo, thus freeing the Indians from state jurisdiction.

Finally, in 1973, Arizona once again sought to extend its tax laws into Navajo country. This time the state attempted to levy a tax on the income of a Navajo woman, Rosalind McClanahan, who worked on the reservation. In *McClanahan v. Arizona State Tax Commission,* the Supreme Court, speaking through Justice Thurgood Marshall, said that Indians and Indian property on a reservation were not subject to state taxation "except by virtue of express authority conferred upon the State by Act of Congress, and that the Navajo treaty precludes extension of state law, including state tax law, to Indians on the Navajo reservation."

Sometime before 1858, the Naachid apparently ceased to function. American military campaigns and the hardships of widespread dispersement of the Navajo people severely inhibited gatherings of this tribal assembly. The Long Walk to Fort Sumner and the subsequent four year confinement of Navajos at "Bosque Redondo" from 1864 to 1868 worked against the practice of keeping the Naachid functional. The evidence suggests that the Naachid was never again reconstituted because most of the older Navajos who knew how to conduct it had died during their oppressive years of imprisonment.

With the Naachid permanently broken, the Navajos turned to individual Naataanii for direction and leadership. General Carleton, the mastermind behind the devastating Fort Sumner experience, had actually planned in the early stages of preparing the fort to further break the Navajo's natural leadership by subdividing the Navajo population (8,000 plus) into twelve villages, to be situated half a mile apart. Each village was to have a chief or headman appointed by the military officer in charge, and one subchief for every 100 Navajos. Carleton's "political organization" plan for the Nation was never implemented, however, because Navajos preferred to live in their extended families and small bands and did not want to live in close proximity with the Mescalero Apache, their enemies, who were also confined at the fort.

When the Navajos were released from Fort Sumner, they recognized a need to reconstitute themselves, politically, socially, and ceremonially. Oral accounts relate that sometime during the fall of 1868, The People, led by their Peace Naataanii and medicinemen, assembled in Window Rock to perform a Blessingway Ceremony. For seven days, thirteen leaders and medicine men fasted and prayed, seeking spiritual guidance and protection. During the ceremony "Sacred Mountain Dirt Bundles" (*Dzil leezh*) were tied together and each of the leaders received a bundle. When the ceremony concluded, each of the leaders was instructed by the medicine man to carry his personal bundle through Window Rock four times. After this, the people dispersed to the four directions to begin their lives anew.

For a period, the Indian agent accepted those Navajo who had emerged from Fort Sumner as the recognized political leadership of the Nation, including Barboncito, Ganado Mucho, Delgadito, Narbona and Mariano. By the early 1880s, the Navajo Indian agent told the Secretary of the Interior that there were four major settlements of Navajos, each under the control of a chief or chiefs: (1) North of Agency, led by Chief Francisco Capitan (population 4,000); (2) East of Agency, Chief Manuelito (population 4,000); (3) South of Agency, Chiefs Mariano and Tsi'naajini Biye' (population 4,000); and (4) West of Agency, led by Head Chief Ganado Mucho (population 4,000).[10]

Gradually, as these leaders died, and with federal policy shifting towards a more coercive form of assimilation, the Navajo Indian agent began acting in a more autocratic fashion. From 1878 to 1910, the "Head Chiefs" of the Navajo people were "appointed" by the Navajo Indian agent and were confirmed by the Secretary of the Interior. Manuelito, who had been appointed in 1870, served until 1884 when the Indian agent replaced him with Henry Chee Dodge, a bilingual, mixed-blood Navajo.

Besides the Head Chiefs, regional Naataanii, also selected by the agent, continued to guide their communities. There were an estimated thirty local headmen functioning throughout the Reservation in 1900. The Indian agent annually assembled the Head Chief and regional leaders to discuss important issues. Clearly, the Navajo Indian agent, living at Fort Defiance by this time, wielded an extreme amount of authority. Valkenburgh pointed out that, "agents deliberately smashed all native power, and those *naat'aanih* who refused to 'play ball', lost all government recognition and, without that, soon lost influence over the people in that region."

Although the agent selected and directed these "Agency Chiefs," Mary Shepardson reported that there remained "the old informal leaders, local headmen, wealthy stock-owners, ceremonial practitioners, and heads of large family groups [who] constituted the defacto leadership of the localities."

By 1900 the Navajo Reservation had nearly quadrupled in size through executive order extensions and it was evident that a single federal agent could no longer oversee the affairs of such a greatly expanded land base. Moreover, the population had doubled and then stood at nearly 15,000. Thus, to regain a better administrative position, Navajo territory was divided into six separate agency jurisdictions, each with its own superintendent, between 1901 and 1934. This included an agency for the Hopi Tribe but which also served Navajos. The agencies were: Western Navajo at Tuba City; San Juan Agency at Shiprock; Navajo Agency at Fort Defiance; Pueblo Bonito at Crownpoint, New Mexico; Leupp Agency at Leupp; and Hopi at Keams Canyon.

According to Robert Young, the subdivision of the Reservation into six separate units, combined with an increase in staff and a smaller land area, "led to the abandonment of the previous system of appointive chiefs. ... By 1910 the use of appointive chiefs was abandoned completely."[11] Young states that:

> In general, after the opening of the present century, with the division of the Navajo country into multiple jurisdictions, federal administration continued to be largely autocratic in its approach and methods, but with ever increasing efforts to reach and influence the people. Concurrently, with the establishment of the six agencies, the tribe came to be viewed, not as one entity, but as six separate and distinct segments, including those members living in the Hopi jurisdiction, each with its own regional interests. The development itself placed a constraint on the evolution of government on a tribal basis.[12]

The Birth of Local Government: 1922–1936

Chapters

The Superintendent of the Leupp Agency, John G. Hunter, is generally credited with the development of what became the Chapter System of government. At first, these community organs were more often referred to as "Livestock Improvement Associations," but that designation changed in subsequent years. Superintendent Hunter recognized a need to reach more Navajos in order to better understand their common problems, particularly those related to livestock and agriculture. His idea was to bring Navajo people together at the local level where representatives of the BIA, in conjunction with returned Navajo students, could be more effective in working with Navajo issues of importance—education, agriculture, housing, and so forth.

Hence, in 1927 Hunter called the first general meeting of Navajos in Leupp, Arizona.[13] The idea of local government spread rapidly and by 1933 over 100 Chapters were operating throughout much of the Reservation. Each Chapter elected a president, vice president, and a secretary/treasurer, and meetings followed parliamentary procedure. Chapter meetings were typically held once a month to discuss projects such as building construction, irrigation and other water projects, roads, livestock improvement, and agricultural practices.[14] The federal government provided materials and funds for these projects and chapter members performed the work. Federal officials also benefitted by Chapters. First, they created opportunities for the concise presentation of government programs and goals. Second, they acted as relay stations to pass information along through the agency. Third, they acted as precincts for the election of council delegates. And finally, Chapters came to be viewed as forums in which local tribal leaders could express their opinions.

Although Chapters were officially established by a federal agent and were heavily subsidized by the government, the idea of local government, as discussed earlier, was certainly not new to the Navajos. In a 1962 interview, Howard Gorman related how the Ganado Chapter began: "Yes, I was there, and all of us thought it was a good idea, for it built upon what was already present, that of organized group meetings. Hunter's idea added some new things, such as the *Robert's Rules of Order,* majority voting, elected officials, and the office of Chairman."

Gorman's comments are supported by Aubrey Williams, Jr., in his classic work, *Navajo Political Process,* where he states that, "The chapters were integrated into pre-existing, local sociopolitical structures which had at their core the extended family structure that functioned as the basic unit of social control among the Navajo."

The First Navajo Tribal Council

As we have described earlier, there was no Navajo National government before the 1920s, except for the brief opportunity generated by the Fort Sumner incarceration. But when oil was discovered on the treaty portion of the Reservation in 1922, the federal government established the semblance of a central Navajo governing authority with which Washington might interact in providing leases for mineral development. Prior to this, interested energy companies had to contact the agency superintendent, who then convened a "general council" of adult Navajos in that agency to consider the companies' requests for leases. But, as Lawrence Kelly noted, "the obvious implication was that the councils were to be subordinate to the government agent," for the Navajos "were not members of any deliberative body which had been in existence prior to that time."

Oil and gas companies, anxious to exploit the perceived mineral wealth of the Reservation, pressured the Department of the Interior and agency superintendents to convene additional "general councils" in both the San Juan (Shiprock) and Southern Navajo (Fort Defiance) Agencies. And although several new leases were granted by the Navajos to the companies, most were rejected.

Rebuffed, the oil companies then exerted more pressure on the Interior Department and the Commissioner of Indian Affairs to take away the inherent leasing power of the Navajos and place it in the hands of a federal representative. The Navajos, however, refused to surrender their right to lease their lands.

Two developments in the fall of 1922 signaled an end to the leasing stalemate. First, the Interior Department changed its policy and now asserted that oil and gas royalties, bonuses, and rentals derived from discoveries *in any part* of the Reservation belonged to the Navajo Tribe *as a whole,* and not "exclusively to those Navajo residents in whose jurisdiction it was found." Second, this policy change resulted in the Interior's creation of a "business council" which was initially composed of three Navajos authorized to deal with lease grants: Henry Chee Dodge, Charlie Mitchell, and Daagha'chii Bikiss. These men were apparently selected by the Secretary of the Interior. However, the legality of this non-representative and non-elected body was immediately questioned because it utterly failed to meet the 1868 treaty requirement of securing the approval of three-fourths of the adult males when any transactions involving Navajo lands occur.

A more representative council had to be devised. Albert Fall, the Secretary of the Interior, on January 3, 1923, proceeded to contact Mr. Herbert J. Hagerman, former territorial Governor of New Mexico, and offered him the position of "Special Commissioner to Negotiate with Indians." Hagerman accepted the appointment as Commissioner to the Navajos, and was granted general authority over the five Navajo agencies. On January 23, the Commissioner of Indian Affairs, Charles Burke, issued a document entitled "Regulations Related to the Navajo Tribe of Indians," which the Navajos had not seen. This document established procedures to create the first Navajo Tribal Council. The council was to consist of one delegate and one alternate from each agency, plus a chair and vice-chair. This body was touted as an organization "with which administrative officers of the Government may directly deal in all matters affecting the tribe." The chair of the council was to be elected by the council delegates at the first meeting and was to be selected from the tribal membership at large. Apparently, once chosen, the chair and vice-chair could have held office indefinitely since no fixed terms were specified. The chair also functioned as a council member as well as the presiding officer following his election. The vice-chair was to be selected from the council's own membership.

If an agency failed to elect a delegate to the council within thirty days, the Secretary of the Interior would fill the position with his own appointment. Furthermore, the Tribal Council could not meet without the commissioner's presence. And, interestingly enough, the Interior Department reserved the right to remove any council member upon proper cause. The document contained no statement of legislative or other formal powers. The council was to serve primarily as a consultative group, though it did have power to consent to leases.

Once these regulations reached the Navajos, they attacked the removal power of the Secretary of the Interior, and objected to the number of delegates and alternates representing each agency. Subsequent to these objections, the regulations were rewritten on April 24. The new laws excluded the removal clause, provided for a forum, interpreters, and a means of succession in the event that the chair or vice-chair positions became vacated. Finally, the number of delegates and alternates to the council was increased from twelve to twenty-four. In other words, there was to be twelve voting delegates and twelve non-voting alternates.

The Secretary of the Interior, nevertheless, maintained tremendous authority over the Tribal Council. He could make appointments when the Navajos refused to do so in a given period of time; meetings could be held only in the presence of a federal representative; and the Council could convene only at the discretion of the Commissioner of the Tribe, who was solely responsible for calling the meetings.

The newly elected councilmen held their first meeting at Toadlena, New Mexico, on July 7, 1923. The council elected Chee Dodge as Chair, but, for some reason, failed to elected a vice-chair. Then they unanimously approved a resolution—drafted in Washington—which gave Commissioner Hagerman the authority to sign all oil and gas leases "on behalf of the Navajo Indians." In effect, their first action essentially eliminated the principal reason the council was organized, which had been to approve leases on behalf of the people. According to Lawrence Kelly, the council apparently agreed to this resolution because they believed that they "would receive government aid in securing new lands." The council would not regain this important power until 1933.

The Tribal Council met annually, usually for two days, and generally functioned as little more than an "advisor" to Commissioner Hagerman during the next decade of its existence. The council was largely a creature of the Secretary of the Interior and certainly not an organization exercising powers of self-government. In April, 1927, the council's regulations were amended to allow council members and executive officers to serve five-year terms, instead of four. The following year, October 15, 1928, a third set of regulations was issued by the Commissioner of Indian Affairs. These included provisions that gave women the right to vote, authorized the Commissioner of Indian Affairs instead of the Commissioner of the Navajo Tribe to call meetings, and re-established the term of office at four years.

There were but two other major changes in the regulations before tribal reorganization began in 1936. On October 3, 1933, under Tom Dodge's chairmanship (Chee Dodge's son), the Tribal Council, in an act of sovereignty, "revoked" and "canceled" the **power of attorney** it had ceded to the federal government at the council's first meeting in 1923. The council also became more outspoken in the kinds of issues it would concern itself with, including chapter organization, employment, education, water projects, tribal resources, health, education, and livestock issues.[15]

Second, on July 10, 1934 the council unanimously voted to give council alternates the right to vote as full-fledged delegates. Thus, the Tribal Council now had twenty-four functioning members and was adamant about issues that other governments concern themselves with.

Navajo Tribal Reorganization: 1936–1938

The subject of Navajo tribal government in the 1930s is closely intertwined and affected by the quality and extent of Navajo lands, erosion cycles, the personalities of certain tribal and federal workers, water development projects like the Boulder, later, Hoover Dam, and, of course, livestock. The

Navajo subsistence system was already in danger by 1930 as evidenced by the William Zeh report. Zeh was a forester for the BIA who, in a detailed report on the overgrazed Navajo range, reported that 1.3 million sheep and goats were living on less than 12 million acres of land. Such large numbers of livestock (horses and cattle were not included in his data) were causing real damage to the land. But Zeh did not recommend massive livestock reduction. Instead, he called for the Reservation to be expanded, urged the elimination of excess horses, and suggested improved breeds of sheep and goats. He only recommended a gradual reduction in the number of goats.[16]

In fact, the winters of 1931–32 and 1932–33 were particularly harsh and thousands of sheep and goats starved, pushing the number of sheep and goats below one million where they remained throughout the 1930s. Simultaneously, Congress authorized the Colorado River Project, whose main cog was Boulder, later Hoover Dam. When completed, the dam created a 150-mile-long lake which protected much of Southern California, created an improved irrigation system, and generated electricity for the Southwest.

But within a few years the U.S. Geological Survey estimated that silt from the San Juan and the Little Colorado Rivers, which course through the Navajo Reservation, would eventually pile up behind the dam and make it useless within a few years. In effect, the Hoover Dam was the catalyst for the drastic **livestock reduction** which would then ensue. According to White, the government "misunderstood the erosion cycle and its causes and blamed it largely on Navajo lands" and acted more to benefit economic development in the Southwest than to protect Navajos.[17] Ultimately, Navajo herds were dramatically reduced from 1,053,498 sheep units in 1933 to 449,000 in 1946 when active reduction was stopped.

In effect, the stock reduction program served as the impetus by which the Navajos people came to see that the decisions of their government, the Navajo Tribal Council (for good or ill), had real import for their lives and pocketbooks. Commissioner of Indian Affairs, John Collier, convinced the Tribal Council to approve and participate in the livestock reduction program with promises that if it did new lands would be added to the Reservation in Arizona and New Mexico. Although some lands were added to Western Navajo, the promised lands were not forthcoming in New Mexico due to powerful non-Indian interests in the state. Gradually, the Navajo people lost what little faith they still had in the Tribal Council.

The council, for its part, was in a profound dilemma. The need for some livestock reduction appeared a reasonable request, and the opportunity to gain additional lands if they did was an important impetus to accept the government's reduction plan. But the council was already feeling pressure from the people that the program was not fair and was leaving many

Navajo families destitute. On the other hand, if they had not supported Collier and his soil conservation program, it was clear that the government intended to carry out stock reduction anyway.

The Navajo Tribe, like most other tribes, was given an opportunity to establish a constitutional form of government in 1934 under the auspices of the Indian Reorganization Act. This major law, discussed in Chapter 3, was the brainchild of CIA, John Collier, and it gave tribes a two-year period to vote on whether they wished to adopt or reject the act's provisions. For many reasons, not the least of which was the government's forced reduction of Navajo livestock, the Navajo people narrowly rejected the act by a vote of 8,197 to 7,679. Collier was deeply hurt by the Navajos' rejection of his measure but he continued to express a need for an overhaul of Navajo government. And as already noted, many Navajos now viewed the Tribal Council with disdain, believing that it had aided and supported the federal government's stock reduction program and did not truly represent the views of the Navajo people.

The last meeting of the original Tribal Council was held November 24, 1936, under acting Chairman Marcus Kanuho.[18] Jacob C. Morgan, the Shiprock council delegate, and the most outspoken opponent of stock reduction, protested the impending breakup of the old Tribal Council. Nevertheless, during this last meeting the council established an Executive Committee charged with calling a constitutional assembly for the purpose of writing and adopting a tribal constitution.

This Executive Committee, led by Chee Dodge, Marcus Kanuho, Henry Taliman, and Father Berard Haile, toured the Reservation throughout the winter, and by February 1937 had a working list of 250 nominees for the constitutional assembly. The Executive Committee ultimately pared this number down to seventy. When the seventy delegates met that spring, their principle objective was to appoint a committee to draft a constitution. Once written, it would be sent to the Interior Department for approval and then sent back to the council and tribal members for ratification.

The constitution was completed later that year. The proposed organic act mirrored those of tribes who had accepted the Indian Reorganization Act's provisions. It laid out the membership requirements and created a council as the legislative body. It was to be composed of 74 delegates, apportioned at the rate of one for every 600 Navajos. It spelled out eligibility criteria for council members and provided for six-year terms of office. The executive branch was to consist of a president and vice-president, who would also serve six-year terms. Importantly, the constitution outlined and delimited the council's powers. These included, but were not limited to, the regulation, use, and distribution of tribal property; the regulation of trade;

the levying of taxes; establishment of inheritance laws; and the hiring of legal counsel.

The constitution also contained a clause, common for that time, which declared that "any resolution or ordinance adopted by the Navajo Council or Executive Committee shall take effect as soon as approved by the Secretary of the Interior."[19] In other words, all the tribes' decisions, had the constitution been adopted, would have had to be approved by the Secretary of the Interior. For a number of complicated reasons,[20] including the fact that Morgan and his associates had become so vehement in their opposition to the constitutional process, the Secretary of the Interior, fearing a permanent political split in the tribe and more hostility to the stock reduction program, rejected the constitution. Instead, the BIA gave the assembly delegates the option of declaring themselves to be the new Tribal Council. The delegates voted themselves into office and later in 1938, the Secretary of the Interior issued a simplified set of by-laws called "Rules for the Tribal Council." These new "rules" (see Appendix E) were sufficient only for the election of the new Tribal Council and executive officers, however. Furthermore, the 1938 "Rules" did not define the scope or limits of the council's authority, nor did the Navajo electorate have any say about the regulations.

Following these latest "rules," the first election was held September 24, 1938 and Jacob C. Morgan was elected Chairman and Howard Gorman was chosen Vice-Chairman. The first Tribal Council meeting was convened on November 8, 1938. The 1938 **by-laws** increased the membership of the council to seventy-four delegates. The Commissioner of Indian Affairs lost the right to appoint delegates but the council meetings still required the presence of a federal official, the superintendent, "who occupied a position beside the chairman in the conduct of Council meetings."[21]

The Council, during the first meeting, chose not to bring forward the Executive Committee. The delegates insisted that all decisions be made by the full council. This was done in part because the previous Executive Committee had approved the hated "grazing regulation." The 1938 "Rules for the Navajo Tribal Council," with important modifications to be discussed later, still constitute the basis for present-day Navajo National government. Robert Young, in his work, *The Navajo Yearbook,* pointed out that:

> There has been a growing tendency on the part of the federal government as well as that of the Tribe, to equate the powers of the Council with those residual sovereign powers remaining in the Tribe although the Tribe has never acted formally to recognize the Council as the governmental organization authorized *by the people* to exercise those powers in their behalf. (Emphasis added.)

Diné Tribal Government: 1940–1989

The 1938 "Rules" were amended several times during this period, but in some important respects the current structure of the Navajo National government remained subject to the influence of the Interior Department. This is reflected in the fact that major **amendments** and changes in the organization or election procedures still require secretarial approval.

During this half century, the Navajo Nation fully entered the wage economy. The Nation was also dramatically affected by World War II. Some 3,600 Navajos served in the military and nearly 15,000 worked in war-related activities. When this global conflict was over most of these Navajos returned to the Reservation to find scant resources and even fewer jobs. Their agitation about these conditions led some Navajos to move permanently to cities in search of employment.

Two other developments were of profound importance in the late 1940s. In 1947, the Tribal Council established an Advisory Committee (formerly the Executive Committee) which, some say, institutionalized Navajo government. Second, the council, also in 1947, entered into a contract with an attorney, Norman Littell, who was to oversee the tribe's legal claims against the United States, the land conflicts with the Hopi Nation, and who also provided general legal services to the Nation.

Three years later Congress stepped forward in an effort to ease the economic suffering of the Navajo and Hopi peoples. In 1950 Congress enacted the Navajo-Hopi Long Range Rehabilitation Act which funneled some 88 million dollars to both tribes for a wide range of socioeconomic programs aimed at economically and socially revitalizing both tribes. Importantly, this measure also authorized the Navajo to adopt a constitution, which, once written, would have to be ratified by the Navajo people. Littell, aware of this provision even while the act was pending, soon had written a draft constitution. In his own words the "constitution has been drafted to give you, the Navajo Tribal Council and the Navajo people, all the power I could get into that constitution under the law."[22]

The 1950s are referred to by some as the time when the Navajo Nation was born. This is arguable, but it is certainly true that many changes occurred that broadened the scope of Navajo government. It represents an era, according to Iverson:

> When Navajo government leaders were engaged in broadening the scope and ambition of tribal government programs and reorganizing the structure of Navajo government in order to carry out these programs. The existence of newly found revenue encouraged these leaders to involve the tribal government in unprecedented fashion ... to

improve the quality of Navajo life. Significant revision of the government's organization included revival of the chapter system and the expansion of the responsibilities of the legislative, executive, and judicial branches.[23]

Changes included:

1950–51:	New Election Procedure Tribal Court system established
1953:	Advisory Committee adopts Navajo Reservation Grazing Regulations
1954:	Tribal Council establishes a Higher Education Scholarship Fund
1955:	Tribal Chapters incorporated into Navajo government
1959:	Tribal Council approves revised Executive Branch of government
1959:	Judicial Branch established—Law and Order Navajo Tribal Utility Authority started

Let us return to the issue of a constitution. In 1953, a more fully developed constitution was completed and sent to the CIA for review and approval. Like the constitutional attempt in 1934, it also was similar to those of Indian Reorganization Act tribes who had approved constitutions. However, several years of negotiating with BIA officials convinced the Tribal Council that "under the language of the Navajo-Hopi Long Range Rehabilitation Act, if the constitution is adopted, it would strengthen the veto power of the Secretary rather than weaken it ... ."[24] This fear of secretarial power would remain an obstacle to the approval of a constitution for a number of years, though ironically the council's foundation itself continues to rest upon secretarial regulations which give the secretary veto power over tribal ordinances in a number of major areas. Thus, the Tribal Council has continued to exercise a growing array of powers through resolutions which remain subject to secretarial veto. In 1962 the tribe's resolutions were codified into a Tribal Code modeled after federal codes. In a broad sense, the codified tribal code was the Navajo Constitution, though it has never been ratified by the tribal electorate.[25]

From 1962, when the Tribal Code was codified, until the civil unrest in 1989, the Navajo government continued to expand in profound ways. The availability of income, both from the federal government and from the extraction of natural resources (i.e., timber, coal, oil, gas, uranium) provided the tribal government with a dose of funds, however tenuous, which enabled the tribe to exercise a growing measure of self-determination.

The Civil Rights movement, which spawned the Great Society and War on Poverty programs of the federal government, taken together, increased the tribe's position nationally and internationally and were also positive developments that facilitated growth within the Nation. For example, in 1965, the Navajo Tribal Council established the Office of Navajo Economic Opportunity (ONEO), which received federal funding from the Office of Economic Opportunity for neighborhood youth corps programs, small business development, headstart programs, and others. Peter MacDonald, a future Chairman, was the first executive director of ONEO. Yet another Great Society program, the Office of Navajo Economic Legal Aid and Defender Society (DNA), was also established under ONEO. Peterson Zah, another future Tribal Chairman/President, headed this organization for a period. Both Zah and MacDonald used these important positions as springboards into tribal leadership. Education also received the focused attention of the Tribal Council, and in 1968 the council officially approved the establishment of Navajo Community College, the first tribally-controlled community college in the nation.

Peter MacDonald was elected Chairman in 1970. He served three consecutive terms before being defeated by Peterson Zah in 1982. MacDonald was reelected in 1986. The MacDonald years began during the so-called Indian Self-Determination period which was intended to allow tribes greater political and economic freedoms to govern their own lives and resources. MacDonald, the first university educated Chairman, was a dynamic speaker and was effective, particularly in his early years, in attracting national attention and prestige to the Nation. There were also a number of impressive and startling changes in Navajo government structure with MacDonald amassing a tremendous amount of power in the executive branch.

Reorganization of the tribal government consisted of two parts: "the revision and alteration of the council committee system and the restructuring of the tribal government framework. Through the first part of reorganization, many new council standing committees became established; in addition, the chairman gained the power to appoint members to all standing committees ... ."[26] The 1971 reorganization also radically revised the executive branch of Navajo government. Five central offices which dealt with business management, operations, and other organizational functions were each headed by a director appointed by MacDonald and serving at his pleasure. Interestingly, this massing of political power in the executive branch and away from the legislative branch was approved by the council with little apparent dissent.

MacDonald's second and third terms were, however, mired in controversy. The chairman was indicted in 1977 on charges of mismanagement of federal funds. Issues like apportionment, the Navajo-Hopi Land Dispute, the controversial creation of a Supreme Judicial Council in 1978, the tribal pension scheme in 1979, and MacDonald's support of Ronald Reagan for president in 1980 only intensified concern over the state of his administration of the Navajo government.[27]

Peterson Zah broke MacDonald's stranglehold on the chairmanship in 1982. Zah emphasized a partnership policy with the Tribal Council, the Navajo people, the Hopi, and with local, state, and federal governments. He also had active economic development initiatives and pushed vigorously for the renegotiation of inequitable energy leases and stressed the importance of education of Navajo youth. In fact, education was his first priority and very quickly the Navajo Tribal Council adopted new educational policies for the tribe and reservation schools.[28]

Reapportionment and tribal government reform, however, were two of the most important issues confronting the Navajo government. A new reapportionment plan was finally adopted on December 6, 1985 (this will be discussed later). And in 1985 the Navajo Nation reorganized its court system through the Judicial Reform Act. This measure created the Navajo Supreme Court and revised the tribal court judge selection process. For our purposes, however, it was Zah's recognition that the tribal government, in general, needed real reform that warrants some attention.

In the fall of 1982 the Navajo Tribal Government Reform Project was begun. It was headed by Mr. Leo Watchman. The functional statement of the Reform Project, as it looked in 1983 was as follows:

> The Navajo Nation will begin a new era in the history of the Navajo people with the development and implementation of reform in the Navajo Tribal Government. Reform in the Navajo Tribal Government must provide for:
>
> 1. The development of a balanced tribal government through the full exercise of the principles of the separation of powers.
> 2. The involvement of the Navajo people at all levels to determine the type of government and to establish appropriate limitations of authority.
> 3. The development of a philosophy for the future of the Navajo people and for the functions of their government.
> 4. The development of appropriate checks and balances within the Navajo Tribal Government to safeguard against the abuse of power.
> 5. The **decentralization** of the Navajo Tribal Government so that local issues are decided by local communities.
> 6. The development of a more responsive, efficient and accountable government to provide services to the Navajo people.

7. The development of a basic Tribal Government structure to be controlled by the vote of the Navajo people.

8. The preservation of the Navajo sovereignty, culture and heritage.

9. The conservation and preservation of the natural resources and to protect the legacy of future Navajo generations.[29]

As we shall see in later chapters, a few of these suggested reforms have been implemented, though the crucial ones—involving the securing of the Navajo people's express involvement and consent—remain unfulfilled.

Despite the stability Zah brought to the Navajo Nation, when his term neared completion, MacDonald once again entered the picture. In an extremely close election, MacDonald had 30,746 votes (carried 54 chapters) to Zah's 30,171 votes (carried 53 chapters); three chapters actually tied in their votes for the two. MacDonald was returned to power and was sworn in on January 13, 1987. MacDonald's inaugural speech seemed to indicate a man who had mellowed somewhat. He emphasized the need for jobs, talked about the importance of education, and, like Zah, stressed partnerships with the business community and the state governments. But he insisted that the Navajo people would continue to hold the federal government accountable as their trustee.

Very soon, however, developments began to spiral out of control. First was the suppression of freedom of the press with the closing of the tribe's newspaper, the *Navajo Times Today,* in February of 1987. (This episode will be discussed in Chapter 11). Second, a special session of the Navajo Tribal Council, called for April 1987, was killed because it lacked a quorum. The purpose of the session was to have been tribal government reform. Third, MacDonald convinced the Tribal Council to purchase the Big Boquillas Ranch just west of the Grand Canyon. It was this final issue, the Big Bo deal, that would be at the vortex of events that led to the 1989 riot in Window Rock in which several Navajos were killed and injured.

Democratization of the Navajo Nation: Title II Amendments, 1989 to Present

By 1989 it was evident that while, theoretically, the Navajo Nation had a three branch government, the actual state of affairs revealed that the executive branch, under MacDonald, was vastly superior to the legislative branch and, in fact, dominated the law-making branch. MacDonald was Chairman, not of the Navajo Nation proper, but of the Navajo Tribal Council. The office of the chair had accumulated vast powers, dating back to the 1950s, an accumulation which grew tremendously under MacDonald's reign.

The chairman, by 1989, headed not only the executive branch, but also held legislative powers greater than those exercised by the Speaker of the House of Representatives, and was also the principal representative of the tribe to the outside world. The chairman presided over all meetings of the Tribal Council, selected all standing committee chairs and members, including those of the powerful mini-Council, the Advisory Committee (which he chaired), that had authority to act for the Council when it was not in session. The Advisory Committee also was empowered to develop an agenda for the Council and could recommend legislation. MacDonald also chaired the Intergovernmental Relations Committee.

The combination of this virtually unlimited executive power with the ample evidence uncovered in U.S. Senate hearings from 1987 to 1989 of MacDonald's leading involvement in the tribe's controversial purchase of the 491,000 Big Bo Ranch (in which he was alleged to have accepted bribes and kickbacks from contractors) led to an intense struggle for power in Window Rock. By early spring of 1989, a majority of the Tribal Council had grown weary of these developments and placed MacDonald on involuntary administrative leave pending the investigation of the allegations against him. Leonard Haskie was appointed as Interim Chairman.

MacDonald and his supporters fought these actions over an eleven week period, despite the fact that the Navajo Supreme Court had upheld the council's power to place a chairman on administrative leave. The conflict eventually escalated into a deadly confrontation which erupted in Window Rock on July 20, 1989 involving MacDonald's supporters, the Tribal Council, and the tribal police. Two Navajos lay dead and ten others were injured in the fighting.[30]

In the fall of 1989 and in later trials, MacDonald was tried and convicted on numerous counts of bribery, instigating a riot, fraud, racketeering, ethics violations, extortion, and conspiracy. He was sentenced to fourteen years in a federal penitentiary. In December of 1989, the Tribal Council, urgently aware of the need to correct those structural problems in Navajo Government that had fostered MacDonald's rise and maintenance of power, set about the task of restructuring the relationship between the executive and legislative branches.[31]

On December 15, 1989, by a vote of 44 to 17, with 13 abstentions, the Navajo Tribal Council enacted a landmark resolution, CD-68-89 entitled, "Amending Title Two (2) of the Navajo Tribal Code and Related Action." This law became operational April 11, 1990. The opening section declares:

> Whereas: 1. Pursuant to 2 N.T.C., Section 101, the Navajo Tribal Council is the governing body of the Navajo Nation; and

2. Recent controversy involving the leadership of the Navajo Nation has demonstrated that the present Navajo Nation Government structure allows too much centralized power without real checks on the exercise of power. Experience shows that this deficiency in the government structure allows for, invites and has resulted in the abuse of power; and

3. The Judicial Branch has been reorganized by the Judicial Reform Act of 1985 ... and treating the Judicial Branch as a separate branch of government has proven to be beneficial to the Navajo Nation and has provided stability in the government; and

4. The lack of definition of power and separation of legislative and executive functions have also allowed the legislative body to overly involve itself in administration of programs thereby demonstrating a need to limit the legislative function to legislation and policy decision making and further limit the executive function to implementation of laws and representation of the Navajo Nation; and

5. There is an immediate need to reorganize the Navajo Nation government by defining the powers of the legislative and executive branches and impose limitations on exercise of such powers; and

6. The number of standing committees of the Navajo Tribal Council has grown to eighteen (18) and some standing committees can be combined ... thereby reducing the number of standing committees to twelve (12) and to provide for a more efficient and responsive committee system; and

7. The reorganization of the Navajo Nation Government as proposed herein is intended to meet the immediate needs of the Navajo people for a more responsible and accountable government and will have no effect on the long term Government Reform Project which will proceed as authorized and directed by the Navajo Tribal Council; and

8. It is in the best interest of the Navajo Nation that the Navajo Nation Government be reorganized to provide for separation of functions into three branches, and provide for checks and balances between the three branches until the Navajo People decide through the Government Reform Project the form of government they want to be governed by ... .[32]

In effect, a number of impressive changes were implemented as a result of this resolution.

- Formal separation of powers between the executive and legislative branches
- Diluted the power of the chief executive by creating the Office of Navajo Nation President and Vice-President who now serve as the Nation's chief executive officers. The president no longer serves as head of the legislative branch
- Created a Speaker of the Council position. This individual presides over the council's deliberations
- Defined and set limits on the powers of the executive and legislative branches
- Reduced the number of standing committees from 18 to 12
- The power to appoint the membership of the legislative committees was taken from the Chairman/President and given to the Speaker of the Council, subject to confirmation by the council

Despite these important and much needed reforms, the Navajo people still were not given the opportunity to have any input in these changes and the Title II Amendments have not yet been taken before the Navajo electorate for their approval. In effect, even as the Navajo National government becomes more democratic, these changes are still taking place without the direct involvement or consent of the Navajo people. Nevertheless, under the Title II Amendments, two Navajo presidents (as of fall 1998) have so far been popularly elected (Zah in 1990 and Albert Hale in 1994) although both Hale and his successor, Thomas Atcitty, were forced out of office for ethical improprieties. Still, the fact that they left office in a peaceful fashion is a testimony to the stability of the current structure of government.

Conclusion

Robert Young noted in 1961 that Navajo National government has neither a constitutional nor a traditional base. This statement is as true today as it was then, although it now has elements of both, as we shall see in later chapters. The 1989 executive/legislative changes were a well-intentioned and generally solid political effort by the leadership of the Nation to institute structural changes to reduce the future likelihood of any single person or branch of government ever amassing so much power that they are unaccountable to the government or the people.

While the Navajo National government, all three formally separated branches, has now emerged as a highly functional political system among the people and competently engages in many programs, activities, and services for the betterment of the Navajo people, it still lacks fundamental political legitimacy because the Navajo citizenry did not create it and still has never duly sanctioned its existence.

Key Terms

Amendments	Live-Stock Reduction
By-Laws	Naachid
Decentralize	Naataanii
Hastói	Natural Community
Hataali	Power of Attorney

Selected Readings

Aberle, David F. *The Peyote Religion Among the Navajo.* 2nd ed. (Norman, Oklahoma: University of Oklahoma Press, 1982).

Francisconi, Michael Joseph. *Kinship, Capitalism, Change: The Informal Economy of the Navajo, 1868–1995.* (New York: Garland Publishing Co., 1998).

Hill, W. W. "Some Aspects of Navajo Political Structure." *Plateau,* vol. 13, no. 2, (October, 1940): 23–28.

Kelly, Lawrence C. *Navajo Indians and Federal Indian Policy, 1900–1935.* (Tucson: University of Arizona Press, 1968).

Navajo Tribe. *Navajo Tribal Council Resolutions, 1922–51.* (Window Rock: Navajo Tribe, 1952).

Parman, Donald C. *The Navajos and the New Deal.* (New Haven: Yale University Press, 1976).

Pollock, Floyd A. *A Navajo Confrontation and Crisis.* (Tsaile, Arizona: Navajo Community College, 1984).

Roessel, Ruth, comp. *Navajo Livestock Reduction: A National Disgrace.* (Tsaile, Arizona: Navajo Community College Press, 1974).

Van Valkenburgh, Richard. "Navajo Government." *American Quarterly,* no. 4, (Winter, 1945): 63–73.

Williams, Aubrey, W., Jr. *The Navajo Political Process.* Vol. 9 (Washington: Smithsonian Contributions to Anthropology, 1970).

Young, Robert W. *A Political History of the Navajo Tribe.* (Tsaile, Arizona: Navajo Community College Press, 1978).

_____. ed. *The Navajo Yearbook: 1951–1961—A Decade of Progress.* (Window Rock: Bureau of Indian Affairs, 1961).

_____. *The Role of the Navajo in the Southwestern Drama.* (Gallup, New Mexico: The Gallup Independent, 1968).

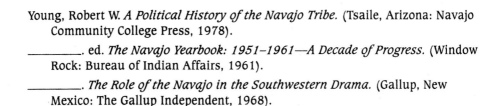

Notes

1 **Hastói** were considered wise elders. **Hataali** were medicine men or singers.

2 W. W. Hill, "Some Aspects of Navajo Political Structure," *Plateau,* vol. 13, no. 2 (October 1940): 24.

3 Ibid., p. 25.

4 As quoted in Bill P. Acrey, *Navajo History: The Land and the People.* (Shiprock, New Mexico: Department of Curriculum Materials Development, 1979): 192–193.

5 Ibid.

6 J. Lee Correll, comp. *Through White Men's Eyes: A Contribution to Navajo History.* (Window Rock, Arizona: Arizona Bicentennial Commission, 1976): 146.

7 Richard Van Valkenburgh, "Navajo Government," *American Quarterly,* no. 4 (Winter 1945): 68.

8 Bill P. Acrey, *Navajo History to 1846: The Land and the People.* (Shiprock, New Mexico: Department of Curriculum Materials Development, 1982): 114. And see J. Lee Correll's account of Antonio Sandoval, another of the so-called Enemy Navajo in "Sandoval: Traitor or Patriot?" Navajo Historical Publications, Biographical Series No. 1 (Window Rock, Arizona: Navajo Tribal Printing Department, 1970).

9 Francis P. Prucha, *American Indian Treaties* (Berkeley, California: University of California Press, 1994): 281.

10 Robert W. Young, *A Political History of the Navajo Tribe.* (Tsaile, Arizona: Navajo Community College Press, 1978): 43.

11 Robert W. Young, "The Rise of the Navajo Tribe," in Edward Spicer and Raymond Thompson, eds. *Plural Society in the Southwest* (Albuquerque, New Mexico: University of New Mexico Press, 1972): 184.

12 Ibid., p. 185.

13 Most authors cite this as the date. However, some suggest that Hunter began Chapters in 1922 and still others say they began in 1924.

14 Sam Bingham and Janet Bingham, *Navajo Chapter.* Revised edition (Tsaile, Arizona: Navajo Community College Press, 1987): 3.

15 Young, "The Rise of the Navajo Tribe," p. 191.

16 Richard White, *The Roots of Dependency: Subsistence, Environment, and Social Change Among the Choctaws, Pawnees, and Navajos.* (Lincoln, Nebraska: University of Nebraska Press, 1983): 253.

17 Ibid., p. 248.

18 Tom Dodge had resigned in May and accepted employment with the BIA.

19 Young, "The Rise of the Navajo Tribe," pp. 203–05.

20 Ibid.

21 Young, "The Rise of the Navajo Tribe," p. 208.

22 Young, "The Rise of the Navajo Tribe," p. 211.

23 Peter Iverson, *The Navajo Nation*, p. 68.

24 Young, "The Rise of the Navajo Tribe," p. 221.

25 Ibid., p. 224.

26 Iverson, *The Navajo Nation*, p. 175.

27 See Peter Iverson's, *The Navajo Nation*, for a relatively unbiased look at these issues, and consult his article entitled "Peter MacDonald," in R. David Edmunds, ed. *American Indian Leaders: Studies in Diversity* (Lincoln, Nebraska: University of Nebraska Press, 1980): 222–241. Also see, Sandy Tolan's, "Showdown at Window Rock," *The New York Times Magazine,* (November 26, 1989): 28, 30–31, 36–40, 74–75 for a more critical, if abbreviated, examination of MacDonald's tenure. But see Peter MacDonald's autobiography, *The Last Warrior: Peter MacDonald and the Navajo Nation,* written with Ted Schwarz (New York: Orion Books, 1993) for a decidedly and not surprisingly pro-MacDonald perspective on these and other issues related to MacDonald's tenure.

28 See, George M. Lubick, "Peterson Zah: A Progressive Outlook and a Traditional Style," in John R. Wunder, ed. *Native American Sovereignty* (New York: Garland Publishing Company, 1996): 241–266 for a good overview of Zah's first term as Chair.

29 Author has copy of this statement.

30 See, U.S. Senate, *Final Report: A Report of the Special Committee on Investigations of the Select Committee on Indian Affairs,* Senate Report 101–216, 101st Cong., 1st sess. (1989), which contains a chapter on the Peter MacDonald corruption scandal. And see, Sandy Tolan, "Showdown at Window Rock," *New York Times Magazine* (November 26, 1989) for a good summary of the events leading to the violence. Also consult the *Navajo Times* for articles about these events.

31 Michael Lieder, "Navajo Dispute Resolution and Promissory Obligations: Continuity and Challenge in the Largest Native American Nation," *American Indian Law Review,* vol. 18, no. 1 (1993): 33–34.

32 CD-68-89. This was a Class "C" Resolution and did not require BIA approval.

Part II

Institutions of Diné Government

Chapter 5

The Framework of Navajo Government Today

Outline   Introduction

Navajo Nation Code: Principles

Navajo Nation Code: Authority

Why Is There a Code and Not a Constitution?

Limits to Navajo Government Power

Attempts at Government Reform

Conclusion

Introduction

On the last page of *Navajo Nation Government,* a booklet produced by the Office of Navajo Government Development, is found a summary statement titled "Hool'a' Agéé Nahat'a bii sila: A Vision for the Future." It reads thus:

> The future of the Navajo Nation government looks bright. As of this writing [1997], the nation is exploring ways to develop better government from the local to national level. The Honorable President, Speaker of the Navajo Nation Council and Chief Justice have caused much of the Nation to look at ways to reaffirm powers and authorities that chapters have always had and at the same time reverse the weight of bureaucracy so that more of the services are provided at the community level with the community in control. ... While the Nation is interested in the development of a more sophisticated form of government, it has to ensure that everything is grounded on the traditions and lessons of the past. For those who read this, please remember the vision of the Navajo ancestors, who endured many challenges throughout their history. At Fort Sumner, during the Long Walk era, the great

leaders of the Diné successfully argued for their return to the sacred homeland. The ancestors of the modern Navajo had a tremendous value for their way of life, tradition, and land. They sustained themselves through the tough times with the hope for their children who would one day carry on their legacy.[1]

This "vision" surely reflects the values and perspectives of the staff of the Government Development office, though there is some question how widespread this sentiment is among Navajo policymakers. For example, in the opening line of the 1989 Title II Amendments, the council expressly declared itself to be "the governing body of the Navajo Nation ... ." Later in the amendments, however, we find the council acknowledging that it will remain "the governing body" until such time as there are amendments which have been "approved by majority vote of all registered voters in all precincts." Of course, in order for the people to have an opportunity to vote for changes they may want in the government, the responsibility lies with the council and the president to initiate the referendum process for the people's voice to be heard. This the council has yet to do on the subject of fundamental governmental reform. And although the Navajo electorate may also initiate a **referendum**, it appears that there is a fundamental lack of knowledge about how this process might be utilized by the people.

The Navajo Nation government, as a result of the reforms instituted in 1989, have a representative/democratic form of government modeled loosely after the American political system (see Figure 5-1). There are, as we saw earlier, important differences between the two systems. The most important difference is that the American people acted to form the American Republic so that sovereignty rests with "the people," whereas the Navajo people have never given their fundamental consent to any of the Navajo government variations from 1922 to the present.

The present governmental structure, established in 1938 by the Secretary of the Interior, is outlined in the six-volume *Navajo Nation Code.* This chapter encompasses the background of the *Code,* and discusses why there is a code and not a tribal constitution.

Navajo Nation Code: Principles

In 1935 Navajos narrowly declined to accept the provisions of the Indian Reorganization Act (1934) which, among other things, would have allowed the Navajo Nation the right to reorganize along constitutional lines. In lieu of a tribal constitution, the Interior Secretary approved a limited set of "Rules for the Navajo Tribal Council," which were written by Commissioner

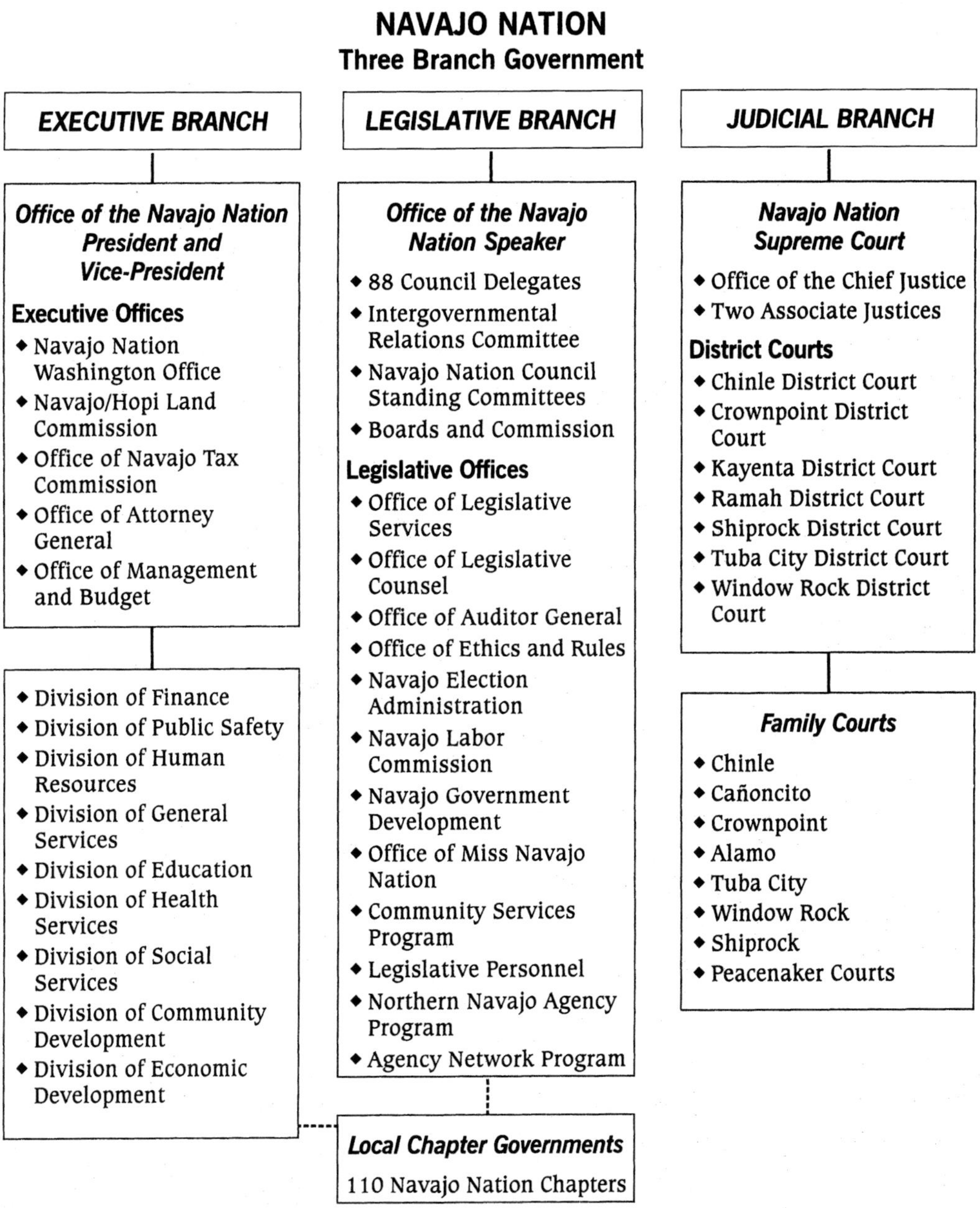

NAVAJO NATION
Three Branch Government

EXECUTIVE BRANCH	LEGISLATIVE BRANCH	JUDICIAL BRANCH

Office of the Navajo Nation President and Vice-President

Executive Offices
- Navajo Nation Washington Office
- Navajo/Hopi Land Commission
- Office of Navajo Tax Commission
- Office of Attorney General
- Office of Management and Budget

- Division of Finance
- Division of Public Safety
- Division of Human Resources
- Division of General Services
- Division of Education
- Division of Health Services
- Division of Social Services
- Division of Community Development
- Division of Economic Development

Office of the Navajo Nation Speaker
- 88 Council Delegates
- Intergovernmental Relations Committee
- Navajo Nation Council Standing Committees
- Boards and Commission

Legislative Offices
- Office of Legislative Services
- Office of Legislative Counsel
- Office of Auditor General
- Office of Ethics and Rules
- Navajo Election Administration
- Navajo Labor Commission
- Navajo Government Development
- Office of Miss Navajo Nation
- Community Services Program
- Legislative Personnel
- Northern Navajo Agency Program
- Agency Network Program

Local Chapter Governments
110 Navajo Nation Chapters

Navajo Nation Supreme Court
- Office of the Chief Justice
- Two Associate Justices

District Courts
- Chinle District Court
- Crownpoint District Court
- Kayenta District Court
- Ramah District Court
- Shiprock District Court
- Tuba City District Court
- Window Rock District Court

Family Courts
- Chinle
- Cañoncito
- Crownpoint
- Alamo
- Tuba City
- Window Rock
- Shiprock
- Peacenaker Courts

Figure 5-1

In December 1989, the Navajo Nation Council enacted Resolution CJA-72-89 which codified the separation of powers between the three branches.

Source: Office of Navajo Government Development. Navajo Nation Government Booklet (Window Rock, Arizona: Office of Navajo Government Development, 1997): 18.

of Indian Affairs, John Collier. These original rules, as discussed in the preceding chapter, still provide the basic framework of Navajo Nation government. Nevertheless, over the last six decades many new laws have been enacted by the Tribal (later Navajo Nation) Council and the Advisory or Executive Committee. These resolutions have considerably expanded the scope and form of Navajo government.

To consolidate and arrange these scattered laws, in 1962, all preceding tribal resolutions and pertinent federal laws were codified—systematically arranged—in two bound volumes under the title *Navajo Tribal Code.* The *Code,* now called the *Navajo Nation Code,* has grown to six volumes. It contains the general and permanent provisions of law and resolutions of the Navajo Nation Council. It is divided into twenty-six titles (Title 25 being reserved), including an appendix which includes the Treaty of 1868, relevant acts of Congress, executive orders, and state disclaimer clauses. Titles include:

Title I—The Nation's General Provisions (e.g., the Navajo Nation Bill of Rights, membership criteria, etc.)

Title II—Navajo Nation Government (e.g., executive, legislative, chapters, etc.)

Title III—Agriculture and Livestock

Title IV—Environment

Title V—Commerce and Trade

Title Va—Navajo Uniform Commercial Code

Title VI—Community Development

Title VII—Courts and Procedures

Title VIII—Decedent's Estates

Title IX—Domestic Relations (e.g., marriage, divorce, adoption, Domestic Abuse Protection Act, etc.)

Title X—Education

Title XI—Elections

Title XII—Fiscal Matters (e.g., appropriations, Navajo Nation Permanent Fund, etc.)

Title XIII—Health and Welfare (Three parts: 1) Health, 2) Welfare, and 3) Government Agencies

Title XIV—Navajo Nation Motor Vehicle Code

Title XV—Labor (e.g., Navajo Nation Labor Commission, Navajo Preference, Workmen's Compensation, etc.)

Title XVI—Land

Title XVII—Law and Order

Title XVIII—Mines and Minerals

Title XIX—Parks and Monuments

Title XX—Professions and Occupations

Title XXI—Public Utilities and Communications (e.g., Navajo Tribal
Utility Authority, Diné Power Authority, KTNN Radio, etc.)

Title XXII—Water (Irrigation Projects, Navajo Nation Water, etc.)

Title XXIII—Conservation and Wildlife

Title XXIV—Taxation (e.g., Hotel Occupancy Tax, Possessory
Interest Tax, etc.)

Title XXV—Reserved

Title XXVI—Local Governance (e.g., Chapters, etc.)

Navajo Nation Code: Authority

Constitutions represent the fundamental law of the United States, states of
the Union, and many tribes. A constitution reflects a system of government
in that it sets forth the people, procedures, and structures that can legiti-
mately create and protect its laws. Constitutions also serve two other broad
and basic functions:

1. They establish the relationship between the people and the government.

2. They represent a grant of power from the people to their leaders.

The *Navajo Nation Code,* however, does not expressly derive its authority
from the Navajo people, since they were not the ones who established the
government. There are, of course, unwritten Diné customs and traditions
that play an important, if limited, role in Navajo government. These customs and traditions should be considered when interpreting the *Code.*

Nevertheless, the real authority for Navajo Nation government still
derives from the July 26, 1938, "Rules," which provided for a governing
body to consist of a chairman (now president), vice-chairman (now vice-
president), and seventy-four delegates (now eighty-eight) elected on a land
management district basis. Once the election procedures were established,
the council was *given recognition as the governing body of the Navajo
Tribe by the Secretary of the Interior.* And as stated earlier, even in the Title
II Amendments, the council merely declared itself to be the governing body,
again without the direct authorization of the Navajo people.

Although the 1989 Amendments did, for the first time, identify what the powers of the council were, they also declared that "all powers not delegated are reserved to the Navajo Nation Council." Compare this last power with the Tenth Amendment to the U.S. Constitution which pronounces that "the powers not delegated to the United States by the Constitution, nor prohibited by it to the States, are reserved to the States respectively, *or to the people.*" (Emphasis added.) Thus, although the council's powers are now defined, they are still not limited and may be expanded by council resolution. The council and the executive branch are not entirely free from constraints, however. We shall discuss this shortly.

Why Is There a Code and Not a Constitution?

The Navajo people, as described earlier, voted against the Indian Reorganization Act largely because they believed that by adopting it more livestock reduction would result. This was probably an erroneous belief, but conflicting reports from Chee Dodge, Jacob C. Morgan, and John Collier and associates, confused Navajos about the true merits of the law. In the preceding chapter, the events of 1936–1937 which gave the Navajos a second chance to secure a tribal constitution were described. That attempt also failed, however, resulting in the 1938 "Rules."

The constitutional question was again raised in 1950 with the passage of the Navajo-Hopi Long Range Rehabilitation Act, which included a provision allowing the Tribe to adopt a constitution. The Tribal Council had one drafted and sent it to the Commissioner of Indian Affairs and the Secretary of the Interior in 1953 for their approval. Simultaneously, however, the discovery of oil in Navajo country in 1953 sparked much debate. The Nation wanted to take advantage of oil and gas development, and had a bill introduced that would have allowed the council to develop minerals in partnership with energy companies without approval of federal officials. Federal officials, however, refused to grant the Navajos the freedom to develop their minerals without federal approval, even though the fervor for the termination of tribes was quite strong.

Norman Littell, General Counsel for the Tribe, then suggested to the Tribal Council delegates that the pending constitution be withdrawn. Littell apparently feared that the Secretary of the Interior would exercise too much authority over the Tribe's affairs, through the veto power of his office. The secretary, of course, could already exercise veto power over all major tribal council resolutions. Nevertheless, the tribal constitution idea was again shelved.

Raymond Nakai, Tribal Chairman from 1963 to 1970, revived the issue during his administration. In fact, one of Nakai's campaign pledges in both elections was the adoption of a constitution. The Tribal Council responded by adopting a resolution calling for "Establishing Procedures for the Adoption of a Navajo Tribal Constitution" in 1968. A constitution was actually submitted to the Tribal Council in November of that year. The Council approved it and originally agreed to send it out for approval by the Navajo people, but it was never actually submitted for popular ratification.

While the idea of a constitution is still discussed, there has been no concerted push to adopt one since 1968. There are a number of reasons for this. First, the Nation's Council has sometimes expressed the view that a constitution would too narrowly define and limit their powers. Many council delegates believe that they alone should exercise all sovereign powers they have currently vested in themselves. Some council delegates also argue that directly involving the Navajo electorate in referendum issues, which a constitution might require, would be too time-consuming and expensive.

But some Navajos also oppose the idea of a constitutional form of government. Much of this opposition comes from elderly Navajo who still associate a constitution with the livestock reduction era. There is also a segment of the population who express First Amendment—separation of church and state—concerns and worry about the impact the new constitutional structure would have on the Nation's explicit desire to protect and enhance Diné culture, traditions, and language. Would a constitution prohibit the tribal government's active role in affirming Navajo religion? If the Navajo Nation supports traditional Navajo culture and religion, is it violating the separation of church and state by supporting one religion—traditional Navajo religion—over say, the Native American Church, Mormonism, or another Christian denomination?[2]

Limits to Navajo Government Power

There are currently four limitations on the powers that may be exercised by the Nation's government—tribal elections, **removal** and recall of elected officials, **Navajo Bill of Rights**, and Secretarial **veto** power.

The first limit, and certainly the most obvious one, is that tribal elections are held every four years. If the president, vice-president, or council delegates fail to meet the expectations of their constituents, they may be voted out of office. The same holds for chapter and other officials on the local level. Navajo Nation judges are the only officials exempt from this, since they are appointed and generally serve for life, like federal judges and justices. However, even appointed Navajo judges may be removed for cause by the Navajo Nation Council if there is evidence presented to the Judiciary Committee that a judge is guilty of malfeasance or misfeasance in office, neglect of duty, or is determined to be mentally or physically incompetent.

The president, vice-president, and council delegates are subject to **removal** for just cause. *Just cause* includes, but is not limited to, insanity, conviction of a felony, excessive absences from council meetings, alcohol addiction, conviction of any misdemeanor involving "deceit, untruthfulness, dishonesty, including but not limited to extortion, embezzlement, bribery ... ," breach of trust duties to the Navajo people, or malfeasance or misfeasance of office.[3] Navajo policymakers must be removed by a two-thirds vote of the council. The president, vice-president, or members of their staff may also be placed on administrative leave when there are reasonable grounds to believe there may have been a breach of trust obligations to the Navajo people by such officials.

Elected officials may also be removed from office, under the second limitation of power, by a successful special recall election. Any five or more registered voters may begin the *recall* process by filing a notarized affidavit which designates them as a petitioner's committee in charge of the recall petition. The petition must contain a two-hundred word statement in which the grounds for the recall are laid out along with the name of the individual being recalled, and the signature, chapter, and census number of each registered voter who voted in the last election for the office in question.[4] Eventually, a special recall election is held if the recall committee collects the required number of signatures—60 percent of voters who cast ballots in the last election for the same office in question.

Third, a Navajo **Bill of Rights** (see Appendix F), originally enacted in 1967, was amended and reenacted as the Navajo Nation Bill of Rights in 1986. This important resolution specifies nine important rights that Navajos and other residents are entitled to. These include, but are not limited to, due process, equal protection, freedom of religion, speech, and press, the right of assembly and petition, freedom from unreasonable searches and seizures, the right to bear arms, the right to trial by jury for certain offenses, and the right to counsel at one's own expense.

The fourth limitation, alluded to earlier, is the Secretary of the Interior's **veto** power over certain council resolutions. Although the United States Supreme Court, in *Kerr-McGee v. The Navajo Tribe* (1985), said the Nation did not need the consent of the Secretary of the Interior to tax companies, the secretary must still sign off on nearly all of the major resolutions of the council, especially those involving trust property. The Interior Department also requires approval of certain committee resolutions, such as business site leases and permits.

In essence, then, the only direct mechanisms that Navajos can exercise to limit their government are to elect accountable candidates and they may, by the recall process, limit individual Navajo politicians. In contrast, the council, even after the Title II Amendments of 1989, still has virtually unlimited authority as the governing body of the Navajo Nation.

This is important to remember because Congress and the Interior Department have not, in recent years, substantially interfered with the internal political affairs of the Nation, although the federal government still claims to have plenary power over all indigenous nations. And although the Navajo Nation lies within the boundaries of three states (Arizona, New Mexico, and Utah), these states are generally barred by treaties, the trust doctrine, tribal sovereignty, and state constitutional disclaimers from intruding into Navajo Nation affairs, especially if such intrusion interferes with tribal self-government or infringes upon a tribal right reserved by treaty or established by federal law.

Attempts at Government Reform

Since Zah's election in 1982 there has been ongoing discussion about the need for fundamental government reform—reform that would genuinely reflect that the consent of the Navajo people formed the basis of Navajo government. As part of the Title II Amendments, the council agreed with this thrust when it established a Commission on Navajo Government Development and the Office of Navajo Government Development. The council declared that "the Commission is a special entity ... with quasi-independent authority to accomplish the Council's project of instituting reform necessary to ensure an accountable and responsible government."

The purposes of the commission included reviewing and evaluating every aspect of the existing structure of government and developing recommendations and proposals for "alternative forms of government for consideration and possible adoption by the Navajo people through a referendum vote."[5] More importantly, the commission had a number of enumerated powers. These included the power to:

1. Develop a series of recommendations and proposals for alternative forms of government for consideration by the Navajo Nation Council and the Navajo People by examining and utilizing the concepts of the separation of powers and the delegation of authority to provide for the appropriate checks and balances in Navajo government; to establish the responsibility of the Navajo government to protect the rights and freedoms of the Navajo People; to establish

limitations on how the Navajo government and its officials may use its powers and to define the powers of the Navajo people.

2. Provide short and long range comprehensive planning, evaluation and development appropriate to further enhance a Navajo Government that will perpetually accommodate the Navajo People by providing for their involvement, promote their general welfare, ensure governmental accountability integrity, justice, domestic order, and retain traditional harmony, cultural respect, heritage, and the protection of personal liberties. ...[6]

The commission's staff set about its task with vigor and engaged in a number of educational activities, such as conducting public surveys and holding public hearings, aimed at drawing knowledge from the public and also educating the public about the potentiality of tribal government reform. The surveys discerned a general distrust of tribal officials and a desire for a more representative National Council. The Navajo public also insisted that the people should be the ultimate judge of what changes tribal government should entail. The people, according to the surveys and hearings, stated that there was a need for a more formalized government that also retained and drew from Navajo culture. Many of the survey's participants supported the idea of a tribal constitution.[7]

Based on this data, in 1993, the project staff prepared and submitted specific recommendations that would, first, have amended the *Navajo Nation Code* to provide for "the Navajo people to consent to be governed by the Navajo Nation government ... ."[8] The project staff, in a seminar presentation to the council in February 1993, stressed that government reform was essential so that the entire government would finally be subject to the will and consent of the Navajo people. Shortly after their presentation, however, the legislators closed the Office of Navajo Government Development, effective March 31, 1993. The council apparently was unwilling at that time to entertain the fundamentally democratic notion that the Navajo government should be subject to the sovereign will of the people.

The Office of Navajo Government Development was revived later, but rather than push for profound changes in the basis of government itself, it focused more narrowly on the idea of decentralizing some authority to local government. Albert Hale, in fact, used the idea of empowering local government as a key to get elected to the presidency in 1994. In generating his "Local Empowerment" plan, he declared that "the local governments must be revitalized with the strength that the basic beliefs of the Diné serving as the foundations of the Navajo Nation." Three years later, in 1998, the council approved the Navajo Nation Local Governance Act. This important measure will be discussed more in the chapter on local government.

Conclusion

The Navajo Nation government has slowly become more democratic over the last decade; on rare occasions it actually took issues of importance directly to the Navajo people in referendum elections to ascertain the will of the people. **Referendum** elections provide that certain tribal resolutions may or may not become law, even though passed by the council, unless the resolution receives the majority approval of adult Navajos in a national election.

The clearest examples of this were the two national referenda in the 1990s centering on whether the people wanted to have tribal sponsored gaming operations within the reservation. Indian gaming as a policy issue will be discussed more in the last chapter. In both cases, the people, largely on moral grounds, voted down the idea of gambling, despite the perception pushed by many in the council that significant revenue would be generated.[9] These referenda were valuable and indicate the evolving presence of democratic traditions in the Nation.

Another possible way for the Navajo electorate to have some say in matters of governance, aside from a full-fledged constitution, is the **initiative** process. Some tribal governments and many state governments provide that the voters may also initiate legislation. (California voters struck down affirmative action and ended property tax through the initiative process.) An initiative means that voters can propose law directly. If a certain percentage of voters favor a proposal, say, the formation of a tribal constitution, it is placed on the election ballot. If it is approved by a majority vote on election day, it becomes law. This mechanism provides a measure of protection against non-responsive elected legislatures.

The Navajo Nation, under Title XI, authorizes registered Navajo voters to petition "to place a referendum measure (an initiative) on a Navajo Nation general or special election ballot where the scope of the referendum affects the entire Navajo Nation and is not limited to a chapter or chapters." In addition chapter members also may, through the referendum process, initiate laws for their chapters through the formal petition process. The referendum process was crafted in April 6, 1990, in the wake of the MacDonald political scandal. Eventually, the referendum/initiative process may prove to be an important means by which Navajo voters secure certain laws or policies not otherwise forthcoming from the Navajo National government. This will only occur, however, if the Navajo electorate is educated about the merits of such a process.

As a result of the political scandal in 1989, the Navajo Nation now has a clearer separation of powers and an evolving sense of checks and balances, two fundamental features of a functional democracy. And the referendum process, begun in 1990, is another positive step in the democratic process. As yet, however, the Navajo people have not fundamentally and organically acted to either create or legitimate their central governing structure. Consequently, while meaningful democratic reforms continue to unfold, these have been initiated from the elected political leadership rather than flowing from the free will of the Navajo people.

Key Terms

Bill of Rights   Removal

Initiative   Veto

Referendum

Selected Readings

Jackson, Charlene D. "Historical Overview of the Navajo Nation's Attempts to Implement a Constitutionally Based Government," (Tucson: Unpublished Manuscript, 1993).

Navajo Nation Code. Titles 1–26 (6 volumes) (New York: Lamb Studio, 1995).

Office of Navajo Government Development. *Navajo Nation Government.* (Window Rock, Arizona: Office of Navajo Government Development, 1997).

Notes

[1] The Office of Navajo Government Development. *Navajo Nation Government.* (Window Rock: Office of Navajo Government Development, 1997): 40.

[2] See Charlene D. Jackson, "Historical Overview of the Navajo Nation's Attempts to Implement a Constitutionally Based Government." (Unpublished manuscript, Univ. of Arizona, 1993). This study provides a thorough description and analysis of the tribe's efforts to establish a constitution.

[3] Navajo Nation Code, Title XI, section 240.

[4] Ibid., section 241.

5 Title II, article 3, section 971, 2.
6 Title II, section 973.
7 Jackson, "Historical Overview of the Navajo Nation's Attempts ..." p. 16.
8 Ibid., p. 17.
9 Eric Henderson and Scott Russell, "The Navajo Gaming Referendum: Reservations About Casino Lead to Popular Rejection of Legalized Gambling," *Human Organization,* vol. 56, no. 3 (1997): 294–301.

Chapter 6

The Navajo Nation Legislature (The Council)

Introduction

The Navajo Nation Council is the heart of the government. The Nation's council delegates and their leader, the Speaker of the Council, constitute the lawmaking branch of the Navajo Nation government. As the Nation's lawmakers, they are concerned with order and stability, justice, protection of cultural values, efficiency, and the delicate balancing of contemporary law with a measure of traditional customs and traditions. Above all, they act as representatives of all the Navajo people and function as decision-makers regarding tribal requests.

What Is a Legislature?

The basic activity of any legislative body is to review requests for action, and say "yes" or "no." The Nation's Council performs many roles, but it is important to remember that *the primary responsibility of the council is to make law.*

The council exercises a number of powers in fulfilling its mandate to make law.

1. It is the governing body of the Navajo Nation and enacts and amends laws.
2. It has all the legislative powers not delegated to any other branch or the people.
3. It has the power to appropriate and expend monies (i.e., approve an annual tribal budget).
4. It represents—through the Intergovernmental Relations Committee —the Navajo Nation's interest in negotiations with all other governments.
5. It confirms the appointments of Division Directors.
6. It establishes all standing committees.
7. It adopts necessary rules, regulations, and procedures for its own conduct.
8. It establishes procedures to regulate the conduct of council members and is authorized to discipline or remove individuals who violate the Nation's laws.
9. It may, by two-thirds vote of the membership, override a presidential **veto** of legislation.

This is not an exhaustive list, of course, and as a practical matter council delegates are expected, if they expect to be reelected, to do constituency related activities (i.e., assist with sanitation matters and irrigation projects, help with financial emergencies at the chapter or individual level, deal with livestock concerns, and so on.)

The Council and Its Delegates

As noted in Chapter 2, unlike the U.S. Congress or the Arizona legislature, both with **bicameral** (a two-house legislature—House and Senate) legislatures, the Navajo Nation Council is a **unicameral** system. The council currently consists of eighty-eight delegates who are elected to four year terms by the registered voters of one of each designated precinct—apportioned among the 110 chapters.

The council holds four regular sessions each year (January, April, July, and October) in Window Rock, Arizona. Special meetings may be called by the speaker, acting on the recommendation of the Ethics and Rules Committee or by written petition of a majority of council delegates. Unlike the president, who is limited to two terms, council delegates may serve an unlimited number of terms. The qualifications to serve as a council delegate are as follows:

1. Be at least 25 years of age
2. Be an enrolled member of the Nation and on the Agency Census roll of the BIA
3. Must not have been convicted of a felony within the last five years
4. Must not have been convicted of certain misdemeanors (e.g., extortion, fraud, theft, child neglect)
5. Must be completely loyal to the Navajo Nation and be competent to hold the oath of office
6. Must be a registered voter in the chapter he/she is elected from
7. Candidates who are already employed by the Navajo Nation must resign and not be gainfully employed again during their tenure in office (except on a school board)
8. Must be able to speak and comprehend Navajo and/or English
9. Cannot be a permanent employee of the federal or any state government (or any subdivision of a state), or be an elected official of the United States or any state (except school board or county office)[1]

Additionally, candidates for council delegate positions must not be under any restraint for holding elective office because of ethical violations of Navajo Nation law.

Council delegates are entitled to a bevy of attractive perks and privileges: an annual salary of $25,000 (compared to the average Navajo salary of a little more than $6,600); group insurance coverage; a hefty per diem and other travel reimbursements; and deferred compensation upon leaving office.

One of the most important changes emerging from the Title II Amendments was the establishment of the Office of **Speaker of the Navajo Nation Council**, a change suggesting a real separation of the executive and legislative powers for the first time in the Nation's modern history. The speaker is selected by the council every two years as the first order of business at the council session in January of odd-numbered years. The speaker must be a member in good standing of the council. He serves at the pleasure of the council. The speaker receives a $30,000 annual salary and by statute is provided a home in Window Rock. The speaker has various statutory responsibilities. These include, but are not limited to:

1. Presides over the council
2. Directs and supervises programs and personnel under the legislative branch, as provided by law
3. Votes only in the event of a tie
4. May call a special session of the council
5. Signs all resolutions approved by the council
6. Serves as the Chair of the Intergovernmental Relations Committee (This important committee consists of the speaker and the chairperson of each standing committee.)
7. Recommends delegates for appointment to standing committees
8. Approves the scheduling of all meetings of standing committees and where the meetings will convene
9. Recommends to the Budget and Finance Committee an annual operating budget and advises the council on the annual budget recommended by Budget and Finance Committee

Committees

The bulk of lawmaking takes place in council **standing committees**. This is appropriate for division of labor and so that individual delegates can develop expertise in particular areas. Nearly all legislative action reflects a committee recommendation. Eventually, however, all council delegates have to vote on each resolution that emerges from the committees. At present there are twelve committees, a reduction from the eighteen existing prior to the Title II Amendments. They are: Budget and Finance, Economic Development, Education, Ethics and Rules, Government Services, Health and Social Services, Human Services, Judiciary, Public Safety, Resources, Transportation and Community Development, and Intergovernmental Relations.

The Speaker of the Council appoints the members of each committee. Each delegate to the council can serve on only one standing committee and one board or commission. The speaker, however, serves only as Chair of the Intergovernmental Relations Committee and cannot serve on any other board or commission. For purposes of parity and distribution, it is required that each of the five Navajo agencies have representation on each committee.

While each committee plays a vital role, the Intergovernmental Relations Committee (IGR) is particularly important because it is chaired by the speaker and consists of the chairs of all standing committees. This committee, has among its powers the authority to coordinate all federal, state, and county programs with other standing committees; serves as the oversight committee for the Office of Legislative Services and other programs and commissions; coordinates all requests for information related to any legislation that might affect the Nation; and authorizes, reviews, and accepts all contracts, grants, and associated budgets with the federal government.

How a Resolution Becomes Law

The way committees are structured within the council is especially significant because the public policy process unfolds there. Generally, the first step in drafting what might ultimately become a **resolution** (a tribal ordinance) is to collect information on the issue. Committee members and their staffers, or the staff of the Office of Legislative Counsel, will research a problem independently, or an issue will be brought to their attention by any number of sources—chapter officials, interest groups, the president's office, or by concerned Navajo citizens.

There are two types of resolutions: those for standing committees, and those for the Navajo Nation Council. Depending on the nature of the proposed legislative action, the number of reviewers may vary. As a general rule, however, there are two mandatory reviewers: The Department of Justice (except for condolences), and the Office of Legislative Counsel. Any resolution involving money must be reviewed by the Controller. And any matter involving intergovernmental affairs must be referred to the IGR committee after the appropriate resolution has gone through the initial review process.[2]

The resolution process was amended in 1997 in an effort to expedite what, according to some, had become a "cumbersome" process that often delayed action on important matters "to the detriment of the Navajo Nation."[3] This change was specifically designed to "reduce the number of days allowed for review, clarify the persons or entities who are mandatory reviewers, clarify the purpose of the review, and create a remedy for the failure to complete review within the limits established ... ."[4]

The resolution eventually adopting the change in procedure outlined the following:

A. The proposed resolution shall be reviewed and signed by the following:
    1. The appropriate Division Director for departments and activities under his or her supervision;
    2. The President or Vice President of the Navajo Nation for resolutions initiated by the Office of the President or by an office within the Executive Branch;
    3. The Attorney General of the Navajo Nation; the Attorney General and the Department of Justice shall not be required to approve any resolutions expressing congratulatory messages, condolences without appropriations, appointments, confirmations and internal budget transfers;
    4. The Controller for all requests affecting financial matters;
    5. The Legislative Counsel to the Navajo Nation Council; the Legislative Counsel to the Navajo Nation Council shall review all resolutions excluded from review by the Attorney General and Department of Justice pursuant to Sec. 164(A)(3);
    6. The Speaker of the Navajo Nation Council for Navajo Nation Council resolutions; and
    7. Chairpersons of Standing committees for committee resolutions.[5]

Reviewers have five working days to study and comment on the proposed resolution. If it is not acted upon (signed) within that period, the measure will be deemed reviewed, approved, and signed. This allows a sponsor to pick up the proposed resolution and proceed with it for eventual committee or council consideration. The purpose of the review process is to ensure that each resolution is legal and to ascertain whether additional clearances and/or investigations are warranted.

Factors Influencing Navajo Lawmakers

While Navajo **political parties** do not exist per se, many Navajo lawmakers identify for ideological purposes as Democrat, Republican, or Independent, and hold liberal, conservative, or moderate views (sometimes some of each) on the role of government in Navajo life. Although there are no extant studies on the political views or governing styles of Navajo politicians, some data are available on the Navajo electorate from which the political leadership is drawn, which provide a general sense of political attitudes.

According to a 1984 National Indian Youth Council study, nearly 70 percent of Navajos identified as Democrats, while only 11 percent identified as Republicans. Another 11 percent considered themselves Independent, and 10 percent expressed no party preference. Seventy-eight (78) percent of the respondents said they voted in Navajo elections, while 67 percent participated in local, state, and federal elections. A great majority, over 81 percent, were registered to vote and noted that they had registered at their local chapters.

Demographic analysis disclosed that Navajos least likely to identify themselves as Democrats were the younger (18–26), more educated (1–3 years of college), and higher income (over $25,000) individuals. Conversely, those most likely to identify as Democrats were the "post high school, trade or business groups, and those with a combined family income between $15,000 to $25,000." Those more active in tribal and general elections were within the 37–66 year age group, were employed, and had a family income over $15,000.[6]

Interest Groups (also known as pressure groups) may also influence the kind of legislation that does or does not get introduced. For example, groups like the Big Mountain Legal Defense/Offense Committee, the Sovereign Diné Nation-Dineh Alliance, and Diné C.A.R.E. (Citizens Against Ruining Our Environment), have each sought to influence the council and other governmental parties regarding land issues. Interest groups will be discussed more in Chapter 10.

Other delegates and staff are often a valuable source of information and will seek to sway their colleagues on particular issues. The *president and vice-president,* because they are elected by voters across the nation, also seek to exert pressure on Council delegates. This, of course, has only been in operation since 1989, since before that time the Navajo chief executive essentially controlled the legislative agenda.

Constituents, the registered voters in each chapter, theoretically represent the group the council delegates are most beholden to. Navajo voters (the **constituents**) elect their representatives and can unelect them if they feel their needs are not being met by their delegate. Finally, each individual delegate holds views inherent to him or her as an individual. It is the interplay of individual political ideology, values, beliefs, and those other forces seeking to influence the decision-making process that makes lawmaking an unpredictable and dynamic process.

Let us look at one central issue, *reapportionment,* to see how the council operates.

Reapportionment—"One Navajo-One Vote"

There are 435 members of the U.S. House of Representatives. Because each state's representation in that body is in proportion to its population, the Constitution provides for a national census every decade to determine the nation's population and to gather other pertinent data. Population shifts are then handled by **reapportionment**—the assignment to a state of a new number of congressional seats—among the states after the census has been completed if population changes warrant a change.

For example, recent population growth has centered in the Sunbelt, Texas, California, and Florida. Those particular areas have gained congressional representatives as a result of their increased population base. Conversely, some states in the Northeast and the Midwest have lost representatives as their population has declined. In effect, each representative is elected from a specific district and each district elects only one representative. The districts within a state must be roughly equal in population.

The Supreme Court, in two landmark cases in the 1960s, *Baker v. Carr* (1962) and *Reynolds v. Simms* (1964), established the principle of "one-person, one-vote," which specified that voting districts had to be structured on the basis of population so that no one person's vote carried more weight than anyone else's.

The Navajo Nation, because of the doctrine of federal plenary power and the fact that Indians are also citizens of the state and the United States, is also subject to what we will call the "one-Navajo, one-vote" standard since only Navajos may vote in tribal elections. The council, in 1974, passed a resolution to begin the reapportionment process based on the "one-Navajo" rule. The following year, the Navajo Nation Election Code declared that "on or before the first Monday of May 1975, and every 10 years thereafter, the Navajo Tribal Council, with the recommendation of the Navajo Board of Election Supervisors, shall designate the number and location of precincts. All such precincts shall be approximately equal in population." (See Figure 6-1.)

Navajo reapportionment became a major political issue because, as a result of the tremendous growth in population and shifts in Navajo demography, some chapters, such as Shiprock, had become very large (7,997 people), while others like Le Chee, with only 463 members, were quite small. The tribal government had been reluctant to institute reapportionment, fearing political repercussions, but by 1976 "federal officials were threatening to sue the Navajos to reapportion."[7]

In that year, the 74 council delegates represented 102 chapters, but the distribution was very uneven. According to the law, and with a total population of 151,627, each delegate should have been representing

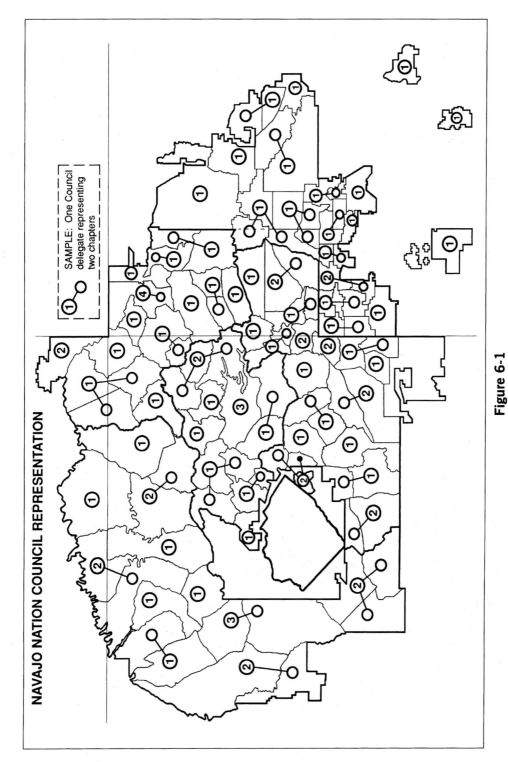

Figure 6-1

Source: Larry Rodgers, ed. Chapter Images: 1992 Edition. (Window Rock, Navajo Nation: Division of Community Development, 1993)

approximately 2,049 people. This was certainly not the case, however.[8] Peter MacDonald, then Chairman of the Council, became embroiled over this issue in 1977; but by 1978 and after great debate, the government arrived at a compromise reapportionment plan which called for an 87 member council, with additional political representation for larger communities like Shiprock, Tuba City, Chinle, and several others, while still maintaining representation for smaller chapters as well. (As the population grew between 1978 and 1990, one additional delegate was added.)

The Navajo Board of Election Supervisors (to be discussed in Chapter 12), created by the council as an independent entity, has—among its many duties—the power to develop and recommend to the council all apportionment plans for election purposes which contain voting precincts that are approximately equal in population. The board's most recent effort at guiding reapportionment was fulfilled in April 1998 when, by way of resolution CAP-35-98, the council adopted reapportionment plan VR3 as recommended by the board for use in the 1998 primary and general elections.

In this law, the council also followed the board's recommendation that voter registration data, rather than the 1990 U.S. Census or the BIA's enrollment information, should be used as the basis on which to construct the Nation's reapportionment plan. The council believed that the voter registration records were "more current, and reflect the entire population of the Navajo Nation, including those who may be absent from time-to-time," but who still participate in Navajo elections. There is a question, however, whether the "one-Navajo, one-vote" rule is being followed if only registered voters are being counted for purposes of allocating political representation.

The board was also required by tribal law to take into account chapter boundaries, district grazing boundaries, and agency borders in forming the new apportionment calculation. Based on 90,887 registered Navajo voters and 88 council delegates, it found the ideal number of registered voters for each council delegate to be 1,033. The board's calculation of the maximum population deviation for reapportionment Plan VR3 was 79.0 percent. That figure was arrived at thus:

Largest Precinct: Houck/Nahata Dzil with 1,507 registered voters

Smallest Precinct: Thoreau with 691 registered voters

Difference between the largest and smallest precinct = 816 registered voters

Ideal number of registered voters for each delegate = 1,033

Calculation: 100 (816/1033) = 79.0%

Translation: Geography, politics, demographic trends, and other limitations in the Navajo Nation have resulted in the creation of precincts ranging from a low of 691 voters per delegate to a high of 1,507 voters. The smallest district, then, has only two-thirds as many registered voters as an ideal district, with the largest district being 1.45 times larger than the target district size. This in some ways mirrors the limitations of district creation for the U.S. House of Representatives. In Congress, the one-person, one-vote standard is also limited by geographic and other considerations. As an example, at-large states such as Wyoming and Montana have district populations ranging from 481,000 in Wyoming, which is slightly over three-quarters the size of an ideal district, to 879,000 people in Montana, which is about 1.45 times larger than an ideal district. Remember, the "ideal district" is the total population divided by 435 seats in the House of Representatives.[9]

The Navajo Nation struggles with reapportionment each time it occurs. One of the problems is that besides the United States legal requirement of reapportionment every ten years, the *Navajo Nation Code* offers little substantive guidance in how reapportionment is to be done.[10] This lack of statutory guidance is complicated by the fact that before any apportionment can take place, a government should first have a clear sense of what the total population is. Unlike the United States, however, which is required by the Constitution to have a decennial census (an official counting of the population, among other purposes), the Navajo Nation has no such law and in the past has generally relied on other data gleaned from voter registration, the U.S. Census, or the BIA.

This lack of a reliable and updated population count has sometimes led to conflict during reapportionment discussions, especially when a Navajo precinct faced the prospect of losing a delegate because of declining population numbers. It has been suggested that an official census conducted by the Navajo Nation well in advance of the reapportionment year would be a significant step forward in preparing a more realistic apportionment plan.

A second issue affecting Navajo reapportionment involves how "precincts" are determined. There is a legal requirement for 88 equal precincts. This requirement involves the currently accepted practice of dividing the 88 districts along chapter lines—based on chapter *membership* and not chapter *boundaries*. Since there are 110 chapters, the complicated task is how to allocate 88 delegates into 88 precincts? Some precincts, because of their size and population, have more than one delegate (e.g., Shiprock has three delegates). Those precincts with more than one delegate serve to confound the proceedings since theoretically each Navajo precinct is supposed to have only one delegate.

This is a difficult process, arguably much more difficult than that faced by states or the federal government since they redraw districts along geographical lines based on actual residency and have bicameral houses (except for Nebraska). In the Navajo Nation, on the other hand, one must take into account chapter membership rather than geographical boundaries for drawing precinct lines; and as discussed earlier, this can be problematic because in many cases Navajos have moved, yet they may still be counted as members of their birth chapters. Each of these factors means that for the foreseeable future the issue of Navajo reapportionment will continue to be a hotly contested issue.

Conclusion

The legislative branch also encompasses a number of important boards and commissions, including the Navajo/Hopi Land Commission, the Eastern Navajo Land Commission, the Navajo Board of Election Supervisors; the Navajo Nation Insurance Commission, and a number of other legislative offices.

It is sufficient to say that as the Navajo Nation enters the twenty-first century, the lawmaking branch appears to have assumed the dominant role in Navajo political affairs.[11] The Title II Amendments inaugurated a clear demarcation between the legislative and executive branches—the judicial branch was not involved. It appears to most knowledgeable insiders that the Navajo Nation Council has gained the upper hand in the separation of powers and checks and balances plan that was outlined in 1989. This is not surprising, in a sense, because for too many years the executive branch dominated the legislative body.

However, it also appears that in its well-intentioned efforts to dilute the extreme power amassed in the executive branch, (through the Title II Amendments and subsequent laws) and the council's steady refusal to recognize that its authority to govern should lawfully derive from the Navajo people has allowed it to become the superior branch of the three coordinate branches of government. Fortunately, the council does not enjoy the commanding power that the executive branch exercised prior to the 1989 changes, but it exercises a significant amount of power nonetheless.

Key Terms

Bicameral	Political Parties
Constituents	Reapportionment

Resolution   Unicameral
Speaker of the Council   Veto
Standing Committee

Selected Readings

Deloria, Vine, Jr. "Congress in its Wisdom: The Course of Indian Legislation,"
in Sandra L. Cadwalader and Vine Deloria, Jr. eds. *The Aggressions of
Civilization.* (Philadelphia, Pennsylvania: Temple University Press, 1984):
106–130.

Fenno, Richard F., Jr. *Congressmen in Committees.* (Boston: Little, Brown, 1973).

Mayhew, David R. *Congress: The Electoral Connection.* (New Haven: Yale
University Press, 1986).

Wilkins, David E. "The 'De-Selected' Senate Committee on Indian Affairs and its
Legislative Record, 1977–1992," *Native American Studies,* vol. 9, no. 1
(1995): 27–34.

Notes

1   Title XI, *Navajo Nation Code,* section 8 (b).

2   Special thanks to Mr. Ronald D. Haven, esq., a staff member of the Office of
Legislative Counsel, who provided the author with the most recent information
available on the resolution process, among other things.

3   CAP-24-97, "Approving the Amendments to 2 N.N.C. Section 164" was
approved by a Council vote of 59–0 on April 22, 1997.

4   Ibid.

5   Ibid.

6   National Indian Youth Council, *Navajo Indian Political Attitudes and Behavior
Poll.* (Albuquerque, New Mexico: October 1984): 23–31.

7   Iverson, *The Navajo Nation,* p. 209.

8   Ibid.

9   Special thanks to Richard Witmer, a former graduate student at the University
of Arizona, for crafting this explanation of reapportionment deviation
calculation.

10 I want to thank Ron Haven of the Office of Legislative Counsel for his critical
comments on this complicated subject.

11 Special thanks to Vivian Arviso for her comments and views on what the
separation of powers meant for the relationship between the president and the
council during Peterson Zah's second run as leader of the Navajo Nation.

Chapter 7

The Navajo Nation Executive
(The President and Vice-President)

Introduction

Throughout history, the Navajo Nation has produced a number of outstanding principal leaders: from Narbona, the Peace Naataanii of the 1840s; to Barboncito, Manuelito and Ganado Mucho—three men who guided their people through wars with the Americans, imprisonment at Bosque Redondo, and the return home after the Treaty of 1868; to Chee Dodge, the first Chairman of the Navajo Tribal Council in 1922; to contemporary leaders like Annie Wauneka (education and health), Tom Tso (Chief Justice of the Navajo Supreme Court), and Claudeen Arthur Bates, who played a key role in tribal government in the wake of the political scandal of the 1980s.

The offices of president and vice-president of the Navajo Nation have only existed in structure for a decade and were, in fact, crafted because of poor and misguided **executive** leadership. Prior to the 1989 Title II Amendments, the chief executive officer was called the chairman of the Navajo

129

Tribal Council. The chair was, legally speaking, the leader of the Tribal Council with the power to preside over the council, appoint all standing committee chairs and members, and serve as chair of the powerful Advisory and Intergovernmental Relations Committees.

It was this virtually unlimited authority in the office of the chairman, combined with Peter MacDonald's unique and powerful personality, which led to the political scandal that rocked the Navajo Nation in 1989. One of the central issues that arose in the wake of that scandalous period was a realization on the part of the council that the position of chair must be split into two wholly separate positions—the speaker of the Council (legislative leader) and the president of the Navajo Nation (executive leader). The Navajo Nation president, therefore, is now the chief executive officer of the executive branch of the Navajo Nation government with full authority to conduct, supervise, and coordinate personnel and programs of the Navajo Nation.

What is Executive Power?

Executive power is concerned with law enforcement: applying or administering laws, agreements, or policies. The executive branch, then, in a government with separation of powers, is that body of individuals beginning with the chief executive officer (whether it be the president of the Navajo Nation, the governor of New Mexico, or the president of the United States) and their supporting bureaucracies who "execute" the nation's or state's laws.

Powers of the Navajo Nation President

The president derives authority from three central sources—the *Navajo Nation Code,* Navajo Nation Council **delegations**, and from traditional Navajo cultural understandings of what the chief leader could or should do to improve the lives of the people. The major powers outlined in the *Code* are summarized below:

> ◆ The president serves as the chief executive officer of the executive branch and has complete authority to conduct, supervise, and coordinate personnel and programs of the Navajo Nation government. The president has a **fiduciary** (trust) responsibility for the proper and efficient operation of all executive branch offices.

- The president represents the Navajo Nation in its relations with all other governments and private agencies and seeks to generate favorable public opinion and goodwill toward the Nation.
- The president is expected to faithfully execute and enforce the Navajo Nation's laws.
- The president negotiates and executes contracts, subject to appropriate legislative committee approval.
- The president appoints supervisory executive personnel.
- The president appoints the members of all boards, commissions, and other entities that are part of the executive bureaucracy.
- The President is required to provide a State of the Navajo Nation report to the council four times a year.
- The president recommends to the Budget and Finance Committee an annual budget for the executive branch and advises the council on the annual budget recommended by the Budget and Finance Committee.
- The president recommends any supplemental **appropriations** to the council for the administration of the executive branch.
- The president exercises those powers delegated to the office by the council.
- The president exercises the veto power over legislation passed by the council (this must be done within ten days after the legislation has been certified by the Speaker of the Council).
- The president speaks and acts for the Nation on all matters relating to the Navajo-Hopi land dispute.
- The vice-president serves as acting president during absences of the Nation's leader.

Presidential Office and Activities

The president (and vice-president) are appointed to four-year terms and may serve, if reelected, two terms. Like the speaker, the government also furnishes a home for the president and the vice-president. The president receives an annual salary of $55,000, the vice-president earns $45,000.

A candidate for president must be an enrolled member of the Navajo Nation and at least thirty years of age. He or she must also have been a resident of the Navajo Nation for three consecutive years before election. Other qualifications are similar to those of delegates—be a registered voter, speak and understand Navajo and read and write English, must not have been convicted of a felony or any of a number of specified misdemeanors within the past five years, and so on.[1]

Vacancies

If, for any reason, the president vacates the position or is unable to perform his/her duties, the vice-president steps in and serves as president for the remainder of the term or until the president's inability to perform his/her duties has been lifted. If a vacancy should take place in both the presidency and vice-presidency, the speaker of the Council serves as president until a special election is held.

The issue of vacancies was tested most recently in 1998 when President Thomas Atcitty was forced to resign because of ethics violations. Kelsey Begaye, speaker of the Council, was sworn in as interim president since Atcitty's vice-president, Milton Bluehouse, Sr., was declared ineligible to assume the presidency because he had been appointed, not elected. Under existing law that was sufficient to make him ineligible. Bluehouse threatened legal action over this interpretation, however, and after discussion the council decided to adopt a resolution clarifying the law to allow any vice-president, whether elected or appointed, to succeed the president in the event of a vacancy. Speaker Begaye voluntarily agreed to step down rather than embroil the Nation in yet another embarrassing incident.[2]

Gifts of Property

Closely related to the discussion of vacancies is the matter of gifts that Navajo presidents receive. The chief executive of any government is often the recipient of gifts and other donations by other heads of state, appreciative businesses, or thankful constituents. Of course, such gifts sometimes are offered for less meritorious reasons—that is to say, the person or interest group who provides the gift expects the recipient, in this case, the president, to look favorably on his or her interests or needs. For example, an energy corporation may lavish gifts, free airplane trips, and other goods on politicians—be they presidents, governors, or chiefs—in the hope that leaders might approve a particular lease for that company, agree to lower taxes or provide some other perquisite for the company. Hence, like any legitimate organization that has policies and rules, the Navajo Nation has instituted regulations about the appropriate manner in which the Nation's elected officials, including the president, must conduct themselves.

These rules concern the appropriateness of behavior while a governmental employee is representing the Navajo Nation.

Government employees are expected to act ethically; that is, they are to follow a set of moral principles and be persons of good character. According to the Nation's **ethics** laws which focus primarily on financial matters, Navajo public officials are to avoid any situation which might result in or create the appearance of any of the following:

1. Using public office for private gain
2. Favoring any special interest group or individual
3. Acting in a manner that creates unnecessary expense for the Navajo Nation or prevents the efficient conduct of the Nation's affairs
4. Making any government decision outside officially prescribed channels
5. Making any government decision that adversely affects the confidence of the Navajo people and the integrity of the government

Under existing law, the president may accept gifts of property "on behalf of the Navajo Nation." If the value exceeds $1,000 the concurrence of the Government Services Committee must be secured. All such gifts become the property of the Nation. Moreover, no Navajo public officials, whether elected or appointed, may receive gifts, favors, or services valued at more that $100 in any year from any person, organization, or group which has or is seeking to do business with the Navajo Nation.

Within the last decade (1989–1999) three of the Nation's presidents were forced out of office over ethics violations ranging from non-recording of gifts and improper use of tribal funds, to bribery, fraud, conspiracy, and racketeering. The ethics of accepting token gifts, however, is seemingly less clear-cut to some. Albert Hale, just after he was ousted from the presidency, maintained that accepting such gifts was a Navajo custom. Others in the tribe insisted that it was corruption and was contrary to tribal law. This raises the question of what constitutes an ethical violation under Navajo Nation law. In other words, should Navajo politicians be held to the same ethical standards as state or federal officials? Is the corruption and scandal that brought down Arizona Governors Fife Symington and Evan Meacham comparable to that which toppled Peter MacDonald? Are the sex scandals which have plagued the Clinton presidency similar to the one which confronted Albert Hale during his abbreviated presidency?

These are important questions, particularly if it is true, as tribal leaders and their constituents often insist, that Indian nations adhere to different cultural values than their non-Indian neighbors. But it is true for another reason. Since the Navajo Nation receives much of its funding from the federal government, many Washington officials insist that Navajo politicians must adhere to American ethical standards whether or not they clash with traditional Diné cultural standards. These cultural issues, combined with blood ties, clan relations, extended families, and traditional medicine power, mean that some ethical questions remain problematic and must still be worked out between the Navajo citizenry and their politicians and between the Navajo Nation and the federal government.

The Executive Bureaucracy

The executive branch is the largest and costliest of the three branches. Nearly 80 percent of the more than $90 million annual budget is spent for the administration and service delivery programs overseen by the executive branch.[3] At the present time the president has under his jurisdiction the following offices: Navajo Nation Washington Office, the Navajo/Hopi Land Commission, the Office of Navajo Tax Commission, the Office of Attorney General, and the Office of Management and Budget. The president is also in charge of the following divisions: Finance, Public Safety, Human Resources, General Services, Education, Health Services, Social Services, Community Development, and Economic Development.

Conclusion

The president of the Navajo Nation is in the enviable position of being the popularly elected leader of the largest reservation-based indigenous nation in the United States. And as noted in the beginning of the text, the Navajo Nation is also larger than a number of internationally recognized sovereign nations. As such, the president's views are sought out on a variety of topics and issues, particularly those centering on tribal sovereignty and self-determination.

Unfortunately, the last decade has been a troubled period for Navajo chief executives and the Nation has had a dramatic and unprecedented amount of turnover in leadership during this period. For just as the president's views are sought out, his favor is also sought by companies, corporations, and others who will sometimes resort to unethical actions in anticipation of gaining the leader's support. The result, as the Navajo Nation learned in 1998 with a succession of four Navajo presidents before the fall election, is often disastrous and embarrassing.

It appears, however, that the 1989 Title II reforms are holding well and the separation of powers and checks and balances, while not perfectly symmetrical, are enabling the government to continue to function relatively smoothly even though individual Navajo chief executives have had some serious ethical problems.

Key Terms

Appropriations   Executive
Delegation   Fiduciary
Ethics

Selected Readings

Iverson, Peter. "Peter MacDonald," in R. David Edmunds, ed. *American Indian Leaders: Studies in Diversity.* (Lincoln: University of Nebraska Press, 1980): 222–241.

Lubick, George M. "Peterson Zah: A Progressive Outlook and a Traditional Style," in John R. Wunder, ed. *Native American Sovereignty* (New York: Garland Publishing, Inc., 1996): 241–266.

Mankiller, Wilma and Michael Wallis. *Mankiller: A Chief and Her People.* (New York: St. Martin's Press, 1993).

Meredith, Howard. *Modern American Indian Tribal Government and Politics.* (Tsaile, Arizona: Navajo Community College Press, 1993). See especially Chapter 7 "Tribal Chairperson."

Trahant, Mark N. "The 1970s: New Leaders for Indian Country," in Frederick E. Hoxie and Peter Iverson, eds. *Indians in American History,* 2nd ed. (Wheeling, Illinois: Harlan Davidson, Inc., 1998): 235–252.

Notes

[1] Title XI, Section 8, *Navajo Nation Code* (1995).

[2] "Navajo Nation Council Names New Interim President—Again," *Tucson Citizen,* July 25, 1988: 3b.

[3] Office of Navajo Government Development, *Navajo Nation Government,* 20.

Chapter 8

The Navajo Nation Judiciary (The Courts)

Introduction

The Navajo judiciary is the youngest of the three branches of government yet, like the court system of the United States, it is unarguably the most respected institution in Navajo Nation government. This is because the traditional form of Navajo tribal organization, like that of most indigenous nations, functioned primarily as an **adjudicatory (judicial)** body, resolving disputes within the nation.[1] It is also because the Navajo courts have more explicitly folded traditional and customary Diné legal values and institutions into the structure of the courts and have fully developed courts—Peacemaker Courts—that are based entirely on Navajo tradition.

For example, two of the most essential concepts in Navajo philosophy are K'e and hozho.[2] K'e, broadly defined, entails one's duty and responsibility for all others, while hozho centers on the idea of harmony. Both of these core ideas have been incorporated into the *Navajo Nation Code of Judicial Conduct.* Furthermore, the Diné clan system is a legal system that is also part of a complicated network that identifies one's mutual obligations in relationships. Traditional Diné common law, then, "fostered a system of justice based on clan relations, harmony, mediation, leadership by reputation and respect, a focus on making victims whole, equality and freedom with responsibility."[3]

Historical Background of the Navajo Nation Courts

Prior to 1892, the Navajo Nation had no formal courts to speak of. The tribal community, led by the Peace Naataanii, relied on the traditional laws and customs to maintain harmony and balance among the people. But in the late 1800s the federal government, intent on "civilizing" Indians, instituted a system of Indian police and courts, controlled by the local Indian agent. The idea was to impose a western legal system on tribal nations.

The first courts were called **Courts of Indian Offenses** and adhered to rigid and very punitive rules established by the BIA. The first Indian offense court in Navajo Country was established in 1892. The three-judge panels were local Indians handpicked by the Indian agent to administer the United States government's laws. According to Tom Tso, the Navajo judges synthesized the Western way with the Navajo way in their deliberations. However, Tso's interpretation of the flexibility of the Navajo judges runs contrary to the actual purpose of the government's policy which was the rapid and forced assimilation of Indians into the Western legal model.[4]

The judges of the Navajo Court of Indian Offenses were, in fact, chosen by the bureau's agents until the late 1950s when the Nation's leaders reclaimed the authority to create their own judicial system by forming the Navajo Tribal Court in 1959 and requested the transfer of law enforcement responsibilities to the Nation. This court system was tightly patterned after the state courts under the assumption that by being so structured they would earn the respect of the state and federal court judges and justices and be able to block the state's efforts to extend its jurisdiction over the reservation under Public Law 280 enacted in 1953.

The judicial branch initially consisted of a Trial Court of seven appointed judges and a Court of Appeals. The appeals court had three judges: the chief justice and two trial court judges. The trial court had jurisdiction over *Law and Order Code* violations committed by Indians and over domestic relations cases.[5]

The next major changes occurred in 1981 when Chief Justice Nelson McCabe initiated a process designed to find ways to integrate Navajo customary law in the Nation's courts. One outgrowth of this project was the creation of the Navajo **Peacemaker Courts** in 1982.[6] In 1985, the council adopted the Judicial Reform Act, which encouraged the use of Navajo **common law** in tribal court decisions and established the Navajo Supreme Court. In fact, in 1991, Navajo common law became the law of preference in the Nation's courts,[7] although Navajo statutory law (*Code*) is also used. Also in 1991, the *Code of Judicial Conduct* was adopted by an administrative order issued by the chief justice. This code relies on Navajo concepts of due process and traditional legal values.[8]

Navajo Nation Court Structure

The Navajo court system is the most complex and sophisticated of Indian court systems and one of the few Indian courts which compiles its decisions in permanent bound volumes. Legal opinions of the Supreme Court and of the trial courts are found in the *Navajo Reporter* and the *Indian Law Reporter.*

As of 1998, the Navajo Nation has seven *judicial districts* (Chinle, Crownpoint, Kayenta, Ramah, Shiprock, Tuba City, and Window Rock) with district and family court divisions. There are seven *district courts* of general jurisdiction and five *family courts* that deal with juvenile issues, divorce proceedings, and probate matters. These court rulings are subject to review by the Navajo Nation *Supreme Court,* which is located in Window Rock. A *small claims court* and the important *Peacemaker Courts* round out the judicial landscape.

The case load of the Navajo courts is increasing tremendously because of severe social and economic problems in the Nation. Chief Justice Robert Yazzie in his "Message" accompanying his quarterly report in 1998, stated that:

> For the first time in years, the criminal caseload is the highest of all case categories. Assault and battery are now the number one crimes, and we know that a great deal of these crimes against persons revolve around family violence. This past fiscal year, there were 3,142 separate civil domestic abuse protection cases. Juvenile assaults are also high. We know that the Navajo Nation jails have very limited space. How can the courts address these issues?[9]

In the second quarter report (January 1, 1998 to March 31, 1998) of the judicial branch, a total of 26,411 cases were heard in just family and district courts. The breakdown was as follows:

Criminal Cases	10,394	39.35%
Traffic Cases	12,234	38.75%
Family Cases	3,714	14.06%
Civil Cases	2,069	07.84%
Total	28,411	100.00%

There are seventeen authorized judges and justices in the Navajo court system—fourteen trial judges and three supreme court justices. A court staff meets the research, administrative, and clerical needs of each judge.

Navajo Supreme Court

This is the court of last resort. It hears all appeals from the Navajo district courts, the family courts, and certain administrative agencies prescribed under the *Code*. The Supreme Court rules only on issues of law raised on the record of appeal.

Navajo District Courts

These courts have personal subject matter jurisdiction over criminal offenses, traffic cases, and all civil actions. In the area of criminal law, the **Major Crimes Act** of 1885 appears to have stripped tribes of jurisdiction over seven major crimes, e.g., murder, rape, arson. Today that list is up to fourteen crimes that the federal government claims jurisdiction over. The U.S. Supreme Court's legally problematic ruling in *Oliphant v. Suquamish* in 1978 stripped tribes of criminal law jurisdiction over non-Indians.

Navajo Family Courts

Family courts have jurisdiction to hear cases involving domestic relations, probates, adoption, paternity, child custody, name changes, grazing, land cases, and others.

Navajo Peacemaker Courts

These courts, more accurately named mediated dispute resolution centers, are based on traditional mediation techniques practiced by Naataanii which involve respect for the mediator (Peacemaker), lectures on religious and traditional values, and an awareness of the dynamics of the community.[10] The theoretical basis of the Peacemaker Courts entails four key elements: structure, enforcement, protection, and choice. As Chief Justice

Raymond Yazzie put it: "Alien ways do not solve people's problems ... Rather, if the Navajo court's institutionalize Navajo justice concepts—equality, talking things out and consent—that will respond to expectations that Navajos already have."[11]

Other Related Institutions

The Navajo Nation Bar Association (NNBA) and the Navajo Nation Council's Judiciary Committee also play important roles in the judicial system.

NNBA   An individual (Navajo or non-Navajo) must be a member of the NNBA in order to practice law before the Navajo courts. In order to join the bar, the applicant must be 21 years of age, of good moral character, have had no serious criminal convictions, and must pass the Navajo Nation Bar exam. Navajos need not have attended law school in order to be a member of the NNBA, since the Navajo courts encourage **lay advocates**, non-law school trained individuals, to practice in the courts. Non-Navajos, however, must be law school graduates. The NNBA, as of fall 1998, had 413 active members.[12]

Judiciary Committee   Under Navajo Nation law, the Judiciary Committee's bold task is to improve the administration of justice in order to serve the interests of the Navajo Nation. It is also charged with working cooperatively with the Navajo Nation's courts and the adjudicatory branches of the states and the federal government. One of its most important functions is to serve as the initial screener, interviewer, and rater of all judicial nominees.

The Committee sends the names of those individuals it deems the most qualified to the president who then makes the selection. The appointee then goes through confirmation hearings before the full council. If confirmed, the judge serves a two-year probationary period during which time he/she is required to attend training provided by the National Judicial College in Reno, Nevada, or the National Indian Justice Center of Oklahoma.

Qualifications for Judicial Appointment

Nominees for judicial posts must be members of the Navajo Nation and at least thirty years of age. They must never have been convicted of a felony, and cannot have committed any misdemeanors within the last year. Candidates are required to have at least a high school education, although individuals with technical training or college degrees are preferred. The individual must also have some legal experience—a minimum of two years in law or a law-related area. They are also required to have a working knowledge of Navajo, federal, and state law. More importantly, the applicants must have a greater level of knowledge of traditional customary law than candidates for executive or legislative offices. They must be bilingual (Navajo/English) and be able to demonstrate "an understanding of the clan system; ... an understanding of religious ceremonies; [and] ... an appreciation of the traditional Navajo lifestyle."[13] Among several other qualifications, each candidate needs to submit a writing sample demonstrating the organizational and communicative skills via the written word. This is crucial since legal opinions are written and used as precedent for future cases.

Tenure of Judges: Cause for Removal

Upon permanent appointment, Navajo judges in good standing may remain in office until retirement, 70 years of age. A judge can be removed if, on the recommendation of the chief justice or the Judiciary Committee, a justice or judge is guilty of malfeasance or misfeasance, neglect of duty, mental or physical incompetence, or if the judge or justice is convicted of a felony in a state or federal court. The accused is then allowed the opportunity to go before the full council to present evidence on his/her behalf. A two-thirds vote of all members of the council is then required to remove the judge.

Salaries

The chief justice receives the same annual salary as the president—$55,000. Associate justices receive $35,000 and district court judges earn $30,000 a year.

Conclusion

In effect, unlike the other two branches, the Navajo judicial branch has two very different systems of justice operating simultaneously yet separately. On the one hand, there is the Western-based **adversarial system** of justice (American); contrasted by the traditional consensus-oriented **alternative dispute resolution** system (Diné).[14] The adversarial system, modeled after the states and federal court systems, has been described as a "vertical" system with a powerful judge controlling affairs from the top down. The

Navajo tradition, most vividly evidenced by the Peacemaker Courts, has been labelled a "horizontal" system, with a group of people gathering as equals to work things out, minus judges and attorneys.[15]

Of course, even the other courts of the Navajo system seek to include traditional concepts and theories and indigenous legal customs in their actions and rulings. Such efforts, however, inevitably leads to some intellectual and practical tension, particularly when verdicts are rendered which the tribal judges hope will be accorded judicial **comity** (the principle in which the courts of one jurisdiction will give effect to the laws and decrees of another, not as a matter of obligation but out of deference and respect) by county, state, and federal courts.

The Navajo courts will no doubt continue to struggle with these issues as well as the rising tide of crime and violence throughout the reservation. But of the three branches, the judiciary has shown the greatest willingness (in part forced on it by federal laws like the Indian Civil Rights Act, but also in part because of their own desire to merge the two systems) to synthesize the best of Diné tradition and knowledge with the most appropriate (and required) of the Western world. It is this ability, rooted in history, that has earned for the Navajo courts and their judges the respect of their people. Increasingly, state, federal, and other tribal courts are also looking to the Navajo courts as a model. As was stated in a Navajo Supreme Court case in 1978, *Halona v. MacDonald,* Navajos have a high regard for their courts because they have a "traditional abiding respect for the impartial adjudicatory process. When all have been heard and the decision made, it is respected. This has been the Navajo way since before the time of the present judicial system. The Navajo People did not learn this principle from the white man ... Whereas once the clan was the primary forum (and still is a powerful and respected instrument of justice), now the People through their Council gave delegated the ultimate responsibility for this to their courts."[16]

Key Terms

Adjudicate	Courts of Indian Offenses
Adversarial System	Judicial
Alternative Dispute Resolution	Lay Advocates
Comity	Major Crimes Act
Common Law	Peacemaker Courts

Selected Readings

Lieder, Michael D. "Navajo Dispute Resolution and Promissory Obligations: Continuity and Change in the Largest Native American Nation," *American Indian Law Review,* vol. 18, no. 1 (1993): 1–71.

Tso, Tom. "Moral Principles, Traditions, and Fairness in the Navajo Nation Code of Judicial Conduct," *Judicature,* vol. 76 (June/July 1992): 15–21.

_____. "The Process of Decision Making in Tribal Courts," *Arizona Law Review,* vol. 31, no. 2 (1989): 225–235.

Wallingford, Jayne. "The Role of Tradition in the Navajo Judiciary: Reemergence and Revival," *Oklahoma City University Law Review,* vol. 19, no. 1 (Spring 1994): 141–159.

Yazzie, Robert. "'Life Comes From it': Navajo Justice Concepts," *New Mexico Law Review,* vol. 24, no. 2 (Spring 1994): 175–190.

Zion, James. "The Navajo Peacemaker Court: Deference to the Old and Accommodation to the New," *American Indian Law Review,* vol. 11 (1985): 89–109.

Notes

1 Deloria and Lytle, *American Indians, American Justice,* p.109.

2 Tso, "Moral Principles, traditions, and fairness ..." p. 17.

3 Jayne Wallingford, "The Role of Tradition in the Navajo Judiciary: Reemergence and Revival," *Oklahoma City University Law Review,* vol. 19, no. 1 (Spring 1994): 142.

4 Tso, "Moral principles, tradition, and fairness ...", p. 16.

5 Iverson, *The Navajo Nation,* p. 76.

6 James Zion, "Navajo Peacemaker Court Manual," (Window Rock, Arizona, 1982).

7 *Navajo Nation v. Platero,* December 4, 1991.

8 Tso, "Moral principles, traditions, and fairness ..."

9 Judicial Branch of the Navajo Nation, Fiscal Year 1998: Second Quarterly Report (Window Rock: April 1998): 2.

10 Wallingford, "The Role of Tradition," p. 147.

11 As quoted in Wallingford, "The Role of Tradition," p. 148.

12 Special thanks to Ms. Andrea Becenti, Executive Director of the NNBA, for providing me with this updated data.

13 Title 7, section 354, *Navajo Nation Code.*

14 Robert Yazzie, quoted in Wallingford "The Role of Tradition," p. 155.

15 Ibid.

16 As quoted in Tso, "Decision Making in Tribal Courts," p. 231.

Chapter 9

Local Governing Jurisdictions

Introduction

A count of non-indigenous government units in the United States in 1992 revealed the following:

1	National Government
50	State Governments
3,043	Counties
19,279	Municipalities
16,656	Townships
14,222	School Districts
33,131	Special Purpose Districts (hospitals, natural resources, fire, etc.)
86,382	Total Governmental Units[1]

This total figure is misleading, however. Indigenous political entities, located throughout the continental United States and Alaska, would add

another 560 governing bodies to the tally. And if we added just those of the
Navajo Nation this would enlarge the total even more. The following gov-
erning units, including the Navajo national government, existed within the
Navajo Nation in 1998.

1	National Government
110	Chapters
1	Township
15	District Grazing Committees
3	Off-Reservation Land Boards/Grazing Committees
41	Off-Reservation Grazing Communities
1	Eastern Navajo Land Board
6	Land Boards (On-Reservation)
5	Agency Councils
183	Navajo National Governmental Units

Historically, as discussed earlier, Diné democracy operated at the
subnational level. That is to say, since there was no overarching national
government, local, and in some cases, regional democratic structures like
the natural outfits and the Naachid, embraced and exercised democracy by
comprehensively meeting the needs of the local community. Today, these
tasks are met by one or more of the just mentioned subunits of Diné government. Presidential candidate Albert Hale, in 1994, ran on a platform of
local empowerment in which the idea was to decentralize authority—take
it from Window Rock and redistribute it to local chapters—so that theoretically the governments closest to the people, the chapters, would have approval authority for rights-of-way, homesite leases, business site permits,
and so forth.

Hale believed that one of the reasons there was so little economic
development on the reservation was the difficulty in getting on-site leases.
As he put it in 1995, "if we cut the bureaucracy down, give the communities the decision-making power, what I envision is a lot more businesses springing up across the Nation in those different communities."[2]
Hale wanted immediate action, but the council adopted a go-slow approach
because it was concerned about how moneys would be allocated and
how prepared many of the smaller chapters were for this amount of self-
determination.

After almost three years of discussion, debate, and several public hearings, on April 20, 1998, the council by a 61-10-3 vote, approved the Local
Governance Act for chapter government administration. It was signed into
law by President Atcitty seven days later. The resolution, after recognizing
that "Navajo Nation Chapters are the foundation of the Navajo Nation
Government," declared that the act addresses the governmental function

of chapters, improves their governmental structure, and more importantly, provides the opportunity for local chapters to make real decisions on matters of local importance. The council required the following of the chapters:

1. All Chapters of the Navajo Nation shall operate under the "Navajo Nation Local Governance Act" upon its enactment by the Navajo Nation Council.
2. All Chapters shall establish and operate under a Five Management System.
3. By the year 2003, all Chapters shall adopt a land use plan based upon a community assessment.
4. The Community Services Coordinators Program and the Commission on Navajo Government Development shall develop a transition plan for the transfer of the Community Services Program to the Chapters and shall present the plant to the Intergovernmental Relations Committee of the Navajo Nation Council for approval.[3]

In addition, the council recognized that all this meant little without funding so it created a permanent local governance trust fund that would be the repository of funds for the chapters, although no specific amount was appropriated. This is a significant piece of legislation but only time will determine how committed the council is to its full implementation and how prepared chapters are to handle the increased stress of local self-determination.

Chapters

The 110 chapter community governing bodies are easily the most recognized and most important unit of local government. Anyone familiar with Navajo politics knows that it is in these small subunits of government that politics is played out in all its beauty and harsh reality. **Chapters** can be efficient units that can quickly assess community needs and mete out appropriate services in a timely way. Conversely, chapters can sometimes be fairly closed and nonresponsive bodies in which a few powerful families dominate political and economic affairs. Other problems have been identified as well at the chapter government level:

It is frequently difficult to achieve a quorum, which is required before business can be conducted.

The chapter secretary/treasurer position is a powerful and important one since this individual handles the financial affairs for the chapter. Such enormous responsibility has sometimes led to mismanagement or misappropriation of monies.

There is some degree of instability in decision making because decisions are sometimes overturned arbitrarily at later meetings.[4]

Thus, there is tremendous variation in how chapters actually operate. Unfortunately, there is little hard comparative data on how the day-to-day operations transpire.

The formation of chapters contrasts with the establishment of the council and the **Grazing Committees**, which were both federally-created institutions created on behalf of Navajos. Chapters, on the other hand, utilized preexisting patterns of political selection and social control as they were formed. Although a federal official, Superintendent John G. Hunter, in 1927 suggested the form and idea for formalized chapters, the content of the chapters was left to the Navajos.[5] Hunter's idea of "town meeting" type of government was easily integrated into the Navajos' existing sociopolitical system, and Navajos had the opportunity—not a common occurrence in those days of oppressive federal policymakers—to accept or reject the idea of establishing a chapter. The formalized Navajo Nation Council and the Grazing Committees, on the other hand, did not initially allow for tribal consent.

Originally, the idea for chapters, from the federal government's perspective, grew out of the need for a local organization through which the government could spread the word about ways to improve farming and livestock enterprises. Once established, the idea spread quickly and by the early 1930s a number of chapters had been established. However, with the advent of the federal government's forced livestock reduction campaign in the 1930s, chapters, which were adamant against such drastic measures, lost federal funding and new chapters were no longer formed. In fact no new chapters were created until the 1950s, when oil revenues gave the Nation the resources to revive the chapter system and formally incorporate it into the National government.[6]

Officially, recognition of chapters as the grassroots political organization came by tribal resolution on June 20, 1955. This measure also provided $78,690 to finance certified chapters. The resolution originally stated that there should be one chapter for each of the seventy-four election communities. Amended in 1958 and 1959, the resolution then provided for the creation of "new" chapters, designated chapter officers, spelled out officer duties, and made provisions for the recall of chapter officials. Today, each chapter has an elected president, vice-president, and secretary.

Chapter officers serve four-year terms. There must be at least one chapter organization in each chapter precinct that elects council delegates.

At least twenty-five community members must be present to convene a chapter meeting. This 25-member quorum stipulation, however, raises the problematic issue of how politically representative chapters are. For example, in chapters with populations ranging from 400 to over 1,000 members, it is possible for a mere handful of individuals to make policy decisions for the entire community. This issue promises to become even more pronounced with the enactment of the Local Governance Act in which chapters will be wielding a significant measure of governing power that will have a direct bearing on the lives and resources of all Navajo chapter members.

Along with the issue of political representation via a small quorum, there is also the issue of membership in a chapter. Under current tribal law, a Navajo belongs to the chapter of his or her birthplace for life, regardless of where he/she actually lives. But as we saw earlier, such an unyielding membership criteria has consequences on issues like political reapportionment, distribution of local resources, and divying up of homesite leases, to name a few.

New chapters may also be formed and certified, but only if the following conditions are met:

1. There is substantial evidence presented to the Council "that the proposed Chapter represents a community group which has existed and functioned as a community for four (4) continuous years.

2. Upon presentation of evidence that the population of the area exceeds 1,000 persons for each of the existing Chapters and that there is a need to establish others.

3. Upon presentation of evidence that the topography or the unique demography of the Chapter area makes it necessary to have more than one Chapter to allow residents access to Chapter meetings."[7]

The most recent Chapter, Nahata Dziil, was formed in 1992 in the recently acquired tribal lands near Sanders, Arizona.

The general functions of chapters are in some respects similar to when they were first established in that they still provide a forum for discussion and dissemination of information, a venue to work out local disputes, and an opportunity to learn how one may acquire services or goods like help with wood hauling, irrigation projects, community farm, etc.[8] They also play an important role in the Navajo electoral process. Every two years the 110 chapters are asked to select individuals to be trained as registrars. These people are trained by the Navajo Nation Election Administration and help register Navajos to vote in tribal elections.[9]

The 1998 Local Governance Act is a landmark piece of legislation. Besides their original powers this act gave chapters many additional powers, including, but not limited to, issuing home and business site leases and permits; acquiring, selling, or leasing chapter property; entering into agreements for the provision of goods and services; retaining legal counsel; and entering into intergovernmental agreements with federal, state, and tribal entities, subject to approval by the Intergovernmental Relations Committee. In addition, under the Act, chapter members may opt for an alternative form of government that would allow chapters "to restructure their current organizational structure by either modifying the roles of the officers or to develop a representative form of government that may include the development of a Council similar to a city council."[10] Chapters are also allowed to collaborate with other chapters to establish regional governments if it is in their interest to do so.

One potential "model" of chapter government, proposed by the Office of Navajo Government Development for consideration, is called the **Chapter Council of Nat'aa**. This type of government synthesizes traditional and modern elements of government. It would include, for example, a position for an elder, a young person, and possibly others with particular skills or aptitudes, say, a rancher, a person with a college or advanced degree, or an environmentalist. According to the plan, the elder would be chosen by a group of elders every two years. Similarly, the young person would be chosen by a group of his peers. The Council of Nat'aa, like a city council, would make decisions on important local matters after having gathered the advice and consent of community members. Furthermore, the council would employ an **Atsilasdai**—executive. This individual, comparable to a city manager, would implement the decisions of the council and would manage the day-to-day operations of the government.[11]

Until the Local Governance Act is funded and implemented, chapters will continue to derive their budgets from investments the Navajo Nation has made on Chapter Claims Trust Funds. These funds are generated from mineral revenues and government claims settlements. The funds are distributed annually based on the number of registered voters in a given chapter.[12]

Township(s)

On November 5, 1985 (CN-86-85), the Navajo Tribal Council approved the plan of operation of Kayenta Chapter officials and established the Kayenta Township Pilot Project (KTPP). This project is administered by a planning board whose goal is to create a 7.5 square mile **township**.

Kayenta is situated in prime tourist territory, near the world famous Monument Valley, and is the host community of Peabody Coal Company, which operates the Black Mesa Mine, one of the largest operations of its kind in the United States. Peabody is a major employer of Navajos.

Although the plan of operation was approved, the township still has not been formally created and technically the "town" of Kayenta still does not exist. Political tension between Kayenta Chapter officials, the National government, and the "township pilot" project supporters has thus far stymied the process.[13] If the township is ever fully established the town's leadership will be able to draft an overall land-use plan, set up a simplified and expedited leasing system, and make laws to govern the new land system. Theoretically, the town government would be able to withdraw land and enact zoning laws (with the permission of local Navajos) to expedite the location of new businesses.

The township would not replace the regular chapter government; instead it would be within the current chapter boundary and would primarily encompass a "downtown" area. It is uncertain at the time of this publication how the 1998 Local Governance Act will impact Kayenta officials' efforts to pursue the township idea.

District Grazing Committees

District Grazing Committees were first established within tribal government in 1952, although the size of the committee and its composition were not clarified until 1953. The 1952 resolution declared that the committees were needed in order to facilitate full Navajo participation at the local level in the administration of reservation grazing regulations. At that time their duties included cooperating with the BIA area director in setting grazing policies, which included the "establishment of **carrying capacities** and other duties which may be delegated to said committees in connection with grazing" (CA-3-52).

Title III of the *Navajo Nation Code* specifies that each land management district shall have one grazing committee composed of one committee member from each certified chapter within that district. District 15 has only one delegate on the Reservation, but is authorized to have a grazing committee of three members. Thus, there are presently seventy-eight district grazing committee members, representing the fifteen on-Reservation land management districts.

A council delegate, following election, is responsible for holding a meeting of the people in the precinct for the purpose of electing a grazing committee member by a majority vote. Grazing committee members serve four year terms. A Committee member must be enrolled in the Nation, be a registered voter of the chapter the candidate seeks to represent, be 21 years of age, be bilingual, and have "demonstrated interest or experience in livestock and range management."

District grazing committees have many duties, including:

1. Organizing and conducting sheep dipping, spraying and dusting, branding, livestock disease prevention, and surplus livestock removal

2. Holding scheduled meetings on transfer and subletting of grazing permits, and cooperating with tribal and bureau conservation programs

3. Preserving forage, land, and water resources of the Reservation

4. Enforcing Navajo Nation Grazing Regulations

5. Educating Navajo people in proper range management methods

6. Mediating land and grazing disputes

7. Other duties as directed by the Central Grazing Committee, or the president's office

The central position in the grazing committee structure is occupied by the Resources Committee (one of twelve standing committees) of the council, which also calls itself the Central Grazing Committee. The Resources Committee has a chair and vice-chair and six members selected by the speaker of the council. Each of the five Bureau of Indian Affairs agencies has a council delegate. Western Navajo (Tuba City Agency), however, because of its more arid climate, has two representatives. Established in 1950, the Resources Committee provides overview services to ensure the most appropriate utilization of Navajo resources and to protect the interests of the Navajo people to enable them to enjoy such resources in a sound and environmentally suitable manner. This body also oversees the activities of the Eastern Navajo Land Board and considers land and grazing disputes on appeal.

Off-Reservation Land Boards

There are three land management districts which lie outside the Navajo Reservation proper; District 15 (a portion is on the Reservation), and District 16 (which includes the satellite reservations of Ramah, Cañoncito, and Alamo) and District 19. These districts are overseen by **Land Boards** which are similar in function to district grazing committees. These boards have a total of twenty members, although this number may be increased by the Government Services Committee if the work justifies it. District 15 has seven representatives, District 16 has nine, and District 19 has four members.

Land Board members must run for election by filing a declaration of candidacy with the Election Administration. Board members serve four-year terms. Their duties, similar to those of the District Grazing Committee, include issuing grazing permits in accordance with the *Off-Reservation Navajo Grazing Code,* arbitrating land disputes, cooperating with tribal and Bureau Range and Land Operations offices, promoting range improvements, and so forth. In 1971 an Eastern Agency Joint Land Board, which consists of all members of the three land boards, was established. This board works under the auspices of the Resources Committee. One of its duties is to act as a Board of Appeals in the event of protests or conflicts from decisions of the three land boards.

Major Irrigation Projects Farm Boards

There are six major **irrigation projects** within the Navajo Reservation: Many Farms, Hogback, Fruitland, Ganado, Red Lake (New Mexico), and Cudei. The Farm Boards for the lake projects—Many Farms, Red Lake, and Ganado—each have a three-member board. The Farm Boards for the river projects—Cudei, Hogback, Fruitland, and San Juan—each consist of one member from each chapter with allotted lands. Only agricultural land-use permit holders are eligible for membership. These lake and river projects have multiple purposes: to encourage proper farming practices, to promote close coordination between farmers and the Division of Natural Resources, to improve economic standards of Navajo farming communities, and to promote the beneficial use of water resources.

Agency Councils

Finally, we will discuss the **Agency Councils**. These are council-of-government-type organizations made up of the Council delegates, chapter officials, and Grazing Committee members. There is one council for each of the five BIA administrative agencies on the Reservation. Agency Council officers include a president, vice-president, and secretary. Councils generally meet four times a year to discuss agency-wide issues such as roads and grazing conditions.

The BIA pays per diem and mileage of executive officers when they meet to discuss the annual bureau budget. The council also provides some funding. *The Agency Council, however, has virtually no authority within the Navajo Nation Council.*

Navajo Governmental Expectations

The lives of Indian people in general, and Navajos in particular, are more regulated than any other racial or ethnic group in the United States. In fact, a jurisdictional quagmire surrounds Navajos who live on federal trust land. This is because Navajo lives and resources are regulated, to a greater or lesser extent, by five very different governing systems:

1. Local Government: Chapters, Townships (potentially), Grazing Committees, Land Boards, etc.
2. County Government (in limited respects)
3. Navajo Nation Government
4. State Governments (Arizona, New Mexico, or Utah, depending on one's residence)
5. Federal Government

Not surprisingly, the National Indian Youth Council political survey revealed that the Navajo Nation government was trusted more than county, state, and federal governments.[14] Navajos expressed the least amount of trust in the federal government. Fifty percent (50%) of those surveyed believed that their government was "somewhat or very representative" of their interests—more so than the federal government. The greatest majority noted that Indian politicians cared more about Indian issues and people than non-Indian politicians, and they echoed the nationwide sentiment that "people don't have any say in government."

The five most serious problems cited by the Navajo respondents, in descending order of magnitude, were:

1. Unemployment
2. Lack of water and electricity in homes
3. Lack of homes
4. Navajo-Hopi Land Dispute
5. Bad road conditions

The largest majority believed the federal government was spending "too little" money to solve these problems: (1) improving roads on the Reservation; (2) home improvement, and (3) new housing construction. On the other hand, the greatest majority felt the federal government was spending far "too much" money on the military.

The questionnaire also contained a set of policy issues that affect Navajos (e.g., alcohol, oil and gas development, police jurisdiction, and business and industry development). Of the six policy statements listed, the greatest number, 83 percent, opposed legalizing liquor sales on the Reservation. Furthermore, 82 percent stated that the penalty for bootlegging should be more severe. Nearly three-fourths (73%) of those polled agreed that the mining industry should do more to increase employment for Navajos and should pay the Nation more for the resources being extracted. The data also convincingly shows that Navajos favor economic development for employment, but not at the risk of their health or the pollution of their environment. Commercial ventures and light industry are preferred over the extraction of non-renewable resources.

Conclusion

Local government, thanks to the council's landmark Local Empowerment legislation in 1998, may finally be on track to reclaim some of the authority and prestige it held historically among Diné people. It is too early, however, to predict how effective that legislation will be, especially in the wake of the difficulties Kayenta Chapter officials have had in trying to establish a functioning Navajo "town."

Because of the recent political scandals and corruption at the national level, one can predict that community leaders will continue their drive for a greater measure of self-determination, though it is debatable how successful they will be in the long run until and unless a constitutional (or equivalent set of principles) form of government is established that genuinely reflects the reality that sovereignty rises from the people and not from the leadership.

Key Terms

Agency Council

Atsilasdai

Carrying Capacity

Chapter Council of Nat'aa

Chapters   Land Board
Grazing Committee   Township
Irrigation Project

Selected Readings

Eck, Norman K. *Contemporary Navajo Affairs.* (Rough Rock, Arizona: Navajo Curriculum Center, 1982).

Etsitty, Duane, comp. *NN Fax 93: A Statistical Abstract of the Navajo Nation.* (Window Rock, Arizona: Division of Economic Development, 1994).

Goodman, James W. *The Navajo Atlas.* (Norman: University of Oklahoma Press, 1982).

Reno, Philip. *Navajo Resources and Economic Development.* (Albuquerque, New Mexico: University of New Mexico Press, 1981).

Rodgers, Larry, comp. *Chapter Images: 1992 ed.* (Window Rock, Arizona: Division of Community Development, 1993).

Notes

1 U.S. Bureau of the Census. *Statistical Abstract of the United States: 1995* (Washington: Government Printing Office, 1997): 297.

2 "A Conversation with Albert Hale," *New Mexico Business Journal,* vol. 19, no. 6 (June 1995): 37.

3 CAP-34-98, April 20, 1998.

4 Office and Commission on Navajo Government Development, "Strategic Implementation Analysis," (unpublished manuscript, Spring 1998): 21.

5 Sam and Janet Bingham, *Navajo Chapters,* revised ed. (Tsaile, Arizona: Navajo Community College Press, 1987): 2.

6 Robert W. Young, *The Role of the Navajo in the Southwestern Drama.* (Gallup, New Mexico: Gallup Independent, 1968): 63–64.

7 Title II, section 4001, *Navajo Nation Code* (1995).

8 Bingham, *Navajo Chapters,* p. 38.

9 Information on elections was provided by Mr. Richie Nez, Executive Director of Navajo Election Administration.

10 Office and Commission on Navajo Government, "Strategic Implementation Analysis," p. 22.

11 Ibid., p. 22–23.

12 Office of Navajo Government Development, *Navajo Nation Government,* p. 36.

13 Larry Rodgers, comp. *Chapter Images: 1992 ed.* (Window Rock, Arizona: Division of Community Development, 1993): 51–52.

14 National Indian Youth Council, *Navajo Indian Political Attitudes and Behavior Poll.* (Albuquerque, New Mexico: National Indian Youth Council, 1984).

Part III

Political Dynamics of Diné Government

Chapter 10

Interest Groups and Diné Politics: From Without and Within

Outline   Introduction

The Navajo Nation "As Subject" to Outside Interest Groups

The Navajo Nation "As Subject" to Inside Interest Groups

The Navajo Nation "Acting As" an Interest Group

Navajo Nation Washington Office

Conclusion

Introduction

American Indian nations have been the focus of more **interest groups** (an organized body of individuals who share some goals and who try to influence public policy, also known as **pressure groups**) and **lobbyists** (a person or group, usually full-time professionals, who seek to influence specific government policies) than any other minority in the United States.

From the longstanding federal policy of forced Navajo assimilation (fueled by Christian reform interest groups); to the pressure from Arizona and Utah to tax Navajo lands or deny tribal members the right to vote; to the efforts of other tribes (e.g., the Hopi Nation and the San Juan Southern Paiute) to challenge the Navajo Nation for lands or other resources; and finally to the Navajo-based interest groups who seek to influence their government—the Navajo Nation government has learned firsthand the power that interest and lobbying groups can wield in American politics and how disastrous or beneficial the result of such formidable force can be on the rights of the Nation.

Equally important, tribes themselves have over the years been active in pushing—as an interest group—to protect or enhance their treaty rights, land rights, resource rights, and civil and political rights. In other words, tribes are sometimes the *subject of interest groups* and sometimes they *function as interest groups* in lobbying states, the federal government, or the world community.

The Navajo Nation "As Subject" to Outside Interest Groups

As discussed in Chapter 4 describing the history of Navajo tribal government, and strange as it may seem, the creation of the Navajo government itself is a direct result of external interest group pressure brought by oil companies in the early 1920s in an effort to expedite the oil leasing process.[1] Before 1921, there was no formal tribal governmental organization to speak of. In fact, there were five distinct Navajo agencies (plus the one the Navajos shared with the Hopi). Each of these agencies functioned as autonomous reservations. As oil and gas discoveries were made in the western states, however, there was a presumption on the part of geologists working with energy companies that the Navajo Reservation probably contained similar resources.

During these years, the calling of an agency-wide Navajo council was quite different than today. As Kelly described it:

> The initiative [for the meeting] came not from the Indians themselves but from the prospectors who were interested in securing leases. The prospectors first applied to the Commissioner of Indian Affairs (CIA) for permission to meet with a council of Navajos. If the permission was granted, the prospectors then presented his credentials to the local agent who issued a call for all adult males to convene at the agency headquarters on a given date. Because of this informal arrangement, once a Council had been held, the Indians disbanded and did not reassemble unless another request for a council was approved.[2]

Companies like Midwest Refining, Western States Oil and Land, Kinney Oil & Refinery, and E.T. Williams Oil, competed vigorously in May 1921 to secure a **lease** to prospect for oil in the San Juan Agency. The assembled Navajos, however, disapproved all the requests and declared that they were opposed to the leasing of their lands.

Over the next several months, the San Juan Navajos and their agent, Evan Estep, were put under tremendous pressure from both the energy companies directly—who offered jobs and water to the Navajos—and the

Commissioner of Indian Affairs (CIA), Charles Burke, who thought it was in the best interests of the Navajos to open their lands for mineral exploration. More importantly, Burke argued that the Navajos should surrender their inherent leasing authority, affirmed in the 1868 treaty, to their agent.

In August 1921, again "in accordance with the Midwest's desire," a second San Juan Council was convened. At this council Midwest got what it had sought—a lease to 4,800 acres near Hogback. The BIA also got what it wanted—the Navajos gave their power of attorney to Estep to negotiate leases on "their behalf."[3] Midwest's success incited a feeding frenzy of other mining companies who began to exert even more pressure on the CIA to call yet another Navajo council. When this gathering occurred in March 1922, nine companies were present. The Navajos, however, rejected all requests for any additional leases. After this meeting CIA Burke, ostensibly the trust agent of the Navajo people, explicitly informed the Navajo's agent that he favored the development of oil, gas, and other minerals and that he wanted Estep to convince the San Juan Navajos to grant general authority to lease their lands to him.

Simultaneously, in an effort to expedite leasing, a Navajo Business Council was formed, consisting of only three Navajos, led by Chee Dodge. The non-representativeness of this committee was grossly evident and the government was forced to create a somewhat more representative council. This three-member council also violated Article X of the 1868 Treaty which calls for the consent of three-fourths of all adult Navajo males before any cession of Navajo lands. Early in 1923, the Secretary of the Interior created a new position, "Special Commissioner to Negotiate with Indians," and named Herbert Hagerman to fill it. A few weeks later, a new directive from the bureau declared Hagerman the "Commissioner to the Navajos" and gave him general authority over all five Navajo reservations. Furthermore, all oil and gas leases hereafter were to be approved by a council of "all the Navajos," and not just those of the San Juan jurisdiction.[4]

The first Tribal Council officially convened in the summer of 1923. Chee Dodge was elected Chairman of the Council. But in its only other business, the council "unanimously approved a resolution, drawn up in Washington, granting the Commissioner to the Navajo Tribe the authority to sign 'on behalf of the Navajo Indians,' all oil and gas leases ... ."[5] The council apparently agreed to cede such a sweeping grant of authority because they had received assurance from government officials that the tribe would receive new lands for their flourishing population. As a result, the very existence of the Navajo Tribal Council owes its existence to the direct and concerted mining interests and high ranking BIA officials intention of having Navajo lands developed.

Interest group pressure from a number of forces, including white ranchers and cattlemen, and New Mexico Territorial and later state legislators, led to congressional acts in the early 1900s which stopped allotments to individual Navajos and made it impossible for the tribal leadership to consolidate the so-called "checkerboard" lands in western New Mexico. Importantly, these forces, with assistance from many others, stripped the president of the United States of the power to add new lands to Indian reservations by executive order. Until the early 1900s, this had been the most effective way in which the Navajo reservation had been expanded.

In 1925, interest groups representing the Grand Canyon used their influence to get Congress to construct Lee's Ferry Bridge (at a cost of $100,000) charged to the Navajo Tribe, although virtually no Navajos lived in the vicinity of the bridge. In the 1930s and 1940s, interest groups from various agencies of the federal government, along with Mexican-American sheepherders and the economic powers that had convinced Congress of the need to construct Boulder (later Hoover) Dam, used their political clout to force livestock reduction on the Navajo people. This action economically and morally devastated the Navajo people and their fragile economy. These developments, of course, led to the newly revised tribal government in 1938.

The discoveries in the 1950s and 1960s of additional oil and natural gas and other resources like uranium, helium, coal and hydroelectric power, funded an expansion of Navajo governmental capacity. Regrettably, they brought additional extended pressure from those interest groups seeking to do the mining in their efforts to negotiate more attractive economic deals with the tribe, or more accurately, with the BIA which acted as trustee of Navajo lands and resources.[6]

For example, companies like Peabody Coal, Kerr-McGee, Pittsburgh & Midway Coal, and others used their powerful influence to secure long-term leases through the BIA in which exceptionally low royalty rates were to be paid to the Navajo Nation. Peabody Coal Company in 1966 negotiated two leases with the Navajo and Hopi Tribes for 40,000 acres on Black Mesa. The Navajo Nation was promised over $2 million per year in royalties for thirty-five years while their oil and gas resources were being depleted. The Interior Department, "under the direction of Stewart Udall, worked with industry and the tribal attorney to convince the council to act immediately, without deliberation."[7]

One must also take into account the role of energy companies, like Peabody, which appeared to have some role in the Navajo/Hopi Land dispute. According to Benedek, "in the early 1970s, the Hopis were actively courting energy companies while Navajo chairman Peter MacDonald was speaking against them."[8] While there appears to be "no convincing evidence of a broad-based conspiracy behind the land dispute it is fairly clear that the energy interests provided the Hopi attorney with an important tool by which to bring attention to the dispute and arguments on why the land should be divided between the two tribes."[9]

The Navajo Nation "As Subject" to Inside Interest Groups

Navajos, like citizens of states, sometimes become disenchanted with their own government and form interest or lobbying groups which seek to pressure their government to create particular policies or to withhold support from policies that run counter to that group's political agenda. Sometimes, Navajos organize simply to pressure the Nation's government in an effort to secure additional funding for their own activities. For example, tribal government employees have marched on the president's office in an effort to secure salary raises. And during the budget session, the council is blitzed by a host of organizations competing for the limited pot of tribal revenues—church groups, chapter officials, sports teams, the local chapter of the American Federation of Labor-Congress of Industrial Organizations (AFL-CIO),[10] Diné College, and others.[11] Unfortunately, there is little in the way of formal research on this important subject, but a number of organizations have been active in Navajo political affairs during this century.

- ◆ **Navajo Returned Students Association** Early 1900s
- ◆ **Native American Church** 1940s to the present. This organization advocates for the rights of church members.
- ◆ **Navajo Codetalkers** 1940s to the present. This organization lobbied for recognition for those Navajos who served in World War II.
- ◆ **Navajo Rights Association** Organization which lobbied on behalf of Raymond Nakai in the 1960s
- ◆ **Coalition for Navajo Liberation** Fought for improved socio-economic conditions for Navajos against expanded mineral development.
- ◆ **Diné Coalition** Navajos who resisted coal gasification in the 1970s
- ◆ **Navajo Construction Workers Association** Organization of skilled Navajos who work at Page Power Plant
- ◆ **Diné C.A.R.E.** (Citizens Against Ruining the Environment) Organized in 1988 in opposition to the dumping of toxic waste on Navajo land. It also fights to protect dwindling Navajo forest lands.

- ◆ **Diné Alliance** A grassroots organization based in Black Mesa, Arizona to resist forced relocation of Diné people from Hopi partitioned lands.
- ◆ **Navajo Uranium Radiation Victims Committee** Organized in 1993 to help Navajo victims of uranium mining.
- ◆ **Dineh Rights Association** Formed in late 1980s. Members support the need for a tribal constitution.

The Navajo Nation "Acting As" an Interest Group

Throughout their history the Navajo people and their leadership have proven adept at representing their distinctive needs to other tribes, the states, the federal government, and increasingly to the international community. Even during the darkest years of the federal government's racist and ethnocentric campaign to crush Navajo identity, the Navajo Nation fought to protect their rights, resources, and beliefs.

As seen throughout the previous pages, from the earliest treaties on record to the 1989 Title II Amendments, the Navajo have struggled to maintain and increase their land base, to meet the social and economic needs of a growing population, and to improve intergovernmental relations with other political entities. A number of important issues serve to distinguish the Navajo Nation and attest to their powers as an "interest group."

First, while most reservations were constricted during the later 1800s and into the early 1900s, the Navajo Reservation actually quadrupled in size because of Navajo lobbying efforts aided by supportive Indian agents. Second, the Navajos retain a measure of aboriginal political institutions through their incorporation of the chapter system of government and Peacemaker Courts. Third, while the Navajo people suffered the brunt of two powerful and traumatic historical episodes—their imprisonment at Fort Sumner in the 1860s and livestock reduction in the 1930 and 1940s—as destructive as these events were, the Navajos emerged from these trying years with an understanding of what nationalism entailed which energized their growth as a collective force in their relations with other tribes and the federal government.

Finally, World War II also had a traumatic effect on Navajos, and rather than face the threat of legal termination of their rights as Indians, the Navajo Nation—lobbying vigorously—pressured the federal government to respond to their needs. As a result, the Nation benefitted from the passage of laws like the Navajo-Hopi Long Range Rehabilitation Act (1950) which helped stabilize the nation socially and economically.

Moreover, the Navajo Nation plays a unique role in national Indian politics. Interestingly, they have never joined the **National Congress of American Indians** (NCAI), the largest and oldest intertribal lobbying group representing over 100 tribes and Alaskan Native villages. Several reasons have been offered to explain their non-participation in NCAI. First, as the largest reservation-based tribe, the Navajo Nation has historically maintained that joining NCAI might in some way be seen as a dilution of their distinctive nation-to-nation relationship with the United States. They believe that their political and demographic status is so unique as to warrant an entirely separate stance vis-à-vis the federal government. There has also, historically, been some uncertainty voiced by Navajo leaders regarding NCAI's stability as an organization. It appears, however, that the Navajo Nation may be softening their heretofore hard-line stance regarding membership in NCAI.[12]

The Navajo Nation, under the leadership of Peter MacDonald, did, however, have a key role in another intertribal organization—the **Council of Energy Resource Tribes** (CERT). In fact, MacDonald was one of the founders of CERT in 1975. At the time of its formation, CERT was an interest group of 25 tribal nations that have substantial amounts of nonrenewable energy supplies (especially coal, uranium, oil, and natural gas) underlying their lands.

Touted as an Indian version of the Organization of Petroleum Exporting Countries (OPEC), the member tribes agreed to "act as a united front to protect their natural resources, to renegotiate their leases, and to demonstrate that their level of expertise was such that they no longer required the Department of the Interior to represent them."[13] Of course, OPEC is a conglomerate of independent nations, and tribes are structurally tied to the federal government via treaties and the trust doctrine which gives them much less actual freedom with their resources. In recent years CERT has scaled back its operations considerably. It now represents 57 tribes who have a more realistic awareness of their political and economic position vis-à-vis the federal government and the world community.

Navajo Nation Washington Office

With the increased amount of federal activity towards Indians in the 1980s, the Navajo Nation Advisory Committee, on August 23, 1984, passed a resolution establishing a permanent office in Washington, DC. The Nation had several reasons in mind when creating this important office:

First, to act as an extension of the Nation's government representing the tribe's interests and concerns to the federal government;

Second, to act as a lobbying presence on behalf of the Nation and to exert influence and control of the Navajo Nation over appropriate federal activities;

Third, to serve as a physical presence with quick access to Congress, the president, the bureaucracy, and to remind the federal government of the nation-to-nation relationship between the Navajo and the United States;

Fourth, to keep track of congressional legislation and federal regulations that may have an adverse or positive impact on the Nation;

Fifth, to act as a distributor to the Navajo Nation government of information concerning federal activities that might affect the welfare of the Navajo Nation and to provide advice, whether solicited or not, regarding possible legislation, regulations, or policy alternatives concerning programs of interest to the Navajo Nation;

Sixth, to participate in the preparation of legislative proposals and testimony that are to be delivered before Congress; and

Finally, to assist other tribal nations with business in Washington.

This office, thus, performs a number of vital roles, none of which is more important than its role as the Navajo Nation's lobbying arm in Washington, DC.

Conclusion

The Navajo Nation has been active as an interest group (both as a nation and as an ethnic group) and has borne the brunt of a number of a number of policies based on the actions and influences of both inside and outside interest groups. As the largest reservation-based indigenous nation, blessed with an enormous land base flush with a wealth of important resources, it is safe to say that interest group activity will continue to be a key factor in the Nation's political affairs.

Key Terms

Council of Energy Resource
    Tribes

Interest Group

Lease

Lobbyist

National Congress of American
    Indians

Pressure Group

Selected Readings

Ambler, Marjane. *Breaking the Iron Bonds: Indian Control of Energy Development.* (Lawrence, Kansas: University of Kansas Press, 1990).

Kelly, Lawrence C. *The Navajo Indians and Federal Indian Policy: 1900–1935.* (Tucson: University of Arizona, 1970).

McCool, Daniel. *Command of the Waters: Iron Triangles, Federal Water Development, and Indian Water.* (Berkeley, California: University of California Press, 1987).

Notes

1 Kelly, *The Navajo Indians,* p. 49.

2 Ibid., p. 49–50.

3 Ibid., p. 51.

4 Ibid., p. 62.

5 Ibid., p. 69.

6 Iverson, *The Navajo Nation,* p. 77–80.

7 Marjane Ambler, *Breaking the Iron Bonds: Indian Control of Energy Development.* (Lawrence, Kansas: University Press of Kansas, 1990): 59.

8 Emily Benedek, *The Wind Won't Know Me: A History of the Navajo-Hopi Land Dispute.* (New York: Alfred A. Knopf, 1992): 138.

9 Ibid., p. 139. See also Hollis Whitson, "A Policy Review of the Federal Government's Relocation of Navajo Indians Under P.L. 93-531 and P.L. 96-305," *Arizona Law Review,* vol. 27, no. 2 (1985): 371–414.

10 The AFL-CIO is a voluntary federation of over a hundred national and international labor unions representing a total of over thirteen million workers.

11 Interview with Ms. Vivian Arviso, August 11, 1998.

12 Interview with Mr. W. Ron Allen, President of the NCAI, August 7, 1998.

13 Donald Fixico, "Mining," in Mary Davis, ed. *Native America in the Twentieth Century: An Encyclopedia.* (New York: Garland Publishing, Co. 1996): 344.

Chapter 11

The Navajo Nation and the Media

Outline Introduction
The Role of the Media
Navajo Nation Media Enterprises
Conclusion

Introduction

The mass media (*print* media—newspapers and magazines, and *broadcast* media—radio and television) plays an increasingly large role as a socialization agent for Navajos just as it does for Americans throughout the United States. Moreover, the **media** also plays an important political role by having some influence over what Navajos hear, what they watch, and what they read. The Navajo Nation is, of course, still more geographically isolated and technologically underdeveloped than other parts of the United States, but through increasing access to and utilization of media, especially television, newspapers, and radio, this is less true than it was even ten years ago.

The Role of the Media

As in many of the areas we have been examining, there is a lack of research data on the actual role the media has on Navajo political attitudes. Fortunately, we have the slightly dated results of the National Indian Youth Council's 1984 political survey of Navajos. While this data is over a decade old, most of the findings appear to have ongoing reliability, although for purposes of this section, the Navajo Nation's radio station, KTNN: "the Voice of the Navajo Nation," had not yet been established when the study was completed. KTNN was set up in 1985 and began broadcasting the following year. By most accounts, KTNN is very popular and (with 50,000 watts) has a daytime range that covers the entire Navajo Nation and beyond. Available evidence indicates that it is now the main source of information for many Navajos and may be the only source for the 6,000 or so listeners who speak only Navajo. We will discuss KTNN a bit later. Let us now review the National Indian Youth Council's 1984 survey results because they still indicate trends that have merit.

When asked how much attention they paid to political advertisements, 46 percent of the respondents said they paid "some or lots" of attention to the ads. Television was the preferred source of news for 36 percent of those surveyed. Of course, a good number of Navajos then and now are still without electricity and therefore have no television or other electrical appliances.

Some 77 percent of the respondents listened to the radio regularly. Again, this figure is probably lower now because of the influence of KTNN. The survey results indicated that television watching and reading newspapers (29 percent read daily) is "positively correlated with age, level of education, employment status, income level, and gender. The more educated, employed, higher income, and younger people read a newspaper and watch the news more regularly."[1] By contrast, the elderly—usually with less formal education—read papers and watched television sporadically. The 1984 results, however, showed that 75 percent of all groups listened to the radio on a regular basis. This figure, again, is most likely higher now that KTNN is in operation.

A final survey question provided results which indicate that media use positively correlates with age, employment, education, and income level. Younger, more educated, higher income Navajos rely more on the media as their source of community information. The older, less educated, lower income, Navajos, on the contrary, still get much of their information through conversations with others or by attending Chapter meetings. Again, KTNN's presence may modify this finding, but by how much we do not as yet know.

Navajo Nation Media Enterprises

The Navajo Times

Article 4 of the Navajo Nation Bill of Rights, enacted in 1967, declares that "the Navajo Nation Council shall make no law respecting an establishment of religion, or prohibiting the free exercise thereof, or abridging the

freedom of speech, or of the press; or the right of people peaceably to assemble, and to petition the Navajo Nation government for a redress of their grievances." This essential set of rights closely mirrors those outlined in the United States Constitution's First Amendment. A key difference, however, is that the Constitution's amendment is just that, a constitutionally established right; whereas Article 4 of the Navajo **Bill of Rights** is a statutory enactment which is subject to modification much more easily than a constitutional right.

The *Navajo Times* was born in the breakthrough decade of the 1950s (birthdate, 1959), when the Navajo Nation began its formal emergence as an indigenous political and economic power. Chapter incorporation, tribal scholarship programs, the establishment of the court system, grazing committee establishment, and significant oil, gas, and uranium discoveries, prompted Robert W. Young to call the 1950s the "golden age" for the Navajo Nation.[2] This "golden age" had a darker side as well, however. The uranium mining has had lasting environmental effects on the land and health of Navajo miners; the Navajo-Hopi Land Dispute entered into a more intensified state; and the slow amassing of power in the executive branch which began in this decade would culminate years later in the deadly riot in 1989.

The *Navajo Times,* like 95 percent of the newspapers in Indian Country, is owned by the Navajo Nation government. Most of the nearly 300 reservation publications serve largely as newsletters touting their tribal government's accomplishments. In other words, most tribal newspapers are organs or instrumentalities of the governing body of the tribe, unlike the vast majority of American newspapers which are independently owned and, under the **First Amendment** to the Constitution, have greater freedom to print what they choose.

However, the *Navajo Times,* published in Window Rock with a 1997 circulation of 17,500, unlike many other tribally-owned newspapers, has throughout its 40 year history sought to assert a greater degree of journalistic autonomy even though the government owns the newspaper and therefore controls a majority of its budget. This was evident as recently as 1996 when the *Times* struggled with whether to run stories which alleged (1) that President Albert Hale had used tribal funds improperly, (2) that the president's wife had been seen beating her stepdaughter, and (3) that his wife was prepared to come forward with allegations that the president was having an affair with his press secretary.[3]

This tension between the tribe as owner and the newspapers' staff—individual journalists committed to publishing the truth even when it does not portray the government's officials in a good light—led at one point to the actual shutdown of the newspaper operations by the government. We shall discuss this momentarily.

As one writer put it, the *Navajo Times* walks a thin line. Indian reporters for tribally owned newspapers "quite possibly have the toughest job in American journalism. For one thing, the [constitutional] First Amendment does not extend to the quasi-sovereign tribal government's in the United States. In addition, state **freedom of information acts**, which allow citizens access to government documents, and sunshine laws, which guarantee access to public hearings, do not apply on the reservation."[4]

As noted above, the Navajo Nation's Fourth Amendment to the Bill of Rights theoretically guarantees **freedom of the press**, but since this is a statutory right it is subject to the interpretation and enforcement of the statute's authors, in this case the government which created the right. *The Navajo Times,* as will be seen by the example below, has experienced its share of encounters with the tribal leaders and sometimes the Fourth Amendment right of freedom of the press has been sacrificed to the governing body's desire.

MacDonald Shuts Down the Paper

Although begun as a monthly newsletter in 1959, by the early 1960s the paper had become a weekly, providing readers with a roundup of tribal press statements, advertisements and announcements, and ample sports coverage. By the early 1980s, with Peterson Zah's election in 1982, there was a significant push to expand the paper's horizons by putting wire service dispatches together with local news reports. The paper became a daily and the name, under the editorship of Mark Trahant, was changed to the *Navajo Times Today.* Even though the paper's circulation climbed from 4,000 to 8,000 and it sought to emulate the coverage of other daily newspapers, it remained a tribal enterprise, beholden to the government for a majority of its funding. As the next tribal election approached in the fall of 1987, Peter MacDonald entered the race to reclaim the chairmanship. The *Times* endorsed Zah, however, and ran headlines and wrote editorials questioning MacDonald's politics.

A month after the election, which MacDonald won by a slim margin, and with the *Times* continuing to challenge MacDonald's administrative policies, MacDonald sent tribal police to shut the paper down. The staff were subsequently fired. MacDonald claimed that the paper was closed because it was losing too much money. The staff, however, saw their firing as politically motivated. Trahant, the former editor, put it this way: "If the paper had indeed been shut down for financial reasons then why was no audit conducted before its closure, why were there no negotiations, and more importantly, why was the entire staff terminated?"[5] The doors remained shut for nearly four months. When it began publishing again, it returned to its pre-Zah format—a weekly publication of local governmental and other events. The *Times'* thrust for a greater measure of journalistic independence had been stifled.

KTNN: The Radio Voice of the Navajo Nation

On September 3, 1985, after five years of planning, the Navajo Nation made a bold decision to establish a new tribal enterprise: KTNN radio station, KTNN (AM Radio)—a 50,000 watt commercial station. Designed to entertain, inform, and educate the Navajo people and visitors to the Navajo Nation, the station broadcasts in both Navajo and English, and reaches a wide audience in the southwest. Because television and cablevision are still relatively uncommon (although satellite dishes dot the Navajo landscape), and the newspaper is still only read by less than a tenth of the people, radios, which many people own and listen to at home and in their automobiles, are important transmitters of information—political, entertainment, and cultural.

Because of the large size of the Reservation, many Navajos spend many hours in their vehicles, thus exposing them to KTNN's airwaves if they happen to prefer that station. The bilingual nature of the programming makes it even more effective as a source of information, particularly for non-English speaking Navajos.

Unlike the *Navajo Times,* KTNN is a semi-independent entity, though it, too, is subject to the Navajo Nation through the Telecommunication Regulatory Commission as well as being subject to the Federal Communication Commission's rules and regulations. Structurally, it is modeled after a commercial private corporation and operates subject to a five member Management Board whose members are selected by the President of the Navajo Nation.[6]

Conclusion

Presumably, some of the same tension that exists between the *Navajo Times* and the government, regarding what news to print, also underlies the relationship between KTNN and its boss, the Navajo government. In fact, since KTNN has become the primary source of political information for many Navajos, especially older Navajo speakers, and is a favorite outlet for campaign advertisements, one can expect that the strain between freedom of speech and allegiance to one's owner will surface from time to time depending on the ideological outlook of the broadcasters and Navajo policymakers.

And as Navajos become increasingly exposed to larger social, economic, and political currents through various media outlets, it will be interesting to see how the Nation's government responds. Will it chose to maintain ownership of the paper and radio station indefinitely, or will it grant them their independence?

Key Terms

Bill of Rights   Freedom of Press

First Amendment   Freedom of Speech

Freedom of Information Act   Media

Selected Readings

Danky, James P., ed. *Native American Periodicals and Newspapers, 1828–1982.* (Westport, Connecticut: Greenwood Press, 1984).

Indian Country Today, published weekly by Tim Giago (Rapid City, South Dakota).

Jones, Matthew L. "Radio and Television," in Mary Davis, ed. *Native America in the Twentieth Century: An Encyclopedia.* (New York: Garland Publishing Co., 1996): 532–533.

Murphy, James E. and Sharon M. Murphy. *Let My People Know: American Indian Journalism, 1828–1978.* (Norman: University of Oklahoma Press, 1981).

News From Indian Country, published bi-weekly by Paul DeMain (Hayward, Wisconsin).

Notes

[1] National Indian Youth Council, *Navajo Indian Political Attitudes and Behavior Poll.* (Albuquerque, New Mexico: NIYC, 1984): 12.

[2] Robert W. Young, *A Political History of the Navajo Tribe.* (Tsaile, Arizona: Navajo Community College Press, 1978): 162.

[3] *Los Angeles Times,* "A Navajo Newspaper Tests the Boundaries," vol. 116, p. A1.

[4] Ibid., p. A24.

[5] *Washington Post,* "Death of a Daily Newspaper: Deficits or Tribal Politics?" by Sarah Helm, 1987.

[6] Title 21, Section 602, *Navajo Nation Code.*

Chapter 12

Diné Voting, Elections, and Campaign Finances

Outline   Introduction

Navojo Voting

Navajo Election Laws

Conclusion

Introduction

American Indians, as described in Chapter 1, are unique in that they are citizens of their own nation and, as of the 1924 Indian **Citizenship** Act, citizens of the United States as well. Gradually and begrudgingly, the states were required to concede that Indian individuals had the right to **vote** in state and local elections. The states of Arizona (1948), New Mexico (1948), and Utah (1956) were three of the last states to grant Indian residents, including Navajos, the right to vote in state elections.

Interestingly, while other racial, ethnic, and gender groups have persistently pushed for entrance into the American polity, tribal nations, because of their sovereign and previously independent status, have generally fought to retain a significant measure of political separateness from the American state. American Indian nations, in other words, remain politically separate from the United States constitutional system, yet the citizens of tribal nations have also been accorded most of the basic rights as American citizens. Indians have citizenship status in three polities—a unique status indeed.

177

Navajo Voting

Because of this unique set of political and historical circumstances, the subject of Indian voting behavior and electoral politics is still relatively unexplored.[1] We do know that as of 1998 over 93,000 Navajos out of a total reservation population of 172,399 were registered to vote in tribal elections. The breakdown by agency reads thus: Ft. Defiance, 24,569; Crownpoint, 20,856; Shiprock, 17,458; Tuba City, 16,967; and Chinle, 13,164.[2] Additionally, some 37,358 Navajos are also registered to vote in federal, state, and county elections, the highest number in Navajo history.[3]

As far as the political behavior of the Navajo Nation government and which candidates it supports in **elections**, a recent study by Corntassel and Witmer identifies three major reasons tribes prefer some candidates over others: (1) a candidate's cultural or ethnological connections (i.e., membership in a tribe); (2) whether the political candidate's views on issues conform to those of the tribe; and (3) the political party of the candidate.[4] After examining data from a number of Arizona and Oklahoma tribes, including the Navajo, results show that "the primary reason for tribal government support of a candidate was due to his/her issue positions," with tribal membership being a distant second.[5] This is certainly evident in the way the Navajo Nation has given its endorsement of Arizona candidates who have supported the Nation's position on issues such as the Navajo-Hopi Land Dispute, the Navajo Indian Irrigation Project and other water developments, and support of Indian treaty rights in general.

Corntassel and Witmer's study also confirmed that the tribes in these two states pay much closer attention to national rather than state or local political candidates, although governors are accorded a measure of intergovernmental respect befitting their positions as chief executives. This supports our earlier discussion about the attitude and importance to the Navajo and other sovereign tribes of the nation-to-nation relationship.

Tribes, of course, including the Navajo Nation, realize that state, county, and local politics are becoming increasingly important and in 1992 thirty-two American Indians were serving in state legislatures, balancing their membership in their Nation and service to the state.[6] Navajos are at the forefront of this relatively recent phenomenon. For example, in 1992, Lynda Morgan, an Eastern Navajo, was elected to the New Mexico State Legislature. Mr. Wallace Charley has also served in the New Mexico state government. James Henderson is currently a senator in the Arizona state government. Henderson, in fact, was preceded in the Arizona legislature by Art Hubbard, Daniel Peaches, and Jack Jackson. Mark Maryboy, at the time of this publication, is a San Juan County official in Utah.

Navajo Election Laws

Indian politics is as intense as that of any other group, maybe more so because of the complicating factors of clan, permanence of community, and kinship. As such, Navajo election laws, procedures, and policies have evolved to keep pace with the evolution of the Navajo Nation government. And, as with other issues we have discussed, many of these changes began in the watershed 1950s decade.

First, there were the revised election regulations of 1950, which amended the 1938 Rules for the Navajo Tribal Council. The new regulations included: registration of voters; a provision requiring the candidates for chair and vice-chair to run on the same ticket; provision for each of the seventy-four election precincts to name a local delegate to the Precinct Nominating Convention; introduction of a paper ballot containing pictures of all candidates; change of the prior requirement that a winning candidate for chairman receive a *majority* of the votes cast to a provision for a *plurality* to win; provision for **absentee ballots**; and established procedures for judges of Navajo courts to be elected rather than selected.[7] (An absentee ballot is a method that allows qualified voters to vote in advance by mail if they anticipate being unable to appear at the polls in person on election day because of military service, illness and so on.)

The BIA, however, had responsibility for conducting the first tribal election under the new procedures in March of 1951. Of 16,000 qualified voters, over 14,000 cast ballots. Sam Ahkeah and John Claw were reelected chair and vice-chair in this important election.

In 1954, the election laws were changed again when the BIA declared that it was no longer interested in participating in tribal election procedures. This time the Advisory Committee, acting on behalf of the tribe, amended the regulations in the fall by establishing the first Board of Election Supervisors whose primary function was to plan and conduct all tribal elections.[8]

As the Nation has grown there have been many other changes in the election procedures. For example, on January 13, 1966, the council created the Navajo Election Commission as a continuing body and delegated to that body the authority to administer all Navajo elections, resolve election disputes, declare vacancies, and certify all elections and candidates.[9] A few months later, the council also authorized the Election Commission to negotiate agreements with county, state, and federal governments to oversee the registration of Navajos for those elections. In 1975 the council established a permanent office for the Election Commission, which has been redesignated the Election Administration Office.

Let us now look generally at the current election laws as codified in the *Navajo Nation Code* in 1995, which contain these and other important changes, especially the important amendments from CAP-23-90, the 1990 Election Code resolution which superseded all prior election rules.

Title 11 of the *Code* is titled "Elections." It entails two chapters. Chapter One outlines the general provisions (e.g., election dates, ballots, terms of office, and qualifications), the process for filing for elections, regulations on primary elections, how elections are to be conducted, the absentee voting process, special election procedures, **campaign** expenses and contributions, removal and recall proceedings, and voter registration, and specifies the powers, duties, and qualifications of the Board of Election Supervisors.

While each of these segments is important, the issue of campaign expenses and contributions—an issue the U.S. Congress is still struggling with—requires some attention because of the potential element of corruption. The *Code* has moderately detailed laws governing such expenses for Navajo elections. Before any election campaign, all candidates must file a report with the Board giving the name(s) of the individual(s) who will serve as their financial agent, or they must declare that they have not authorized anyone to serve in this capacity.

Candidates are also required, within 30 days of the election's conclusion, to file a "sworn and signed itemized statement of receipts and expenses" which details the money or other things of value the candidate has received during the course of the campaign. Failure to provide this list will preclude the winning candidate from taking office and will subject that person to a fine of not less than $300 or more than $500.

There are also express limitations on how much candidates may spend in both the primary and general elections. Presidential and vice-presidential candidates can spend a maximum of $1.50 per registered voter. In 1998 there were 93,014 registered voters throughout the Nation. Thus, candidates for the chief executive post are authorized to spend a grand total of $139,521 in primary and general elections. For the offices of council delegate, chapter official, or other elected officials, candidates are also allowed a maximum of $1.50 per registered voter "within the election district" the candidate is running from. A candidate violating these campaign expenditure limits is guilty of an offense punishable by a fine of no less than $300 but no more than $1,000, by a jail term of no more than six months, or both.

Radio and television time that is donated on an equal basis to all qualified candidates is not factored into the **expenditure** limitations but must still be reported. Finally, the law explicitly decrees that it is unlawful for any nonmember of the Nation or any corporation "to make any contributions of money or anything of value for the purpose of campaigning or influencing a Navajo election." However, local radio or television stations may make free air time available so long as equal time is offered to all other candidates. Non-Navajo individuals who break this law will be expelled from the Reservation and corporations who violate the law will be barred from any lease, right-of-way, or franchise for at least one year but not more than five years.

Chapter Two of the Election law charts the **referendum** process. The referendum procedure was one of the most important changes in the Navajo election law in 1990 and added yet another element of democratic reform to the structure of Navajo government. The referendum is a procedure for submitting proposed laws directly to the people for ratification. A petition signed by an appropriate percentage of registered voters can force a newly passed law onto the ballot or it could be placed on the ballot by the recommendation of the council or the president. The procedure has been used only twice (as of 1998). On both occasions it involved whether the Navajo electorate wanted to offer Nation-sponsored gambling. In both cases the people rejected the government's arguments about the need for such business activity. We will discuss gaming more in Chapter 13.

The other referendum vote, this on an "alternative form of government" (e.g., whether the Nation should adopt a constitution, maintain its current system but incorporate traditional culture and language, or add a preamble to the existing *Code* which would begin with "We the Diné), was originally set for August 4, 1992. Leo Watchman, then chairman of the Navajo Government Reform Project, and his office had been holding public hearings throughout the Nation to get the people's input on the kind of government they wanted.

The council had given the Reform Project explicit instructions to seek recommendations and proposals on ways to better utilize the separation of powers doctrine, checks and balances idea, and delegations of authority concepts, and to explore "limitations on how the Navajo government and its officials may use its powers, and to define the powers of the Navajo people."[10] The referendum vote, however, never took place.

President Zah, in his spring State of the Nation quarterly report in 1992, urged the council to at least place the Title II Amendments before the people in a referendum vote. His calls went unheeded by the council and to date the Navajo people have never had an opportunity to vote on the Title II Amendments or to express their collective voice regarding alternative forms of government.

Conclusion

The Navajo electorate, like that of any sovereign, is a fluid entity. And since hard data is not easily attainable, it is too early to tell whether the politically embarrassing developments involving the Navajo presidency in 1998 will have a lasting impact on the Navajo people's willingness to participate in tribal politics. All in all, while some individual lawmakers have engaged in unethical behavior and have paid the price by being removed or forced out of office, the recent rules and regulations governing elections and ethics appear to be working well.

Key Terms

Absentee Ballot	Expenditure
Campaign	Referendum
Citizenship	Vote
Election	

Selected Readings

Deloria, Vine, and Clifford M. Lytle. *American Indians, American Justice.* (Austin, Texas: University of Texas Press, 1983).

Engstrom, R. and J. Barrilleaux, "Native Americans and Cumulative Voting: The Sisseton-Wahpeton Sioux," *Social Science Quarterly,* vol. 72 (1991): 388–393.

McCool, Daniel, "Indian Voting," in Vine Deloria, Jr. *American Indian Policy in the 20th Century.* (Norman: University of Oklahoma Press, 1985): 105–133.

Ritt, Leonard, "Some Social and Political Views of American Indians," *Ethnicity,* vol. 6 (1979): 45–72.

Notes

[1] See Daniel McCool, "Indian Voting," in Vine Deloria, Jr. ed. *American Indian Policy in the 20th Century.* (Norman: University of Oklahoma, 1985): 105–133; O. J. Svingen, "Jim Crow, Indian Style," in Roger Nichols, ed. *The*

American Indian: Past and Present. (New York: McGraw Hill, 1992): 268–277; and Jeff Corntassel and Richard C. Witmer, II, "American Indian Tribal Government Support of Office Seekers: Findings from the 1994 Election," *Social Science Journal,* vol. 34, no. 4 (1997): 511–525.

2 Data from the Navajo Election Administration, courtesy of Mr. Richie Nez, Executive Director.

3 Ibid.

4 Corntassel and Witmer, "American Indian Tribal Governments," p. 515.

5 Ibid., p. 518.

6 Judy A. Zelio, "Indian Legislators Break New Ground," *State Legislatures,* vol. 18, no. 3 (March 1992): 18–20.

7 Robert Young, *A Political History,* p. 135.

8 Ibid., p. 146.

9 Resolution CJA-2-66, courtesy of materials sent to the author by Richie Nez.

10 *Navajo Times,* December 12, 1991, p. 1–2.

Chapter 13

A Diné Policy Portfolio

Outline   Introduction

Navajo-Hopi Land Disputes

Navajos and Tribally-Sponsored Gambling (Gaming)

Taxation and the Navajo Nation

Conclusion

Introduction

The Navajo Nation government, as we have seen throughout this text, is confronted by a barrage of critical issues that push it hither and yon. We have already dealt with many of these—the Navajo Nation's relationship with the federal government; the Nation's struggle with democratization; and the political corruption scandals of Chairman Peter MacDonald which led to the latest surge of democratic reforms. But even this surge has not yet led to the ultimate step in the process of democratization—when the Navajo policymakers concede that the Navajo people are the legitimate fount of Navajo sovereignty.

There are, of course, many other issues that animate the Navajo political spectrum. Some of these are listed in the attached Timeline (Appendix A) which identify many of the important events, personalities, and issues that have driven Navajo political, social, economic, and cultural life.

In this concluding chapter we will describe and discuss three of the ongoing public **policies** of importance to the Navajo Government—land disputes, gaming, and taxation. Suffice it to say, there are many others, and entire texts could be written about each of these. For example, a quick review of just the most recent Navajo president's annual reports reveals discussion, commentary, and concern about issues such as:

- ◆ The rising tide of juvenile crime
- ◆ The quality and quantity of water
- ◆ Matters relating to Navajo education
- ◆ The relationship of the Nation to the states and the federal government
- ◆ Eastern Navajo land consolidation
- ◆ Taxation matters
- ◆ Lack of quality housing
- ◆ Ongoing disputes—both land and religious—with the Hopi Nation and the San Juan Band of Southern Paiute
- ◆ The rights of off-reservation Navajos
- ◆ Health care
- ◆ Economic development
- ◆ Environmental issues around deforestation, coal and uranium extraction
- ◆ Special problems of Navajo veterans and
- ◆ The retention and application of traditional Navajo culture and philosophy.

I have chosen to focus on three particular topics for this portfolio. The first, the Navajo-Hopi Land Disputes, entail past, present, and future intertribal possibilities. The second, Indian gaming, is a potential issue of great economic and moral importance. The third, taxation, has important economic connotations and indicates that the Nation has evolved as a government into a more self-determined entity.

Navajo-Hopi Land Disputes

Of the many issues confronting the Navajo government, this may easily be the one most recognized by parties inside and outside the Nation. The disputes arise from an exceedingly complicated set of situations with roots dating back to at least 1882, if not before. The land tension involves not only the two tribal governments (and their legal staffs) but many other parties who have been involved over the years, including various agencies of the federal government, state governments, corporate interests, individual ranchers and landowners, cities, and two other little-discussed tribes—the San Juan Band of Southern Paiute and the Zuni Indians of New Mexico.

The conflicts have spawned countless federal and state lawsuits, several congressional laws, many tribal resolutions, a new federal agency (the Navajo-Hopi Relocation Commission), and needless to say, heartbreak on the part of those Navajo and Hopi (over 9,000 Navajo and 100 Hopi) who were required by federal law to relocate. The relocation of members of both tribes constituted the largest relocation (forced for some, voluntary for others) of any racial/ethnic group since the Japanese relocation during World War II. It is also the most expensive Indian relocation, costing at least $330 million by 1997. A wealth of literature[1] has also been generated by the conflicts between the tribes and others, though the reader is cautioned to read material presented from both tribes' perspectives before drawing any conclusions.

Background of the Disputes

Briefly, the issue is this. After the Navajo Reservation was created in 1868, a later Hopi Reservation located southwest of the Navajo Reservation, was established in 1882 through an executive order issued by President Chester A. Arthur. This order set aside 2.5 million acres for the Hopi and "such other Indians" the Secretary of the Interior might see fit to settle there. As the Navajo population expanded, and with it their land base, gradually the boundaries of the Navajo Reservation came to engulf the Hopi Reservation; and Navajo people settled within the 1882 executive order Hopi Reservation lands.

Even as this land conflict began to loom, another arose in 1934 when Congress added about 234,000 acres of land to the Navajo Reservation in the Western Agency. This acreage, just east of Tuba City, happened to include the Hopi Nation's westernmost village, Moencopi. This time the language of the congressional act was the reverse of the 1882 executive order. The law stated that the land was for the benefit of Navajos and "such other Indians as are already settled thereon." The Hopi, however, claimed the entire area as compensation for Navajo occupancy elsewhere within the 1882 Hopi Reservation.[2]

This formed the basis of what would become known as the **Bennett-Freeze** area, named after Commissioner of Indian Affairs, Robert Bennett who, in 1966 at the urging of Secretary of the Interior Stewart Udall, placed severe limitations on construction and development in the 1934 disputed lands. Any future development would require the consent of both tribes and all revenue from the land would go into a special account to be held until the respective rights of both tribes could be determined.

The construction freeze has left an indelible mark on the over seven hundred families living in the contested area. Although originally developed as "a means of encouraging negotiation over an age-old dispute ... the Bennett Freeze gradually developed into an intrusive and burdensome policy ... forcing [the Indians] to live in poverty by denying them the right to enlarge, to maintain, and even to repair their homes."[3]

The construction ban was temporarily lifted in 1992 by federal judge Earl Carroll. However, it was reinstated yet again before it was finally lifted in 1996 after the two tribes reached an agreement. However, the freeze remained on some 700,000 acres the Hopi Nation claims. Congress then got involved when Representative Hayworth introduced H.R. 2934 on November 13, 1997 which would legislatively repeal the Bennett-Freeze, thus ending what Hayworth called "a gross treaty violation with the Navajo Nation ... ." As of this writing (fall 1998) this bill had not been enacted.

The land problems between the two tribal nations festered throughout the middle part of the twentieth century. Delicate negotiations between the tribal councils and their attorneys failed and a court settlement, which called for joint use and occupancy by the two tribes, also failed to settle the profound differences between the Navajo and Hopi governments. The Hopi, for their part, demanded a **partition** of the 1882 Reservation that would clarify and affirm their land rights. The Navajo Nation, for its part, wanted its members to be able to remain where they were in the disputed area and preferred buying out the Hopi Nation's interests.

Congress responded in 1974 with P.L. 93-541,[4] which provided for partition—a 50-50 division of the 1.8 million acres of land between the two tribes. An independent, temporary relocation commission was established by the law to oversee the **relocation** of the affected tribal members who, after land division, were found to be on the "wrong side of the line." Houses and relocation expenses were to be provided by the federal government. Relocation was scheduled to be completed by 1986.

Human conflicts like this which include issues of property rights (land, livestock, water, coal); religious freedom concerns (access to sacred shrines and eagle gathering areas and use of eagle parts); corporate involvement; and the psychological, emotional, and formal disruptions and violence they generate; rarely conform to governmental timetables. Although the vast majority of Navajos and all Hopis have been relocated, as of 1998 the process was not yet complete. The incompletion stems from the persistent resistance of some two to three hundred Navajos (the figures vary) who refuse to leave the lands they feel culturally and religiously connected to: lands that the Hopi Nation has legally owned since 1882 and been spiritually and culturally linked with for many more centuries.

The fierce resistance of this group of Navajos led Congress in the fall of 1996 to enact yet another law, P.L. 104-301, the Navajo-Hopi Land Dispute

Settlement Act, which implemented the Accommodation Agreement that had been worked out over the previous five years. The Land Dispute Act ratified the settlement of four claims of the Hopi Nation against the federal government and provided the necessary authority for the Hopi to exercise jurisdiction over their lands by issuing 75-year lease agreements to the Navajos still residing on Hopi-partitioned lands. The Hopi are to be paid $50 million by the United States for lost rents and to enable the tribe to buy new lands.[5]

The Navajo Nation Council had already enacted resolutions in 1994 and 1995 which opposed the **Accommodation Agreement** in its original form because, according to the Nation, it did not protect the religious rights of the Navajo residents. While morally opposed to relocation, then-President Albert Hale noted in a speech on February 1, 1997 that changes in the Accommodation Agreement, implemented with the passage of Public Law 104-301 in 1996 and spearheaded by the Navajo residents themselves, guaranteed them religious protection. As such, he declared that "this agreement represents the only remaining means to establish their legal basis for continued residency on Hopi Partitioned Lands. Will they accept what their fellow Navajo neighbors have negotiated? I submit to all my people: the Navajo Hopi Partition Lands residents should sign the Accommodation Agreement."

The council, however, in a special session later in February, reaffirmed its earlier resolution "opposing the Accommodation Agreement in its present form" and recommended an extension of the March 31, 1997 deadline. The council also expressed "adamant opposition" to forced eviction of Navajos.[6] Navajo residents were given until March 31, 1997 to sign the 75-year leases (renewable for another 75 years) with the Hopi Nation, though the ones who refused to sign were not evicted immediately. If they agreed to relocate, the federal government was required under the 1996 law to pay for their moving expenses and build them a home, a process which takes anywhere from six months to more than a year.

Navajos and Tribally-Sponsored Gambling (Gaming)

Since the 1980s, many tribal governments have introduced legalized gambling as a means of generating revenue to offset dramatically decreased federal funding and developing their own economic base. In fact, tribes were encouraged by the Reagan administration to pursue tribally-owned Indian gambling enterprises as one means to counterbalance the severe cuts in federal expenditures his administration had implemented. After an important Supreme Court decision in 1987, *California v. Cabazon Band of*

Mission Indians,[7] which held that states could not enforce their civil/ regulatory gaming laws to prohibit gaming on Indian lands, Congress stepped forward the following year and enacted the Indian Gaming Regulatory Act (IGRA).[8]

This act had three broad goals: (1) promote tribal economic development, self-sufficiency, and strong tribal government; (2) provide a regulatory base to protect Indian gaming from organized crime; and (3) establish a National Indian Gaming Commission. The act separated Indian gaming into three classes. Class I was strictly social gambling. This was solely under tribal jurisdiction. Class II included bingo, pull tabs, and so forth. This type was subject to tribal jurisdiction, with federal oversight. It also had to be legal under existing state law. Class III, the most potentially lucrative, included keno, lottery, pari-mutuel, slot-machines, casino games, and banking card games. This class required a tribal ordinance, permission from the Indian Gaming Commission, and the state had to permit the activity. In fact, tribes were required to conduct Class III gaming in conformance with a **tribal-state compact.** If state law, such as in Utah, did not allow Class III gaming, tribes were denied the chance to engage in the same.

States were required under the act to make a "good faith" effort to negotiate a tribal-state compact with those tribes who wanted to pursue these gaming ventures. The act authorized a tribe to bring suit in federal court against a state in order to force performance of that duty if the state refused to act in good faith and in good time to work out a compact. This final provision, however, was changed when the Supreme Court ruled in *Seminole Tribe of Indians v. Florida*[9] in 1996 that the Eleventh Amendment to the Constitution prevents Congress from authorizing suits by tribes against states absent state consent.

In fact, the IGRA gave states a voice—for the first time—over internal economic issues that previously were left solely to the discretion of the tribes and their trustee, the federal government. The requirement that tribes have to negotiate a compact with a state for Class III gaming operations, in effect, provided state officials with powerful leverage over a tribal nation's internal economic decisions.

States, with only a few exceptions (e.g., General Allotment Act of 1887, Public Law 280 of 1953, terminated tribes), have rarely had any direct say, much less veto power, over internal tribal decisions. Several reasons account for this. First, the doctrine of tribal sovereignty recognizes the right of tribal nations to manage their own affairs without state interference. Second, the nation-to-nation treaty relationship from which states were precluded from participation provides tribes a measure of protection from state intrusion. And third, many western states—including Arizona and New Mexico—were required to insert "disclaimer" clauses in their constitutions in which they assured the federal government that they would never attempt to interfere in tribal affairs and would never attempt to tax Indian trust lands. Despite this wealth of protection, however, the ideology of states' rights activism has grown tremendously in the last ten years and Congress and the Supreme Court are more often siding with states when they are competing with tribes.

For some tribes, such as the Mashantucket Pequot of Connecticut, the Cabazon Band of Mission Indians of California, or the Ak-Chin Community of Arizona, Indian gaming (as the business has come to be called) has brought in billions of dollars, provided jobs for tribal members, and generally enabled the successful tribes to attain a level of economic self-sufficiency they had not enjoyed since before the days of European colonialism. Indian gaming has also generated jobs, revenues, and other economic benefits for local and state economies as well.

For other tribes, however, such as the Mohawk and Oneida of New York, while gaming has generated significant revenue, it has also led to severe intra-tribal tension, sometimes leading to violence and has produced other negative social consequences as well. More importantly, it has generated a severe backlash in many state governments and among more established gambling interests in Las Vegas and New Jersey. States and the players in Vegas and Jersey are envious of the riches—both actual and perceived—that tribes are enjoying. The backlash has worked its way into the Congress where bills are pending that would reduce the tribes' gaming options, and into the Supreme Court where recent decisions have restricted the sovereignty of tribes while uplifting the sovereign powers of states.[10]

As of 1998, 188 of the 560 tribal entities were operating 285 gaming facilities in twenty-eight states. In Arizona alone, seventeen tribal nations have gaming operations (e.g., Cocopah, Ft. McDowell Mohave-Apache, Gila River, Hualapai, San Carlos and White Mountain Apache, and the Pascua Yaqui). In 1993 the Ft. McDowell tribe announced profits of $41 million, which was split thus: $12.3 million for tribal government operations; $15.6 for economic development; $2 million for community welfare; $410,000 for contracts with local governments; $410,000 for local charity; and $10.3 million for per capita (individual) payments to tribal members—averaging about $12,000 per person.[11] The only tribes in Arizona which do not have gaming in 1998 are the Havasupai, the Hopi, the San Juan Southern Paiute, and the Navajo Nation.[12]

Navajos Reject Gaming

Historically, Navajos, like most social groups, enjoyed a number of informal gambling rituals. For example, the shoe game is still very popular and certainly gambling was done on horse- and footraces. Card games were and still are played quite frequently at Squaw Dances and other gatherings.[13] This type of gambling is very different from the type of state or tribally-sanctioned gaming that is backed by the force of law and designed to generate revenue for governmental purposes. From a governmental perspective, the Navajo Nation passed a resolution in 1977 which criminalized gambling if the person engaging in it "intends to derive an economic benefit other than personal winnings" from the endeavor. However, seemingly in anticipation of tribal-sponsored gambling, this law was amended in 1993 by providing an "exception" to the offense section. Resolution CN-81-93 declared that "it shall not be unlawful for any person to engage in the activities constituting this offense if done as part of an economic initiative of the Navajo Nation Government, or as a gaming licensee of the Navajo Nation Government."[14] In a footnote to this law, it was stated that the effective date of this amendment was "subject to enactments of a comprehensive statutory scheme to control gaming within the Navajo Nation by the Navajo Nation Council."

Despite the council's optimism, however, and with so many tribes having already ventured into gaming as a prime economic generator, why has the Navajo Nation not joined in the process? More specifically, why has the Navajo Nation electorate, in two separate tribal referenda—1994 and 1997—explicitly rejected the establishment of Indian gaming within the Reservation?

According to research conducted by Henderson and Russell, the Navajo people rejected the gaming referendum in November 1994 by a vote of 28,073 (No) to 23,450 (Yes), largely because of moral concerns. It appears that these concerns outweighed the perceived potential for revenue because, "unlike other tribal casinos which generally attract predominantly non-Indian patrons, the proposed casinos in the Navajo Nation would be patronized by large numbers of Navajos."[15] Not easily dissuaded, the council pushed forward and in November of 1997 authorized yet another national referendum by Resolution CAP-26-97 during the spring session. Once again, Navajos in a closely contested vote of 18,097 (No) to 15,224 (Yes), rejected the measure. While no scientific research has been done on the second referendum, in all likelihood the Navajo turned away from gaming for reasons similar to those in 1994—concern about the social welfare of tribal members. As Richie Nez, Executive Director of the Navajo Election Administration put it: "No matter how you educate people, especially the older people, they still associate gambling with alcoholism, and all other vices ... They just don't see any good coming out of it."[16]

This issue pits the general social and moral concerns of the Navajo electorate against the financial and economic concerns of a majority of those in the government who believe that the Nation is losing out on millions of dollars and thousands of permanent jobs. Gaming is an issue that promises to be revisited in the future by the council and by the Nation.

An interesting question is: Why has the council twice placed this issue before the people using the referendum process, yet refused to put the question of a tribal constitution, one of the proposed alternative government ideas, or even the Title II Amendments, before the people for their consideration? Certainly, economic considerations are vitally important to the Nation as their nonrenewable natural resource endowment (especially coal and gas) continues to decline, which directly reduces the revenues coming into the tribal treasury. The question of governmental legitimacy is, from the standpoint of what constitutes the actual basis of tribal sovereignty, one could argue, even more vital to the character of the Nation.

Taxation and the Navajo Nation

Euro-Americans and taxes have coexisted uncomfortably since the beginning of the American Republic. "Taxation without representation," after all, was one of the catalysts sparking the American Revolution, since American colonists resented the idea of being forced to pay taxes to a distant government, Great Britain, in which they had no actual representation. Americans then and now, including Indian peoples, knew, as Chief Justice John Marshall stated in *McCulloch v. Maryland* in 1819, that "the power to tax involves the power to destroy." Furthermore, anyone holding a job is aware, because of hefty tax deductions, of the truth in of the famous expression: "In this world nothing can be said to be certain, except death and taxes."

But taxes are also the lifeblood of most non-Indian governments and are becoming increasingly important to tribal governments as well. Taxes raise the revenues required to hire employees, to provide essential services (libraries, roads, schools), and to conduct government affairs. Of course, **taxation**, like many issues we have been discussing, touches Indian lives and reservation lands in a different way than it touches other Americans. For example, the U.S. Constitution, in the section describing how United States representatives were to be elected to Congress, required each state, when it counted its citizens for purposes of congressional apportionment, to exclude "Indians not taxed." This same expression is also found in section two of the Fourteenth Amendment, which was ratified and proclaimed in 1866. This expression was included because, as we learned in Chapter 1, Indians were not citizens of the United States when the Constitution was drafted and most had still not been enfranchised as late as the 1860s when the Fourteenth Amendment was ratified. Indians remained citizens of their own sovereign nations.

The passage of several laws, including the 1924 Indian Citizenship Act, altered the status of individual Indians vis-à-vis federal taxes. And after some court cases in the 1930s, 1940s, and 1950s, it was determined by the federal government that individual Indians, as citizens of the United States, were indeed required to pay federal income taxes unless a treaty or statute exempted them.[17]

Tribal governments, however, as sovereign entities, are generally exempt from paying most federal taxes and nearly all state taxes. In fact, the Internal Revenue Service has determined specifically that tribes are exempt from federal income taxes. But the immunity tribes have from some taxation is not nearly as secure as the immunity states enjoy from federal taxation. Tribes periodically face concerted attempts by certain state and federal legislators to require them to pay taxes, notwithstanding tribal sovereign status. States do not face such taxation assaults by the federal government.

The Power of the Navajo Nation to Tax

Until the 1970s the Navajo Nation did not collect taxes to finance its operations although, as we have shown, the Nation was clearly entitled to collect taxes. Ironically, while the Nation was not collecting taxes, state governments were using the state's taxing authority and were earning sizable sums of money by taxing certain businesses operating within Navajo lands. In fact, in a study done by Michael Benson in 1975, Benson learned that besides paying applicable federal taxes, Navajos were also paying taxes to support the state governments of Arizona, New Mexico, and Utah. They were even contributing to six county governments in those three states—Apache, Coconino, and Navajo in Arizona; Mckinley and San Juan in New Mexico, and San Juan in Utah. Benson further noted that:

> State and county governments collect taxes on property located in the Navajo Nation and on income derived from activities in the Navajo Nation. They directly tax the incomes and property of non-Navajos who live, work or conduct business in the Navajo Nation. They collect a lot of taxes 'indirectly' from Navajos and non-Navajos by taxing wholesalers who supply Navajo Nation retailers with such commodities as gasoline and cigarettes.[18]

What was particularly frustrating, as this report showed, was that non-Navajo governments were receiving far more money *in taxes* from the development of Navajo Nation resources than the Navajo Nation was securing in income from royalties and lease arrangements from those same resources. For example, in 1972 the Navajo Nation received $1.4 million in royalties for the coal that was used at the Four Corners Power Plant. By contrast, the state, county, and local governments were earning $7.2 million from taxes on that same coal.[19]

As a result of this kind of disparity and with the growing realization that the Nation's mineral resources were not inexhaustible, in 1974 the Navajo Government enacted a resolution establishing a "Navajo Tax Commission." The MacDonald administration was slow in getting the Commission started, but it was eventually set up and began the process of devising a taxation program to correct the evident taxation inequities. The Commission's work led to two tribally-approved tax ordinances in 1984: (1) a *Possessory Interest Tax;* and (2) a *Business Activity Tax.* We will discuss these momentarily. The taxes were immediately challenged by individuals and companies subject to them, although, as noted above, one of the inherent powers of any sovereign is the power to tax. Tribal governments, therefore, have the legal right to tax their citizens, non-citizens residing on their land, and businesses and corporations doing business within their lands. As the Supreme Court said in 1982 in *Merrion v. Jicarilla Apache Tribe:*

> The power to tax is an essential attribute of Indian sovereignty because it is a necessary instrument of self-government and territorial management. This power enables a tribal government to raise revenues for its essential services. The power does not derive solely from the Indian tribe's power to exclude non-Indians from tribal lands. Instead, it derives from the tribe's general authority, as sovereign, to control economic activity within its jurisdiction, and to defray the cost of providing governmental services by requiring contributions from persons or enterprises engaged in economic activities within that jurisdiction.[20]

Notwithstanding this important decision, the Navajo Nation taxes continued to be challenged by companies like Kerr-McGee Corporation. Ultimately, in 1985, the Supreme Court ruled in *Kerr-McGee Corporation v. The Navajo Tribe*[21] that the Nation possessed the sovereign power to enact and impose tax laws without approval by the Interior Department.[22]

The Possessory Interest Tax (PIT) requires any owner of a lease granted by the Navajos to pay an annual tax on the value of the lease site and natural resources thereunder at a rate of between one and ten percent. The Business Activity Tax (BAT) requires anyone who is engaged in production activities on the Reservation to pay a tax on the gross receipt from such activities at a rate of between four and eight percent. Both ordinances have been amended several times and other taxes have since been enacted as well.

In 1985 the Council established an *Oil and Gas Severance Tax,* a tax imposed on the severance, producing, or taking from the soil, of products within the Nation at the rate of between three and eight percent. In addition, in 1992 the council created a *Hotel Occupancy Tax* which "imposed on a person who, under a lease, concession, permit, ... pays for the use or possession or for the right to the use or possession of a room or space in a hotel costing $2 or more each day." The tax rate was initially five percent, but in 1994 it was increased to eight percent.

The council, in 1995, instituted two new measures to generate revenue for the tribal coffers: a *Tobacco Products Tax & Licensing Act* (a forty cents per pack tax is assessed on tobacco sales) and a *Fuel Distributors Licensing Act* (taxing any person or business delivering fuel on the Reservation). The Tax Commission is also in the early stages of discussing the need for a *Gross Receipts Tax* which, if ever enacted, would impose on the gross receipts of any person engaged in trade, commerce, manufacture, power production, or any other productive activity, a tax at a heretofore unspecified rate. This tax would exempt the sale of gasoline, church-sponsored activities, prescription drugs, wages, food stamps, etc.[23]

These currently approved taxes and license fees (as of 1998) generate an average of $30 million a year for tribal government operations. The BAT brings in $15 million, the PIT $10 million, the Oil and Gas Severance about $4 million, and Hotel Occupancy about $1 million. The remainder comes in from the tobacco and fuel taxes.[24]

Significantly, the taxes are imposed on Navajo citizens as well as non-Navajo business activities, although the Navajo Nation itself is exempt from being taxed. As the amount of nonrenewable resources continues to decrease, taxation and the revenues it produces will become even more important to the Nation's economy.

Conclusion

If this sampling of policy issues is any indication of what the future holds for the Navajo Nation government, then it is clear that the Navajo people and their elected and appointed representatives face a future, as in the past and present, that is full of both promise and tension. Promise because as we have seen, the Diné people are particularly adept at finding creative ways of taking care of themselves, their resources, and managing their affairs with others. Tension, however, because internal conflicts, a gradually diminishing pool of natural resources, and the inconsistent nature of Navajo political relation with counties, states, and the federal government, mean that consistent harmony is not likely. This is understandable. But the continuing move toward full democracy, which intensified with the Title II Amendments of 1989, means that the Nation is heading in a positive direction.

Of course, the Navajo people still have not had nor have they taken the opportunity via a referendum/initiative to express their collective will about what shape Diné democracy should be, and this must be rectified. But even after this is accomplished, assuming that it will be, everything will not be settled. Democracies, we have learned, are not perfect governments. It is up to successive Navajo generations to nurture and strengthen the foundation of Navajo government.

Perhaps former Chief Justice Tom Tso, as he neared retirement, put it best when asked by a reporter what he thought his primary contributions to the Navajo court system had been. Tso responded by saying:

> I don't know if I've done anything extraordinary. Basically, I did my job, which was to hear and to cite cases—giving everybody a fair shake. I've tried to be very fair about the procedures and to make decisions based on the facts and the laws. I guess what I am trying to say is, that during all of my years on the bench, I just tried to do what a judge should be doing. There is no significant magic. I've had a lot of resources and a lot of cooperation from the leadership and the staff and we just did our jobs. We tried to look to Navajo customs, tradition and culture, and we found that many of our decisions and laws were influenced by those traditions.[25]

This statement by a highly respected Navajo jurist exemplifies the strength, hindsight, and foresight of the Diné spirit which entails cooperative living; respect for tradition, culture, and language; a focus on fairness and integrity; and the pursuit of justice.

Key Terms

Accommodation Agreement	Relocation
Bennett-Freeze	Taxation
Partition	Tribal-State Compact
Policy	

Selected Readings

Barsh, Russel Lawrence. "Issues in Federal, State, and Tribal Taxation of Reservation Wealth: A Survey and Economic Critique," *Washington Law Review,* vol. 54 (June 1979): 531–586.

Benedek, Emily. *The Wind Won't Know Me: A History of the Navajo-Hopi Land Dispute.* (New York: Alfred A. Knopf, 1992).

Cornell, Stephen and Joseph Kalt, eds. *What Can Tribes Do? Strategies and Institutions in Indian Economic Development.* (Los Angeles: American Indian Studies, 1992).

Deloria, Vine, and Clifford M. Lytle. *The Nations Within: The Past and Future of American Indian Sovereignty.* (New York: Pantheon Books, 1984).

Feher-Elston, Catherine. *Children of Sacred Ground: America's Last Indian War.* (Flagstaff, Arizona: Northland Publishing Co., 1988).

Guyette, Susan. *Planning for Balanced Development: A Guide for Native American and Rural Communities.* (Santa Fe, New Mexico: Clear Light Publishers, Inc., 1996).

Lane, Ambrose I., Sr. *Return of the Buffalo: The Story Behind America's Indian Gaming Explosion.* (Westport, Connecticut: Bergin & Garvey, 1995).

Notes

[1] See, e.g., Jerry Kammer, *The Second Long Walk: The Navajo-Hopi Land Dispute* (Albuquerque, New Mexico: University of New Mexico Press, 1980); David M. Brugge, *The Navajo-Hopi Land Dispute: An American Tragedy* (Albuquerque, New Mexico: University of New Mexico Press, 1994); Emily Benedek, *The Wind Won't Know Me: A History of the Navajo-Hopi Land Dispute* (New York: Alfred A. Knopf, 1992); and Maureen Trudelle Schwarz, "Unraveling the Anchoring Cord: Navajo Relocation, 1974 to 1996," *American Anthropologist,* vol. 99, no. 1 (March 1997): 43–55. See also Hollis A. Whitson, "A Policy Review of the Federal Government's Relocation of Navajo Indians Under P.L. 93-531 and P.L. 96-305," *Arizona Law Review,* vol. 27 (1985) for a dated but fairly objective account of the policy implications of this conflict. And see Catherine Feher-Elston, *Children of Sacred Ground* (Flagstaff: Northland Publishing Company, 1988).

[2] Iverson, *The Navajo Nation,* p. 195.

[3] John D. Moore, "Justice Too Long Delayed on the Navajo Reservation: the 'Bennett Freeze' As a Case Study in Government Treatment of Native Americans," *Harvard Human Rights Journal,* vol. 6 (Spring 1993): 222–229.

[4] 88 Stat. 1714.

[5] U.S. Congress, Senate Report, "Providing for the Settlement of the Navajo-Hopi Land Dispute, and for other purposes," Senate Report #104-363 (Washington, DC: Government Printing Office, 1996).

[6] CF-19-97.

[7] 480 U.S. 202.

[8] 102 Stat. 2475.

[9] 116 S.Ct. 1114.

[10] See, e.g., the 1996 *Seminole* case, *Alaska v. Native Village of Venetie Tribal Government* (1998), *South Dakota v. Yankton Sioux Tribe* (1998), and *Strate v. A-1 Contractors.*

[11] Heidi L. McNeil, "Indian Gaming: Prosperity and Controversy," in Malcolm Merrill, ed. *American Indian Relationships in a Modern Arizona Economy.* 65th Arizona Town Hall (Phoenix: Arizona Town Hall, 1994): 120.

[12] Loa M. Schell, comp. and ed. *1995–1996 Tribal Directory of the 21 Federally-Recognized Indian Tribes of Arizona.* (Phoenix: Arizona Commission of Indian Affairs).

[13] Eric Henderson and Scott Russell, "The Navajo Gaming Referendum: Reservations About Casinos Lead to Popular Rejection of Legalized Gambling," *Human Organization,* vol. 56, no. 3 (1997): 294–301. Much of this section of this chapter derives from this excellent article.

[14] Title 17, Section 421, *Navajo Nation Code.*

[15] Henderson and Russell, "The Navajo Gaming Referendum ..." p. 294.

[16] Ibid., p. 297.

[17] See, *Carpenter v. Shaw,* 280 U.S. 363 (1930) and *Squire v. Capoeman,* 351 U.S. 1 (1956).

[18] Michael Benson, *Sovereignty: the Navajo Nation and Taxation,* (Window Rock: DNA-People's Legal Services, Inc., 1976): 20.

[19] Ibid., p. 26.

[20] 455 U.S. 130, 139 (1982).

[21] 105 S.Ct. 1900.

[22] See, Robert W. Hanula, "The Navajo Tax System," *Arizona Bar Journal* (Dec–Jan. 1988): 6–9.

[23] Interview with Amy Alderman, an attorney for the Navajo Tax Commission, August 1, 1998.

[24] Ibid.

[25] Tom Tso, "Interview," *Arizona Attorney,* vol. 28, no. 9 (May 1992): 10.

Appendices

APPENDIX A
Timeline of Diné Political History

APPENDIX B
Chairmen (Presidents) of the Navajo Nation

APPENDIX C
Treaty Between The United States of America and
The Navajo Tribe of Indians (1849)

APPENDIX D
Treaty Between The United States of America and
The Navajo Tribe of Indians (1868)

APPENDIX E
Rules for the Navajo Tribal Council (1938)

APPENDIX F
Navajo Nation Bill of Rights

APPENDIX G
Resolution of the Navajo Tribal Council
(Amending Title Two (2) of the Navajo Tribal Code
and Related Actions)

APPENDIX H
Resolution of the Navajo Tribal Council
(Repealing 2 N.N.C. Section 4001 Et. seq., the Enacting of the
"Navajo Nation Local Governance Act" for Navajo Nation Chapters,
Chapter Officials and Chapter Administration)

Appendix A

Timeline of Diné Political History

First World (Black)

Creation of First Man and First Woman; place of Spirit and Holy People.

Second World (Blue)

First Man and First Woman see birds, large insects, and animals. First Man performs ceremonies to lead the beings from the Second World when quarreling begins.

Third World (Yellow)

Sacred mountains and rivers are formed. Turquoise Boy, White Shell Woman, and Coyote are present. Coyote introduces deception and trickery into this world. First four Naataanii (Chiefs) appear.

Fourth World (Glittering World)

First Man and First Woman create four sacred mountains. Following the instructions of Talking God, the first Sweat House and Hogan are constructed. Changing Woman creates the first four clans; the people are settled within the four sacred mountains by the Holy People.

900–1400 A.D.

Navajo oral accounts combined with archaeological, linguistic, and tree-ring data place the Navajos in the Southwest.

1583

Antonio de Espejo encounters Querechos (Navajos) in northwestern New Mexico. This is, reputedly, the first recorded contact between Navajos and Spaniards.

1626

Father Zarate Salmeron provides the first known documented reference to the Navajos as a distinct tribal group.

1630

Fray Alonso de Benavides refers to the Navajos as "very great farmers for that is what 'Navajos' signifies—'great planted fields.' " Benavides also refers to them as Navajo Apaches, or simply Apaches.

1630–1860s

Spaniards begin slave raids against the Navajos after 1630. This practice precluded any lasting peace between Navajos and the Spaniards, or between the Diné and the Mexicans or the United States in the early years.

1645

Navajos negotiate a military alliance treaty with Jemez Pueblo Indians. The two tribes conspire to drive out the Spaniards.

1680

Some Navajos ally with various Pueblo communities and drive the Spaniards of out of Pueblo territory in the Great Pueblo Revolt. Later, when the Spaniards regain control over most of the Pueblos in 1696, many individual Pueblo Indians flee to Navajo country and are adopted.

1692

Hopis state that some Apaches (probably Navajos) are nearby.

1706

First peace treaty between the Navajos and Spain. (This, and all subsequent treaties except the 1868 treaty, is negotiated by some, but not all, major Navajo leaders. The Navajos have no central political authority that speaks for or controls all Navajos. The Naachid is active, but the council's decisions affect only the participating clans.)

1720–1750

Period of comparative peace between the Navajos and Spaniards. Navajo livestock and trade in baskets, skins, etc., prospers.

1749

Spaniards establish two Catholic missions in Navajo country: Encinal and Cebolleta. Several Navajos are Christianized. The Navajos, however, rebel and drive the missionaries out in 1750. They fear that they may be enslaved like many Pueblos.

1750s

Spanish government begins to issue land grants to its citizens. Many of these grants overlap with Navajo territory. The uneasy peace ends.

1772

Navajos establish military alliance with Gila Apaches to war against the Spaniards.

1786

The Navajos are said to be subdivided into five divisions: San Mateo, Cebolleta, Chuska Mountain, Ojo del Oso, and Canyon de Chelly.

The Spaniards, in an attempt to break up the Navajo and Gila Apache alliance, negotiate an agreement with a group of Navajos. The Spaniards "select" a Navajo, Don Carlos, to be "Head Chief" of all Navajos. The Spaniards even pay Don Carlos an annual salary of 200 pesos, alleging that Carlos is "elected with the consent of all the Nation."

1805

Treaty between the Spaniards and Navajos. The massacre of over 100 Navajos the preceding year forces several Navajo bands to sue for peace.

1819

A fourth and last treaty is concluded between the Spaniards and the Navajos. This agreement, like those before it, is written in Spanish and contains a provision that establishes the position of "General" among the Navajos. Joaquin, the leader of a Navajo band which had split from the main tribe, is appointed "General."

1821

Mexico declares independence from Spain.

1822

A delegation of thirteen Navajo Peace Naataanii are killed by Mexicans at Jemez Pueblo. The delegation had approached the Mexicans seeking peace.

In August, the first of six peace treaties is concluded between several Navajo bands and the Mexican Governor, Facundo Melgares.

1823

A second peace treaty is negotiated at Paguate Pueblo.

1824

At Jemez Pueblo, a third treaty is signed between the two peoples.

1839

Chief Cayutano and several other Navajo headmen negotiate a fourth treaty with the Mexicans.

1840

Navajos hold a Naachid west of Canyon de Chelly. This is conducted, in part, to bring about peaceful relations between the Navajos and the Spaniards.

1841

At the Pueblo of Santo Domingo, several Navajo headmen and the Mexican Governor negotiate a fifth peace treaty.

1844

The sixth and final peace agreement between the two peoples is concluded.

1846

Colonel Stephen Watts Kearny marches into Santa Fe, New Mexico, claiming the capital for the United States.

In November, over 500 Navajos and nearly 100 Americans meet at Fort Wingate, New Mexico, to establish treaty relations. (This is the first of nine treaties between the two peoples).

1848

Treaty of Guadalupe Hidalgo is negotiated between the United States and the Republic of Mexico. Under its terms, Navajos and other Indians in the Southwest are placed "under the jurisdiction of the United States." (No tribes were represented at the negotiations.)

A second treaty is concluded between the Navajos and the United States.

1849

On September 9, a third treaty is signed by the Navajos and the federal government. (Of the nine treaties concluded between the United States and the Navajo Nation, only two were ratified by the U.S. Senate: the 1849 and 1868 treaties.)

1851

In March, Sandoval, a Navajo headman of the Cebolleta band, captures eighteen Navajos and scalps several others. Sandoval and his group had waged war and made slave raids against other Navajos for many years. His descendants eventually settle at Cañoncito, New Mexico, and are labeled Diné Ana'ii ("Enemy Navajo") by other Navajos.

A fourth treaty is apparently concluded between the United States and Navajos, although there is no extant copy of this arrangement.

Fort Defiance is established at Canyon Bonito. (This is the first military fort constructed in Navajo country by any foreign nation.)

1853

Henry Linn Dodge is appointed the first Navajo Indian Agent.

1855

Treaty of Laguna Negra is concluded. Zarcillos Largos is replaced by Manuelito as "Head Chief" of the Navajo Tribe.

1858

An armistice (temporary truce) is signed on November 20.

On December 25, the temporary truce is replaced by the Bonneville Treaty.

1859(?)

Last Naachid reportedly held.

1861

An eighth treaty is negotiated between the Navajos and the United States.

1864–68

Navajos are imprisoned at Bosque Redondo, New Mexico (Fort Sumner).

1868

A final treaty between the Navajos and the United States is concluded at Fort Sumner, New Mexico. This agreement is ratified by the U.S. Senate on July 25. It establishes a permanent reservation for the Navajos, among other things.

1872

Navajo police force is organized by Thomas Keams. The force is led by Manuelito.

1878–86

The size of the original treaty Reservation is increased by five major land annexations. (Additional lands are added into the early 1930s.)

1882

A presidential executive order establishes a 2.4 million acre reservation for "the use and occupancy of the Moqui (Hopi) and other Indians as the Secretary of the Interior may see fit to settle thereon." This acreage forms the basis of what becomes the Navajo-Hopi Land Dispute.

1884

Henry Chee Dodge is appointed Head Chief of the Navajos.

1901–11

The federal government creates five Navajo agencies (mini Navajo Reservations) to improve its administration of Navajo affairs: Southern (Fort Defiance), Northern (San Juan, later Shiprock), Western (Tuba City), Western extension (Leupp), and Eastern Navajo or Pueblo Bonito (Crownpoint).

1921

Oil is discovered in San Juan Agency.

1922

The federal government creates a "Business Council," composed of Chee Dodge, Charlie Mitchell, and Dugal Chee Bekiss, ostensibly to negotiate oil leases on behalf of the Navajo Tribe.

1923

The federal government replaces the nonrepresentative "Business Council" with the Navajo Tribal Council. Chee Dodge is elected the first Navajo Tribal Chairman.

Herbert Hagerman is appointed "Special Commissioner to the Navajo Tribe."

1927

The Tribal Council's regulations are revised—tenure of office is changed from four to five years.

John G. Hunter, Superintendent of the Leupp Agency, institutes the Chapter House system of local government.

1928

Dashne Clah Cheschillege is elected Navajo Tribal Chairman; Maxwell Yazzie, Vice-Chairman.

Tribal Council regulations are again revised—women are given the right to vote.

1932

Thomas Dodge, Chee Dodge's son, is elected Tribal Chairman; Marcus Kanuho serves as Vice-Chairman.

1934

Navajo people reject the Indian Reorganization Act in a close vote.

Congressional legislation adds 243,000 acres of land to the Navajo Reservation and redefines the boundaries of the tribe's land. This acreage, east of Tuba City, included the Hopi village of Moencopi, leading to yet another land dispute—the Bennett-Freeze area.

1934–1940s

The federal government enforces the disastrous livestock reduction program.

1936

Tom Dodge resigns as Tribal Chairman. Marcus Kanuho serves as Interim Chairman until government reorganization begins.

Nineteen land management districts are created by the federal government.

Formation of a Navajo Constitutional Assembly.

District Six, a 499,248-acre section within the 1882 Hopi Reservation is recognized as encompassing all of the lands exclusively occupied by the Hopi people.

Window Rock, Arizona, becomes the center of Navajo government.

1937

Henry Taliman is selected Tribal Chairman; he serves until 1938.

Navajos submit a tribal constitution to the Secretary of the Interior for approval. The Secretary rejects the document.

1938

Secretary of the Interior issues a new set of by-laws, in the place of the constitution, called "Rules for the Tribal Council." These rules, despite important modifications, still form the general framework of Navajo National government.

Jacob C. Morgan is elected Navajo Tribal Chairman; Howard Gorman is his Vice-Chair.

1940

The Navajo Tribal Council enacts a resolution outlawing peyote use on the Reservation. The Native American Church challenged this resolution in federal court on grounds that it was an unconstitutional violation of their First Amendment right to freedom of religion. In *Native American Church Inc. v. Navajo Tribal Council* (1959), a federal court held that the First Amendment applied only to Congress and the states and that "no provision in the constitution makes the First Amendment applicable to Indian nations ... ."

1941

District Six is expanded to 631,194 acres; some Navajo families are forced to relocate and are never compensated or provided with replacement homes.

1941–1945

Over 3,500 Navajos serve directly in World War II. An additional 10,000–12,000 are employed in war related jobs.

1942

Chee Dodge is re-elected as Chairman of the Tribal Council; Sam Ahkeah is Vice-Chairman.

1946

Sam Ahkeah is elected Chairman; Chee Dodge is elected Vice-Chairman.

1947

Chee Dodge, eighty-seven years of age, dies.

The Tribal Council creates an Advisory Committee (sometimes referred to as the Executive Committee).

Norman Littell becomes the Navajo Nation's first attorney.

1948

The Arizona Supreme Court in *Harrison and Austin v. Laveen* concedes that Arizona Indians have the right to vote.

1950

Congress enacts the Navajo-Hopi Long Range Rehabilitation Act which authorizes an appropriation of $88,570,000 for the social, economic, health, education, and other needs of the two tribes.

1951

Sam Ahkeah is re-elected Chairman of the Tribal Council. John Claw is Vice-Chair. Claw later resigns and is replaced by Adolph Maloney.

1953

Navajo Tribe submits another tribal constitution for Secretarial (Interior) approval. It is never approved.

1954

Navajo Tribe assumes control of its own election process.

1955

Paul Jones is elected Tribal Chairman; Scott Preston, Vice-Chairman.
    Navajo Tribal Council officially recognizes tribal Chapters, and establishes criteria for the certification of new Chapters.

1958

Congress passes Public Law 85-547, which authorizes the Navajo and Hopi Tribal Councils to participate in a lawsuit to determine their respective rights and interests in the 1882 executive order "territory." A three-judge federal court is given jurisdiction to oversee this process. This act also "vested" title to the land in both tribes.

1959

Navajo Tribal Council enacts rules to govern chapter elections.
    Navajo Tribe assumes control of law and order functions on the Reservation.
    Navajo Judicial Branch is established.
    The Executive Branch of the Navajo Tribe is reorganized.

Position of Executive Secretary is created. J. Maurice McCabe, the only man to hold the post, is recognized by some commentators as the "architect" of modern Navajo government.

Paul Jones is re-elected Tribal Chairman; Scott Preston, Vice-Chairman.

1962

Navajo Tribal Code is published. This two-volume set bound all preexisting laws, regulations, and policies of the Tribal Council, applicable federal laws, and pertinent state laws. (By 1995 the *Code* had expanded to six volumes.)

In *Healing v. Jones,* a federal district court rules that the Hopi Tribe has exclusive title to District Six but that both tribes have "joint, undivided, and equal interests as to the surface and sub-surface including all resources appertaining thereto, subject to the trust title of the United States" to the remaining 1.8 million acres of the 1882 Reservation outside District Six. This acreage became known as the Joint Use Area (JUA). The ruling was affirmed by the Supreme Court in 1963. Judge Hamley described this land controversy as "the greatest title problem of the West."

1963

Raymond Nakai is elected Navajo Tribal Chairman; Nelson Damon, Vice-Chairman.

1965

The Office of Navajo Economic Opportunity is created.

1966

Dinebeiina Nahiilna Be Agaditahe "Attorneys who contribute to the economic revitalization of the people" (D.N.A.). An extensive legal services program within the Office of Navajo Economic Opportunity, begins operation.

Commissioner of Indian Affairs, Robert L. Bennett, and Secretary of the Interior, Stewart Udall, impose a construction ban on development in the 1934 Act area. This action prohibits construction without a permit issued by both tribes. This becomes known as the Bennett-Freeze area.

1967

Raymond Nakai and Nelson Damon are re-elected to their posts.

Navajo Tribal Council enacts the Navajo Bill of Rights.

1968

Congress enacts the Indian Civil Rights Act. This law imposed most of the provisions of the U.S. Bill of Rights on tribal governments.

Another Navajo constitution is written. Like all its predecessors, it was never submitted to the Navajo people for approval.

1970

Peter MacDonald is elected Navajo Tribal Chairman; Wilson Skeet, Vice-Chairman.

1972

In *United States v. Kabinto* a federal court rules that the United States is within its right as trustee of the Hopi Tribe to evict 16 Navajos, declared "trespassers," from District Six.

1974

Peter MacDonald and Wilson Skeet are re-elected to their positions.

Congress enacts Public Law 93-531, the Navajo-Hopi Land Settlement Act. The most significant provision gave the U.S. District Court of Arizona jurisdiction to partition the Joint Use Area (JUA) and directed a 50-50 division of the lands between the two tribes. An independent, temporary Navajo-Hopi Indian Relocation Commission was established to facilitate the relocation of Navajo and Hopi residents who, after partition, found themselves to be on the other tribe's lands. Incentives were provided for "voluntary relocation" prior to the 1986 deadline for final removal.

1977

U.S. District Court Judge James Walsh concurs with the recommendations of the federal mediator who had suggested a partition line dividing the JUA between the two tribes. The placement of the partition line would result in the relocation of 3,495 Navajo and approximately 40 Hopi.

1978

Navajo Tribal Council creates a Supreme Judicial Council. This quasi-judicial body could hear cases on appeal from lower courts. It was immediately criticized and was finally repealed in 1985.

Peter MacDonald is re-elected to an unprecedented third term. Frank Paul is MacDonald's running mate.

1980

Navajo and Hopi Indian Relocation Amendments Act is passed by Congress. These amendments authorize the payment of attorneys' fees for both sides in the continuing litigation, increase authorizations for the operating expenses of the Relocation Commission, and give each tribe jurisdiction over the lands partitioned to it, among other things.

1982

Peterson Zah is elected Tribal Chairman; Edward T. Begay is Vice-Chairman.

1985

Navajo Tribal Council approves reapportionment plan.

In *Kerr McGee Corp. v. Navajo Tribe of Indians,* the United States Supreme Court holds that the Navajo Tribe's right to tax is an essential element of sovereignty and that it is not necessary for the Tribe to secure the approval of the Interior Department before implementing taxes.

The Tribal Council approves the creation of a Navajo Supreme Court.

President Reagan designates former Interior Secretary, William Clark, as his personal representative to encourage the Hopi and Navajo tribes to settle the land dispute. After seven months, however, Clark determines that it is unlikely the tribes can negotiate a peaceful settlement of their differences.

1986

Original deadline, under the 1974 law, for Navajos to have been relocated from Hopi partitioned land passes with approximately one-half of Navajos certified for voluntary relocation benefits not yet relocated. Other Navajo families insist they will not relocate.

1987

Peter MacDonald elected Chairman of the Nation for an unprecedented fourth term. Johnny R. Thompson is chosen Vice-Chairman.

The *Navajo Times Today* is shut down by tribal officials on February 19.

MacDonald convinces the Tribal Council that the purchase of the Big Boquillas "Big Bo" Ranch (just south of the Grand Canyon) will help rejuvenate the Navajo Nation's economy. The Council agrees and in April it approves the purchase in a lopsided vote. It was purchased by the tribe on July 9 for $33.4 million dollars, just minutes after Byron "Bud" Brown, a Scottsdale developer and MacDonald friend and another associate paid a California company $26.2 million for the same ranch. The Tribal Council approved the sale with its members unaware of the double escrow or the fact that the tribe was paying $7 million more than the ranch was actually worth.

Navajo Economic Summit held in July at Tohatchi, New Mexico.

Senate Select Committee on Indian Affairs establishes a Special Committee on Investigations to uncover "fraud, corruption and mismanagement in American Indian affairs, no matter where or to whom it led." As part of the committee's mandate, it is also called to examine Indian tribal governments to ascertain the degree of corruption in those institutions. The committee pays special attention to Peter MacDonald's leadership.

1989

The Senate Committee's investigation of political corruption in Peter MacDonald's administration, centered around the "Big Bo" land purchase and other deals, leads to intense conflict in the Nation. A majority of the Tribal Council become dissatisfied with MacDonald's leadership and organize against him. MacDonald agrees to leave office peacefully if the Council will furnish him with a legal defense fund. The Council refuses and on February 16 MacDonald resigns. However, the next day he reneges and decides to fight his ouster. The Council, by a 49 to 13 vote, then places MacDonald on involuntary administrative leave without the defense funds he demanded. This leads to a series of events, culminating in a deadly confrontation which erupts in Window Rock on July 20, (two Navajos were killed and ten were injured) pitting supporters of Peter MacDonald against the Tribal Council, tribal police, and others.

Leonard Haskie is selected as Interim Chairman by the Tribal Council. Irving Billy is designated Vice-Chair.

On December 15 the Navajo Nation Council reorganizes the Navajo government through amendments to Title Two of the *Navajo Tribal Code*. The amendments will take effect April 1, 1990. Among other things, the Title Two Amendments split the position of Chairman into two new positions, the Speaker of the Council and the President of the Navajo Nation. These changes install the doctrine of separation of powers by dividing and clearly demarcating the legislative and executive functions. The judicial branch is already independent.

1990

MacDonald is tried and convicted in the Navajo court and later in federal courts of several counts of bribery, instigating a riot, fraud, racketeering, extortion, conspiracy, and ethics violations. He is sentenced to a 14-year term in Pennsylvania. Because of poor health he is later transferred to a Federal Medical Center in Fort Worth, Texas, a minimum security prison.

Nelson Gorman is elected first Speaker of the Navajo Nation Council.

Congress enacts the Radiation Exposure Compensation Act, Public Law 101-426 on October 16. This measure provides $100,000 in "compassion payments" to uranium miners—many of whom were Navajo—and who were diagnosed with cancer or other respiratory ailments linked to uranium mining—or to the families of the uranium miners who had died. The law includes an apology to the miners. "The Congress," it was declared, "apologizes on behalf of the Nation to the individuals described in subsection (a) and their families for the hardships they have endured." This was only the second time the United States government had ever apologized for its misdeeds. A similar apology had been included in the compensation act for the Japanese-Americans who had been wrongly imprisoned during World War II.

1991

Peterson Zah is elected President of the Navajo Nation. Marshall Plummer is Vice-President.

In December the Nation's Council formally exchanges land patents and deeds involving 100,000 acres in the Eastern Navajo Agency. This clears title uncertainty for over 200 Navajo families who had been considered "unauthorized occupants."

1992

Agreement-in-Principle reached as a result of mediation between the United States, the Hopi Tribe, and the Navajo Nation. Terms resolve cases between the tribes and the United States and provide a vehicle for the Navajo families to remain on Hopi partitioned lands. Approved by the United States and the tribal governments, opposition to the agreement from state and surrounding communities begins.

1993

In the spring a deadly and traumatic "mystery illness" appears in the southwest, initially striking down several young Navajo men and women. The disease ultimately kills 27 people from all walks of life and various ethnic groups. The scientific community eventually determined that the cause of death was the hantavirus carried by deer mice. Many Navajo experts agree that deer mice are the illness-bearers, but they believe the true cause is a breakdown of proper spiritual relations in the Diné world.

1994

June 1 is designated "Navajo Nation Treaty Day" by presidential executive order.

A new chapter, "Nahata Dziil," is formed in the newly acquired lands located near Sanders, Arizona. This is the 110th Chapter.

Navajo electorate defeat a measure to legalize gaming by a vote of 28,073 to 23,450.

1995

Albert Hale is inaugurated as President. Thomas Atcitty is elected Vice-President.

1996

Fannie Mae, the United States largest source of home mortgage funds, signs a landmark agreement on June 19 that will allow the first-ever secondary market-supported conventional mortgage lending to Navajos living on trust lands. Until now, mortgage lending on Indian trust lands had been limited to programs using government guarantees or insurance programs.

In October Congress enacts Public Law 104-301, the Navajo-Hopi Land Settlement Act. This act ratified the U.S.-Hopi Settlement and Accommodation Agreement. The Hopi tribe is granted 75-year leasing authority over the remaining Navajos, if they decide to stay.

Two Navajo deities reportedly visit Irene Yazzie, a 96-year-old Navajo, warning that the Diné are in grave danger if they continue to forsake tribal traditions. Many Navajo visit Ms. Yazzie's hogan to pray and sprinkle corn powder in the footprints said to have been left by the deities. There is disagreement in some quarters, however, about how authentic the visitation is.

U.S. Supreme Court lets stand a Utah Supreme Court ruling, *Mark Maryboy v. Utah State Tax Commission,* that allows the state to tax the income earned by Indians who are elected state officials (Maryboy was a San Juan County official), but who live and conduct most of their duties on reservations.

U.S. District Judge Earl Carroll formally lifted the construction ban on about half of the 1.7 million acres in the "Bennett-Freeze" area after the two tribes reached agreement in a bitter fight over the land. The Hopi Tribe had recently acknowledged that the land was no longer in litigation. The ban, however, remained in effect on 700,000 acres the Hopi Tribe, and later the San Juan Band of Southern Paiute, claims. Judge Carroll must decide whether Hopis and Paiute have a historical and religious presence there.

1997

Navajo families living on Hopi designated land who refused to sign a 75-year lease under the 1996 Accommodation Agreement by the midnight deadline of March 31 will not face immediate eviction. Navajo families who do not sign leases have 90 days to decide whether they want to be moved at the federal government's expense.

A congressional bill to repeal the Bennett-Freeze administrative order is introduced in November. The language of the bill states that the "Bennett Freeze is a gross violation of treaty obligations to the Navajo Nation."

1998

Albert Hale is forced to resign his presidency in February amid charges of ethical and financial misdeeds. He faces criminal charges from a special prosecutor looking into accusations that he misspent tribal money, accepted illegal gifts from companies with tribal contracts, and that he had a sexual affair while in office. Thomas Atcitty is sworn in to serve out the remainder of Hale's term.

In April the Navajo Nation Council enacted into law the "Navajo Nation Local Governance Act." This measure addresses the governmental functions of Chapters, improves their structure, and provides the opportunity for local Chapters to make decisions over local matters.

Less than four months after Albert Hale is forced out of office, President Thomas Atcitty is also removed after he was accused by the Ethics and Rules Committee of violating tribal ethic laws for having accepted corporate gifts. Speaker of the Council, Kelsey Begaye, is sworn in as Interim President, but within two days, the council is forced to select a new Interim President, Mr. Milton Bluehouse

(Atcitty's Vice-President), after he warned that he would take legal action unless he was named president.

1999

Kelsey Begaye, the former Speaker of the Council and Interim President, is inaugurated as President. Dr. Taylor MacKenzie is elected Vice-President.

2000

The U.S. Census reports that 269,202 people reported themselves as Navajo, with an additional 28,995 individuals claiming to be Navajo in combination with one or more other races.

A tribal referendum was held to determine whether to maintain the size of the Navajo Nation Council at 88 members or to reduce it to 24 members. Although a clear majority of those voting were in favor of the reduction, the measure did not pass because less than 50 percent of the total number of registered voters had cast ballots.

2001

In a major case with adverse consequences for tribal sovereignty, the U.S. Supreme Court held in *Atkinson Trading Company, Inc. v. Shirley* that the Navajo Nation lacked authority to impose a tax on nonmember guests of a hotel located on non-Indian fee land within the exterior boundaries of the Navajo Reservation.

Five Navajo uranium miners or their widows were each presented checks for $50,000 at a ceremony in Shiprock, New Mexico. The checks were lump-sum payments awarded through a new federal compensation program for uranium miners who suffered physical and emotional ailments or died as a result of their work in the industry beginning in the 1950s.

The Navajo Nation Council adopts a 3 percent sales tax. It is estimated that it will generate more than $6 million a year for the Nation and the local chapters. The tax goes into effect April 1, 2002.

In April, the Navajo Nation joins forces with several tribes from Montana and Wyoming to form the Council of Large Land-Based Tribes. This is an association of First Nations that have land bases of more than 100,000 acres.

In one of his last actions as president, Bill Clinton commutes (but does not pardon) the remaining sentence of former Navajo Nation President, Peter MacDonald. MacDonald had been in prison since 1992 after his conviction for crimes that culminated in a deadly riot in 1989.

U.S. President George W. Bush on July 29 presents congressional gold medals to four of the five living Navajo codetalkers and to relatives of the other twenty-four codetalkers.

The Navajo Board of Election Supervisors and the Navajo Election Administration is involved in a major battle with the Council, with criminal charges being brought against eight of the election supervisors for failure to conduct chapter election in August 2000.

The Navajo Nation Council passes a resolution that authorizes gaming, but only for the Canoncito Band of Navajos who live on lands off the reservation and west of Albuquerque. The resolution also amended the Nation's Code by decriminalizing gaming "if done pursuant to a gaming compact." However, President Kelsey Begaye later vetoed the measure, asserting that the Navajo people in two tribal referenda had expressed their views against gaming. After two unsuccessful attempts to override Begaye's veto, a compromise gaming ordinance was finally approved by the Council and signed into law by President Begaye in October.

The Navajo Nation seeks to take over the delivery of health care administration from the Indian Health Service. Although the Navajo electorate voted in a referendum against the government's proposed plans, the tribe's leadership continues to support the idea of eventually running the nation's health services.

Two Navajo women, Marcella Ben-King and Lorene Ferguson, are appointed during the year to the Navajo Supreme Court. This is the first time women have served on the Nation's high court.

Dorothy Fulton is picked to be the Navajo Nation's first female police chief. She oversees a reservation plagued with a high vehicular death rate and a crime rate that has increased significantly in recent years.

In *Navajo Nation v. United States,* a federal court of appeals reverses and remands an earlier claims court ruling in 2000, holding that the secretary of interior had indeed breached his fiduciary (trust) duties to the Navajo Nation with respect to coal mining royalties and that the Nation was entitled to monetary relief.

2002

After years of research, surveys, and public hearings, the Navajo Nation Government Development Commission organizes the first Navajo Nation Statutory Reform Convention to discuss and vote on twenty-six proposed amendments aimed at reforming the Nation's government to make it more democratically accountable.

Incumbent President Kelsey Begaye, Vice-President Taylor McKenzie, and fifteen other presidential hopefuls are vying for the offices of president and vice-president.

The Navajo Nation Council adopts a reapportionment plan for use in the 2002 elections, but the resolution is subsequently vetoed by President Begaye on the grounds that it "fails to properly and adequately designate precincts which are equal in population."

Derrick Watchman, a Navajo, seeks the Democratic Party's nomination for the newly created 1st Congressional District in Arizona. If Watchman is elected, it will be the first time Arizona has sent an Indian to Congress.

Navajo Nation President Kelsey Begaye vetoed a Council resolution that would have allowed the Baca-Prewitt Chapter to engage in gaming. Currently, only the Canoncito Band of Navajos near Albuquerque have been granted an exception to the tribe's gaming ban.

Joe Shirley, Jr., and his running mate, Frank Dayish, Jr., defeated the incumbent Kelsey A. Begaye and his vice-president, Taylor McKenzie, by an unofficial vote of 31,754 to 24,166 on November 5, 2002.

Appendix B

Chairmen (Presidents) of the Navajo Nation

Chairmen	Term
Chee Dodge	1923–1928
Dashne Cheschillege	1928–1932
Thomas Dodge	1932–1936
Marcus Kanuho (interim)	1936–1936
Henry Taliman	1937–1938
Jacob C. Morgan	1938–1942
Chee Dodge	1942–1946
Sam Ahkeah	1946–1954
Paul Jones	1955–1963
Raymond Nakai	1963–1970
Peter MacDonald	1970–1982
Peterson Zah	1982–1987
Peter MacDonald	1987–1989
Leonard Haskie (interim)	1989–1991

Presidents	Term
Peterson Zah	1991–1994
Albert Hale	1995–1998
Thomas Atcitty	1998
Kelsey Begaye	1998
Milton Bluehouse (interim)	1998
Kelsey Begaye	1999

Appendix C

Treaty Between The United States of America and The Navajo Tribe of Indians

Concluded September 9, 1849
Ratified by the Senate September 9, 1850
Proclaimed by the President September 24, 1850

The following acknowledgements, declarations, and stipulations, have been duly considered, and are now solemnly adopted and proclaimed by the undersigned: that is to say, John M. Washington, Governor of New Mexico and Lieutenant-Colonel commanding the troops of the United States in New Mexico, and James S. Calhoun, Indian agent, residing at Santa Fe, in New Mexico, representing the United States of America, and Mariano Martinez, Head Chief, and Chapitone, second Chief, on the part of the Navajo tribe of Indians.

I.   The said Indians do hereby acknowledge that, by virtue of a treaty entered into by the United States of America and the United Mexican States, signed on the second day of February, in the year of our Lord eighteen hundred and forty-eight, at the city of Guadalupe Hidalgo, by N. P. Trist, of the first part, and Luis G. Cuevas, Bernardo Couto, and Mgl Artistain, of the second part, the said tribe was lawfully placed under the exclusive jurisdiction and protection of the government of the said United States, and that they are now, and will forever remain, under the aforesaid jurisdiction and protection.

II.   That from and after the signing of this treaty, hostilities between the contracting parties shall cease, and perpetual peace and friendship shall exist; the said tribe hereby solemnly covenanting that they will not associate with, or give countenance or aid to, any tribe or band of Indians, or other persons or powers, who may be at any time at enmity with the people of the said United States; that they will remain at peace, and treat honestly and humanely all persons and powers at peace with the said States; and all cases of aggression against said Navajoes by citizens or others of the United States, or by other persons or powers in amity with the said States, shall be referred to the government of said States for adjustment and settlement.

III.   The government of the said States having the sole and exclusive right of regulating the trade and intercourse with the said Navajoes, it is agreed that the laws now in force regulating the trade and intercourse, and for the preservation of peace with the various tribes of Indians under the protection and guardianship of the aforesaid government, shall have the same force and efficiency, and shall be as binding and as obligatory upon the said Navajoes, and executed in the same manner, as if said laws had been passed for their sole benefit and protection; and to this end, and for all other useful purposes, the government of New Mexico, as now organized or as it may be by the government of the United States, or by the legally constituted authorities of the people of New Mexico, is recognized and acknowledged by the said Navajoes; and for the due enforcement of the aforesaid laws, until the government of the United States shall otherwise order, the territory of the Navajoes is hereby annexed to New Mexico.

IV.   The Navajo Indians hereby bind themselves to deliver to the military authority of the United States in New Mexico, at Santa Fe, New Mexico, as soon as he or they can be apprehended, the murderer or murderers of Micente Garcia, that said fugitive or fugitives from justice may be dealt with as justice may decree.

V.   All American and Mexican captives, and all stolen property taken from Americans or Mexicans, or other persons or powers in amity with the United States, shall be delivered by the Navajo Indians to the aforesaid military authority at Jemez, New Mexico, on or before the 9th day of October next ensuing, that justice may be meted out to all whom it may concern; and also all Indian captives and stolen property of such tribe or tribes of Indians as shall enter into a similar reciprocal treaty, shall, in like manner, and for the same purposes, be turned over to an authorized officer or agent of the said States by the aforesaid Navajoes.

VI.   Should any citizen of the United States or other person or persons subject to the laws of the United States, murder, rob, or otherwise maltreat any Navajo Indian or Indians, he or they shall be arrested and tried, and, upon conviction, shall be subjected to all the penalties provided by law for the protection of the persons and property of the people of the said States.

VII.   The people of the United States of America shall have free and safe passage through the territory of the aforesaid Indians, under such rules and regulations as may be adopted by authority of the said States.

VIII.   In order to preserve tranquility, and to afford protection to all the people and interests of the contracting parties, the government of the United States of America will establish such military posts and agencies, and authorize such trading-houses, at such time and in such places as the said government may designate.

IX.   Relying confidently upon the justice and the liberality of the aforesaid government, and anxious to remove every possible cause that might disturb their peace and quiet, it is agreed by the aforesaid Navajoes that the government of the United States shall, at its earliest convenience, designate, settle, and adjust their territorial boundaries, and pass and execute in their territory such laws as may be deemed conducive to the prosperity and happiness of said Indians.

X.   For and in consideration of the faithful performance of all the stipulations herein contained, by the said Navajo Indians, the government of the United States will grant to said Indians such donations, presents, and implements, and adopt such other liberal and humane measures as said government may deem meet and proper.

XI.   This treaty shall be binding upon the contracting parties from and after the signing of the same, subject only to such modifications and amendments as may be adopted by the government of the United States; and, finally, this treaty is to receive a liberal construction, at all times and in all places, to the end that the said Navajo Indians shall not be held responsible for the conduct of others, and that the government of the United States shall so legislate and act as to secure the permanent prosperity and happiness of said Indians.

In faith whereof we, the undersigned, have signed this treaty, and affixed thereunto our seals, in the valley of Cheille, this the ninth day of September, in the year of our Lord one thousand eight hundred and forty-nine.

J. M. Washington, [L.S.]
   Brevet Lieutenant-Colonel Commanding.

James S. Calhoun [L.S.]
   Indian Agent, residing at Santa Fe.

Mariano Martinez, his x mark, [L.S.]
   Head Chief.

Chapitone, his x mark, [L.S.]
   Second Chief.

J. L. Collins.

James Conklin.

Lorenzo Force.

Antonio Sandoval,   his x mark.

Francisco Josto,   his x mark.
   Governor of Jemez

Witnesses—

H. L. Kendrick, Brevet Major, U.S.A.

J. N. Ward, Brevet lst Lieut. 3d Inf'ry.

John Peck, Brevet Major U.S.A.

J. F. Hammond, Assistant Surg'n U.S.A.

H. L. Dodge, Capt. comd'g Eut. Rg's.

Richard H. Kern.

J. H. Nones, Second Lieut. 2d Artillery.

Cyrus Choice.

John H. Dickerson, Second Lieut. lst Art.

W. E. Love.

John G. Jones.

J. H. Simpson, First Lieut. Corps Top. Engrs.

Appendix D

Treaty Between The United States of America and The Navajo Tribe of Indians

Concluded June 1, 1868
Ratification Advised July 25, 1868
Proclaimed August 12, 1868
ANDREW JOHNSON
PRESIDENT OF THE UNITED STATES
OF AMERICA

TO ALL AND SINGULAR TO WHOM THESE PRESENTS SHALL COME, GREETING:

Whereas a Treaty was made and concluded at Fort Sumner, in the Territory of New Mexico, on the first day of June, in the year of our Lord one thousand eight hundred and sixty-eight, by and between Lieutenant General W. T. Sherman and Samuel F. Tappan, Commissioners, on the part of the United States, and Barboncito, Armijo, and other Chiefs and Headmen of the Navajo tribe of Indians, on the part of said Indians, and duly authorized thereto by them, which Treaty is in the words and figures following, to wit:

Articles of a Treaty and Agreement made and entered into at Fort Sumner, New Mexico, on the first day of June, 1868, by and between the United States; represented by its Commissioners, Lieutenant General W. T. Sherman and Colonel Samuel F. Tappan, of the one part, and the Navajo nation or tribe of Indians, represented by their Chiefs and Headmen, duly authorized and empowered to act for the whole people of said nation or tribe, (the names of said Chiefs and Headmen being hereto subscribed,) of the other part, witness:

ARTICLE I.

From this day forward all war between the parties to this agreement shall for ever cease. The government of the United States desires peace, and its honor is hereby pledged to keep it. The Indians desire peace, and they now pledge their honor to keep it.

If bad men among the whites, or among other people subject to the authority of the United States, shall commit any wrong upon the person or property of the Indians, the United States will, upon proof made to the agent and forwarded to the Commissioner of Indian Affairs at Washington city, proceed at once to cause the offender to be arrested and punished according to the laws of the United States, and also to reimburse the injured persons for the loss sustained.

If bad men among the Indians shall commit a wrong or depredation upon the person or property of any one, white, black, or Indian, subject to the authority of the United States and at peace therewith, the Navajo tribe agree that they will, on proof made to their agent, and on notice by him, deliver up the wrongdoer to the United States, to be tried and punished according to its laws; and in case they willfully refuse so to do, the person injured shall be reimbursed for his loss from the annuities or other moneys due or to become due them under this treaty, or any others that may be made with the United States. And the President may prescribe such rules and regulations for ascertaining damages under this article as in his judgment may be proper; but no such damage shall be adjusted and paid until examined and passed upon by the Commissioner of Indian Affairs, and no one sustaining loss whilst violating, or because of his violating, the provisions of this treaty or the laws of the United States shall be reimbursed therefor.

ARTICLE II.

The United States agrees that the following district of country, to wit: bounded on the north by the 37th degree of north latitude, south by an east and west line passing through the site of old Fort Defiance, in Cañon Bonito, east by the parallel of longitude which, if prolonged south, would pass through old Fort Lyon, or the Ojo-de-oso, Bear Spring, and west by a parallel of longitude about 109° 30′ west of Greenwich, provided it embraces the outlet of the Cañon-de-Chilly, which cañon is to be all included in this reservation, shall be, and the same is hereby, set apart for the use and occupation of the Navajo tribe of Indians, and for such other friendly tribes or individual Indians as from time to time they may be willing, with the consent of the United States, to admit among them; and the United States agrees that no persons except those herein so authorized to do, and except such officers, soldiers, agents, and employees of the government, or of the Indians, as may be authorized to enter upon Indian reservations in discharge of duties imposed by law, or the orders of the President, shall ever be permitted to pass over, settle upon, or reside in, the territory described in this article.

ARTICLE III.

The United States agrees to cause to be built at some point within said reservation, where timber and water may be convenient, the following buildings: a warehouse, to cost not exceeding twenty-five hundred dollars; an agency building for the residence of the agent, not to cost exceeding three thousand dollars; a carpenter shop and blacksmith shop, not to cost exceeding one thousand dollars each; and a school-house and chapel, so soon as a sufficient number of children can be induced to attend school, which shall not cost to exceed five thousand dollars.

ARTICLE IV.

The United States agrees that the agent for the Navajos shall make his home at the agency building; that he shall reside among them and shall keep an office open at all times for the purpose of prompt and diligent inquiry into such matters of complaint by or against the Indians as may be presented for investigation, as also for the faithful discharge of other duties enjoined by law. In all cases of depredation on person or property he shall cause the evidence to be taken in writing and forwarded, together with his finding, to the Commissioner of Indian Affairs, whose decision shall be binding on the parties to this treaty.

ARTICLE V.

If any individual belonging to said tribe, or legally incorporated with it, being the head of a family, shall desire to commence farming, he shall have the privilege to select, in the presence and with the assistance of the agent then in charge, a tract of land within said reservation, not exceeding one hundred and sixty acres in extent, which tract, when so selected, certified, and recorded in the "land book" as herein described, shall cease to be held in common, but the same may be occupied and held in the exclusive possession of the person selecting it, and of his family, so long as he or they may continue to cultivate it.

Any person over eighteen years of age, not being the head of the family, may in like manner select, and cause to be certified to him or her for purposes of cultivation, a quantity of land, not exceeding eighty acres in extent, and thereupon be entitled to the exclusive possession of the same as above directed.

For each tract of land so selected a certificate containing a description thereof, and the name of the person selecting it, with a certificate endorsed thereon that the same has been recorded, shall be delivered to the party entitled to it by the agent, after the same shall have been recorded by him in a book to be kept in his office, subject to inspection which said book shall be known as the "Navajo Land Book."

The President may at any time order a survey of the reservation, and, when so surveyed, Congress shall provide for protecting the rights of said settlers in their improvements, and may fix the character of the title held by each. The United States may pass such laws on the subject of alienation and descent of property between the Indians and their descendants as may be thought proper.

ARTICLE VI.

In order to insure the civilization of the Indians entering into this treaty, the necessity of education is admitted, especially of such of them as may be settled on said agricultural parts of this reservation, and they therefore pledge themselves to compel their children, male and female, between the ages of six and sixteen years, to attend school; and it is hereby made the duty of the agent for said Indians to see that this stipulation is strictly complied with; and the United States agrees that, for every thirty children between said ages who can be induced or compelled to attend school, a house shall be provided, and a teacher competent to teach the elementary branches of an English education shall be furnished, who will reside among said Indians, and faithfully discharge his or her duties as a teacher.

The provisions of this article to continue for not less than ten years.

ARTICLE VII.

When the head of a family shall have selected lands and received his certificate as above directed, and the agent shall be satisfied that he intends in good faith to commence cultivating the soil for a living, he shall be entitled to receive seeds and agricultural implements for the first year, not exceeding in value one hundred dollars, and for each succeeding year he shall continue to farm, for a period of two years, he shall be entitled to receive seeds and implements to the value of twenty-five dollars.

ARTICLE VIII.

In lieu of all sums of money or other annuities provided to be paid to the Indians herein named under any treaty or treaties heretofore made, the United States agrees to deliver at the agency house on the reservation herein named, on the first day of September of each year for ten years, the following articles, to wit:

Such articles of clothing, goods, or raw materials in lieu thereof, as the agent may make his estimate for, not exceeding in value five dollars per

Indian—each Indian being encouraged to manufacture their own clothing, blankets, etc.; to be furnished with no article which they can manufacture themselves. And, in order that the Commissioner of Indian Affairs may be able to estimate properly for the articles herein named, it shall be the duty of the agent each year to forward to him a full and exact census of the Indians, on which the estimate from year to year can be based.

And in addition to the articles herein named, the sum of ten dollars for each person entitled to the beneficial effects of this treaty shall be annually appropriated for a period of ten years, for each person who engages in farming or mechanical pursuits, to be used by the Commissioner of Indian Affairs in the purchase of such articles as from time to time the condition and necessities of the Indians may indicate to be proper; and if within the ten years at any time it shall appear that the amount of money needed for clothing, under the article, can be appropriated to better uses for the Indians named herein, the Commissioner of Indian Affairs may change the appropriation to other purposes, but in no event shall the amount of this appropriation be withdrawn or discontinued for the period named, provided they remain at peace. And the President shall annually detail an officer of the army to be present and attest the delivery of all the goods herein named to the Indians, and he shall inspect and report on the quantity and quality of the goods and the manner of their delivery.

ARTICLE IX.

In consideration of the advantages and benefits conferred by this treaty, and the many pledges of friendship by the United States, the tribes who are parties to this agreement hereby stipulate that they will relinquish all right to occupy any territory outside their reservation, as herein defined, but retain the right to hunt on any unoccupied lands contiguous to their reservation, so long as the large game may range thereon in such numbers as to justify the chase; and they, the said Indians, further expressly agree:

1st.   That they will make no opposition to the construction of railroads now being built or hereafter to be built, across the continent.

2nd.   That they will not interfere with the peaceful construction of any railroad not passing over their reservation as herein defined.

3rd.   That they will not attack any persons at home or travelling, nor molest or disturb any wagon trains, coaches, mules or cattle belonging to the people of the United States, or to persons friendly therewith.

4th.   That they will never capture or carry off from the settlements women or children.

5th.   They will never kill or scalp white men, nor attempt to do them harm.

6th. They will not in future oppose the construction of railroads, wagon roads, mail stations, or other works of utility or necessity which may be ordered or permitted by the laws of the United States; but should such roads or other works be constructed on the lands of their reservation, the government will pay the tribe whatever amount of damage may be assessed by three disinterested commissioners to be appointed by the President for that purpose, one of said commissioners to be a chief or head man of the tribe.

7th. They will make no opposition to the military posts or roads now established, or that may be established, not in violation of treaties heretofore made or hereafter to be made with any of the Indian tribes.

ARTICLE X.

No future treaty for the cession of any portion or part of the reservation herein described, which may be held in common, shall be of any validity or force against said Indians unless agreed to and executed by at least three-fourths of all the adult male Indians occupying or interested in the same; and no cession by the tribe shall be understood or construed in such manner as to deprive, without his consent, any individual member of the tribe of his rights to any tract of land selected by him as provided in article 5 of this treaty.

ARTICLE XI.

The Navajos also hereby agree that at any time after the signing of these presents they will proceed in such manner as may be required of them by the agent, or by the officer charged with their removal, to the reservation herein provided for, the United States paying for their subsistence en route, and providing a reasonable amount of transportation for the sick and feeble.

ARTICLE XII.

It is further agreed by and between the parties to this agreement that the sum of one hundred and fifty thousand dollars appropriated or to be appropriated shall be disbursed as follows, subject to any conditions provided in the law, to wit:

1st. The actual cost of the removal of the tribe from the Bosque Redondo reservation to the reservation, say fifty thousand dollars.

2nd. The purchase of fifteen thousand sheep and goats, at a cost not to exceed thirty thousand dollars.

3rd. The purchase of five hundred beef cattle and a million pounds of corn, to be collected and held at the military post nearest the reservation, subject to the orders of the agent, for the relief of the needy during the coming winter.

4th. The balance, if any, of the appropriation to be invested for the maintenance of the Indians pending their removal, in such manner as the agent who is with them may determine.

5th. The removal of this tribe to be made under the supreme control and direction of the military commander of the Territory of New Mexico, and when completed, the management of the tribe to revert to the proper agent.

ARTICLE XIII.

The tribe herein named, by their representatives, parties to this treaty, agree to make the reservation herein described their permanent home, and they will not as a tribe make any permanent settlement elsewhere, reserving the right to hunt on the lands adjoining the said reservation formerly called theirs, subject to the modifications named in this treaty and the orders of the commander of the department in which said reservation may be for the time being; and it is further agreed and understood by the parties to this treaty, that if any Navajo Indian or Indians shall leave the reservation herein described to settle elsewhere, he or they shall forfeit all the rights, privileges, and annuities conferred by the terms of this treaty; and it is further agreed by the parties to this treaty, that they will do all they can to induce Indians now away from reservations set apart for the exclusive use and occupation of the Indians, leading a nomadic life, or engaged in war against the people of the United States, to abandon such a life and settle permanently in one of the territorial reservations set apart for the exclusive use and occupation of the Indians.

In testimony of all which the said parties have hereunto, on this the first day of June, eighteen hundred and sixty-eight, at Fort Sumner, in the Territory of New Mexico, set their bands and seals.

W. T. Sherman,
  Lt. Gen'l, Indian Peace Commissioner.

S. F. Tappan,
  Indian Peace Commissioner.

Barboncito, Chief.   his x mark.

Armijo.   his x mark.

Delgado.   [no mark or signature]

Manuelito.	his x mark.
Largo.	his x mark.
Herrero.	his x mark.
Chiqueto.	his x mark.
Muerto de Hombre.	his x mark.
Hombro.	his x mark.
Narbono.	his x mark.
Narbono Segundo.	his x mark.
Ganado Mucho.	his x mark.

COUNCIL.

Riquo.	his x mark.
Juan Martin.	his x mark.
Serginto.	his x mark.
Grande.	his x mark.
Inoetenito.	his x mark.
Muchachos Mucho.	his x mark.
Chiqueto Segundo.	his x mark.
Cabello Amarillo.	his x mark.
Francisco.	his x mark.
Torivio.	his x mark.
Desdendado.	his x mark.
Juan.	his x mark.
Guero.	his x mark.
Gugadore.	his x mark.
Cabason.	his x mark.
Barbon Segundo.	his x mark.
Cabares Colorados.	his x mark.

Attest:

Geo. W. G. Getty,
  Col. 37th Inf'y, Bt. Maj. Gen'l U.S.A.

B. S. Roberts,
  Bt. Brg. Gen'l U.S.A., Lt. Col. 3rd Cav'y.

J. Cooper Mckee,
  Bt. Lt. Col. Surgeon U.S.A.

Theo. H. Dodd,
  U.S. Indian Ag't for Navajos.

Chas. McClure,
  Bt. Maj. and C.S. U.S.A.

James F. Weeds,
  Bt. Maj. and Asst. Surg. U.S.A.

J. C. Sutherland,
  Interpreter.

William Vaux,
  Chaplain U.S.A.

Appendix E

Rules for the Navajo Tribal Council

July 26, 1938

CHAPTER I   How the tribal council is set up

SECTION 1. The Tribal Council shall be the governing body of the Navajo Tribe.

SECTION 2. The Tribal Council shall consist of 74 delegates.

SECTION 3. The 74 members of the Tribal Council shall be elected by the people of the several districts in accordance with the population of each district.

SECTION 4. Cañoncito District and Puertocito District and Ramah District shall each elect one delegate.

SECTION 5. Districts 2, 5, 11, 13, 16 and 19 shall each elect three delegates.

SECTION 6. Districts 1, 3, 4, 7, 8, 9, 10, 14 and 15 shall each elect four delegates.

SECTION 7. District 12 shall elect five delegates.

SECTION 8. Districts 17 and 18 shall each elect six delegates.

SECTION 9. Each delegate shall serve for a term of four years.

SECTION 10. No person shall serve as a delegate unless he or she is a member of The Navajo Tribe above the age of 30.

SECTION 11. No person shall serve as a delegate if he is in the permanent employment of the United States except as a judge, interpreter, teacher, or Indian Assistant, or if he is in the employment of any State or any private employer with business interests on the Navajo Reservation. (See Amendment, Order No. 1912, attached.)

SECTION 12. If any delegate, after his election enters such employment he shall immediately resign his office.

SECTION 13. If any delegate is unable to attend the meetings of the Tribal Council for one year, he shall immediately resign his office.

SECTION 14. If any delegate fails to resign his office in accordance with these rules, a notice shall be sent him and he shall be given a chance to come before the Tribal Council and show cause why he should not resign.

SECTION 15. When the accused delegate has been heard, the Council shall vote on his case, and if two thirds of the votes are cast for his removal, he shall be removed from office.

SECTION 16. In the same manner, a delegate may be removed if he misrepresents the action of the Tribal Council, or accepts any bribe, or commits any act of disloyalty toward the Tribal Council.

SECTION 17. If any vacancy arises in the Council, the Council shall order the people to elect another delegate to serve the remainder of the term.

CHAPTER II How the executive committee is set up

SECTION 1. The delegates of each district shall choose one among them as chief delegate; if they cannot agree among themselves, the Chairman of the Tribal Council shall make the choice.

SECTION 2. All the chief delegates shall compose the Executive Committee.

SECTION 3. The Executive Committee shall act in the place of the Tribal Council between the meetings of the Tribal Council.

SECTION 4. The Executive Committee shall refer all matters of very great importance to the Tribal Council, but matters of lesser importance the Executive Committee shall act upon in its own discretion.

CHAPTER III How the offices of the tribal council are set up

SECTION 1. There shall be one Chairman of the Navajo Tribal Council, and he shall hold office for a term of four years.

SECTION 2. When the Chairman of the Tribal Council has served four years, he may be elected for a second term, but he may not be elected for a third term.

SECTION 3. The Chairman of the Navajo Tribal Council may yield the chair to the Vice-Chairman in order to take part in the sessions of the Tribal Council. He may make recommendations and appoint committees. He shall be the Chairman of the Executive Committee, and he may advise and assist the Government on any action or policy adopted by the Tribal Council.

SECTION 4. There shall be one Vice-Chairman of the Navajo Tribal Council, and he shall hold office for a term of four years.

SECTION 5. When the Vice-Chairman of the Navajo Tribal Council has served four years, he may be elected for a second term, but he may not be elected for a third term.

SECTION 6. The Vice-Chairman of the Navajo Tribal Council shall serve as Chairman of the Navajo Tribal Council when the Chairman is unable to perform his duties.

SECTION 7. No person shall serve as Chairman or as Vice-Chairman of the Navajo Tribal Council unless he is a member of the Tribe, 35 years old or older.

SECTION 8. No person shall serve as Chairman or Vice-Chairman of the Navajo Tribal Council unless he has during the last three years before the time of election lived on the land of the Navajos, that is to say, on tribal or allotted land within the boundaries of the Navajo Reservation, or on land of a restricted allotment or homestead, or on purchased or exchanged land or on public domain outside of said exterior boundaries, or in the immediate vicinity of the reservation, and in the case of such non-resident that he has participated continuously and actively in the affairs of the tribe for the three years prior to his taking office. The Tribal Council shall, by majority vote, decide whether such continuous active participation in tribal affairs on the part of the candidate has taken place and shall so certify.

SECTION 9. A Chairman or Vice-Chairman may be removed from office for the same causes and in the same manner as a delegate may be removed from office.

SECTION 10. If a vacancy should occur in the office of Chairman or Vice-Chairman, the Tribal Council shall appoint a member of the Council as successor to serve the remainder of the term.

CHAPTER IV   How the tribal council is elected

SECTION 1. Elections shall be held not less than 20 days nor more than 40 days before the end of the Council's four-year term, at such time and places as may be designated by the General Superintendent acting under instructions from the Commissioner of Indian Affairs.

SECTION 2. All members of the tribe over 21 years of age shall be entitled to vote.

SECTION 3. At least 30 days before the election date, the District Supervisor shall require the qualified voters in each election community in his district, at a general meeting called for that purpose, to nominate not more than three qualified candidates, for the office of delegate from the election community.

SECTION 4. At such meeting each voter may cast one vote, and the three persons receiving the largest number of votes shall be considered candidate for delegate from the election community.

SECTION 5. At this same meeting there shall be elected in the same manner not more than three election Judges to serve at the community polling place in the general election.

SECTION 6. At this same nomination meeting, each candidate will draw for the color which will designate his ballot.

SECTION 7. All candidates for delegates and election judges shall be certified to the General Superintendent by the District Supervisor not later than ten days after the nominations takes place.

SECTION 8. The General Superintendent shall cause to be posted in public places, in each election community, its certified candidates for Tribal delegate, and the color of each candidate's ballot.

SECTION 9. The General Superintendent shall cause to be sent to the polling place in each community ballots and ballot boxes.

SECTION 10. Voting shall commence at each designated polling place at 7:00 a.m. and end at 6:00 p.m.

SECTION 11. It shall be the duty of the election judges to guard the polling places, to pass on the eligibility of voters, and to count the ballots at the close of voting.

SECTION 12. It shall be the specific duty of the election judges receiving the largest number of votes to issue the ballots.

SECTION 13. A government representative designated by the District Supervisor shall be present at each community polling place to act as referee and assistant to the judges.

SECTION 14. The election judges or the Government representatives shall not influence any voter in behalf of any candidate.

SECTION 15. Immediately after the end of the voting day, the election judges, in the presence of the Government representative, shall count the ballots cast.

SECTION 16. The results of the election, together with the sealed ballot boxes containing the ballots cast in the election, shall be certified and forwarded by the judges to the General Superintendent who shall in the presence of at least four members of the Executive Committee, including the Chairman and Vice-Chairman of the existing Tribal Council, open the ballot boxes and announce the names of the elected delegates and Tribal officers.

SECTION 17. All elections shall be by majority vote. In case no one candidate receives a majority of the votes cast, the voters of the election committee shall re-vote on the two highest candidates not later than sixty days after the General Election.

CHAPTER V   How officers of the tribal council are elected

SECTION 1. The 74 election communities shall be divided into four provinces.

SECTION 2. At least thirty days before the General Election, members of the existing Tribal Council from each province shall call a nominating convention at a place designated by the General Superintendent.

SECTION 3. At such nominating convention, each voter within the province shall be entitled to cast one vote.

SECTION 4. Each province shall nominate one candidate for Chairman of the Tribal Council.

SECTION 5. The candidate receiving the largest number of votes shall be certified to the General Superintendent as the province candidate for Chairman of the Tribal Council.

SECTION 6. Members of the existing Tribal Council shall act as a nominating committee and certify candidates to the General Superintendent.

SECTION 7. When the candidates for Chairman have been certified to the General Superintendent, they shall be called to Window Rock for a drawing of the colors to designate their ballots.

SECTION 8. The ballots drawn by the candidates for the Office of Chairman shall be so marked as to avoid confusing them with the ballots of tribal delegates.

SECTION 9. The Candidate for Chairman receiving a majority of votes in the general election shall be the Chairman of the Navajo Tribal Council. If no one candidate receives a majority of the votes, a revote shall be taken on the two highest candidates not later than 60 days after the General Election.

SECTION 10. The candidate for Chairman receiving the next largest number of votes in the general election shall be the Vice-Chairman of the Navajo Tribal Council.

CHAPTER VI   The meetings of the tribal council

SECTION 1. The place of meeting of the Navajo Tribal Council shall be the House of the Tribal Council at Window Rock.

SECTION 2. The expenses of two meetings during the first year after the election of the Tribal Council and of one meeting during each other year shall be paid from tribal funds, if available. The Council itself must arrange to meet the expenses of any additional meetings.

SECTION 3. Meetings of the Tribal Council shall be called by the Commissioner of Indian Affairs, upon at least seven days' notice, whenever a majority of the members of the Executive Committee shall request such a meeting.

SECTION 4. The Chairman of the Tribal Council shall designate a Secretary, and the General Superintendent shall make available clerical assistance, to make a proper record of the proceedings of Council meetings. One or more official interpreters shall be designated by the Chairman with the concurrence of the General Superintendent.

SECTION 5. The Executive Committee shall meet at the call of its Chairman, upon at least seven days' notice, at the House of the Tribal Council at Window Rock. The Chairman shall be required to call a meeting whenever a majority of the members shall request such a meeting. No business shall be transacted at any meeting of the Executive Committee unless a majority of its members shall be present.

SECTION 6. The Chairman or, in the case of his absence, inability or unwillingness to act, the Vice-Chairman of the Tribal Council is authorized to sign or countersign resolutions, contracts or commitments approved by the duly authorized representatives of the Tribe.

CHAPTER VII

SECTION 1. All regulations heretofore promulgated relating to the Navajo Tribal Council which are found to be inconsistent with these rules are hereby revoked as to such inconsistencies.

(Signed) E. R. Fryer, General Superintendent of the Navajo Agency.

Recommended for Approval:

(Signed) John Collier, Commissioner of Indian Affairs

Approved: July 26, 1938

(Signed) Harold L. Ickes, Secretary of the Interior

Amendments approved September 17, 1938, and March 27, 1939.

Navajo Nation Bill of Rights

The Navajo Nation Council Amended and reenacted the Navajo Nation Bill of Rights, by Navajo Nation Council Resolution CD-59-86.

The Bill of Rights are:

1. **Other rights not impaired; deletion or abridgement only by public referendum.**

   The enumeration herein of certain rights, shall not be construed to deny or disparage others retained by the people. No provision of this Chapter, the Navajo Nation Bill of Rights, shall be abridged or deleted by amendment or otherwise, except by referendum vote of the Navajo electorate, in accordance with applicable provisions of the laws of the Navajo Nation.

2. **Equality of rights not abridged by entitlements, benefits or privileges; nor affirmative action necessary to support rights of the Navajo People to economic opportunity.**

   Recognition, enactment, lawful implementation and enforcement of provisions for specific entitlements, benefits and privileges based upon membership in the Navajo Tribe or in other recognized Tribes of Indians and affirmative action in support of Navajo or other Indian preference in employment and business contracting or otherwise necessary to protect and support the rights of Navajo people to economic opportunity within the jurisdiction of the Navajo Nation, shall not be abridged by any provision herein nor otherwise be denied.

3. **Denial or abridgement of rights on basis of sex: equal protection and due process of Navajo Nation law.**

   Life, liberty and the pursuit of happiness are recognized as fundamental individual rights of all human beings. Equality of rights under the law shall not be denied or abridged by the Navajo Nation on account of sex nor shall any person within its jurisdiction be denied equal protection in accordance with the laws of the Navajo Nation, nor be deprived of life, liberty or property, without due process of law. Nor shall such rights be deprived by any bill of attainder or ex post facto law.

4. **Freedom of religion, speech, press, and right of assembly and petition.**

The Navajo Nation Council shall make no law respecting an establishment of religion, or prohibiting the free exercise thereof, or abridging the freedom of speech, or of the press; or the right of people peaceably to assemble, and to petition the Navajo Nation government for a redress of grievances.

5. **Searches and seizures.**

The right of the people to be secure in their persons, houses, papers, and effects, against unreasonable searches and seizures, shall not be violated, and no warrants shall issue, but upon probable cause, supported by oath, or affirmation, and particularly describing the place to be searched, and the persons or things to be seized.

6. **Rights to keep and bear arms.**

The right of the people to keep and bear arms for peaceful purposes, and in a manner which does not breach or threaten the peace or unlawfully damage or destroy or otherwise infringe upon the property rights of others, shall not be infringed.

7. **Rights of accused; trial by jury; right to counsel.**

In all criminal prosecutions, the accused shall enjoy the right to a speedy and public trial, and shall be informed of the nature and cause of the accusation; shall be confronted with the witnesses against him or her; and shall have compulsory process for obtaining witnesses in their favor. No person accused of an offense punishable by imprisonment and no party to a civil action at law, as provided under 7 NNC Sec 651 shall be denied the right, upon request, to a trial by jury of not less than six (6) persons; nor shall any person be denied the right to have the assistance of counsel, at their own expense, and to have defense counsel appointed in accordance with the rules of the courts of the Navajo Nation upon satisfactory proof to the court of their inability to provide for their own Counsel for the defense of any punishable offense under the laws of the Navajo Nation.

8. **Double jeopardy; self-incrimination; deprivation of property.**

No person shall be subject for the same offense to be twice put in jeopardy of liberty, or property; nor be compelled in any criminal case to be a witness against themselves; nor shall private property be taken nor its lawful private use be impaired for public or governmental purposes or use, without just compensation.

9. Cruel and unusual punishments; excessive bail and fines.

Excessive bail shall not be required, nor excessive fines imposed, nor cruel and unusual punishment inflicted.

Appendix G

Resolution of the Navajo Tribal Council

Amending Title Two (2) of the
Navajo Tribal Code and Related Actions
CD-68-89
Class "C" Resolution
No BIA Action Required.

WHEREAS:

    1. Pursuant to 2 N.T.C., Section 101, the Navajo Tribal Council is the governing body of the Navajo Nation; and

    2. Recent controversy involving the leadership of the Navajo Nation has demonstrated that the present Navajo Nation Government structure allows too much centralized power without real checks on the exercise of power. Experience shows that this deficiency in the government structure allows for, invites and has resulted in the abuse of power; and

    3. The Judicial Branch has been reorganized by the Judicial Reform Act of 1985, Resolution CD-94-85, and treating the Judicial Branch as a separate branch of government has proven to be beneficial to the Navajo Nation and has provided stability in the government; and

    4. The lack of definition of power and separation of legislative and executive functions have also allowed the legislative body to overly involve itself in administration of programs thereby demonstrating a need to limit the legislative function to legislation and policy decision making and further limit the executive function to implementation of laws and representation of the Navajo Nation; and

    5. There is an immediate need to reorganize the Navajo Nation government by defining the powers of the legislative and executive branches and impose limitations on exercise of such powers; and

    6. The number of standing committees of the Navajo Tribal Council has grown to eighteen (18) and some standing committees can be combined and Navajo-Hopi Land Committee moved back to a Commission thereby reducing the number of standing committees to twelve (12) and to provide for a more efficient and responsive committee system; and

7. The reorganization of the Navajo Nation Government as proposed herein is intended to meet the immediate needs of the Navajo People for a more responsible and accountable government and will have no effect on the long term Government Reform Project which will proceed as authorized and directed by the Navajo Tribal Council; and

8. It is in the best interest of the Navajo Nation that the Navajo Nation Government be reorganized to provide for separation of functions into three branches, and provide for checks and balances between the three branches until the Navajo People decide through the Government Reform Project the form of government they want to be governed by; and

9. The Intergovernmental Relations Committee by Resolution IGRNV-01-89, Exhibit "C" attached, has recommended the Title Two (2) amendments.

NOW THEREFORE BE IT RESOLVED THAT:

1. The Navajo Tribal Council hereby amends Title Two (2) of the Navajo Tribal Code as provided in Exhibit "A" attached hereto and incorporated herein by reference.

2. The Navajo Tribal Council further directs and authorizes the Legislative Counsel to codify the Title Two (2) amendments and to insert the proper language in the Code to reflect the amendments.

3. The Navajo Tribal Council further directs and authorizes that the Title Two (2) amendments adopted herein shall become effective April 1, 1990; except that the Plans of Operation of the Intergovernmental Relations Committee of the Navajo Tribal Council, Navajo Nation Commission on Navajo Government Development and the Office of Navajo Government Development, Office of Legislative Counsel, Office of Legislative Services, the Navajo Board of Election Supervisors and Navajo Election Administration shall become effective immediately upon passage of this resolution. The salary provided in 2 N.T.C. Section 106(a) of the amendments shall become effective on January 1, 1990.

4. The Navajo Tribal Council further repeals and declares null and void rules, regulations and laws or parts thereof which are inconsistent with the provisions of Title Two (2), Navajo Tribal Code, as amended herein.

5. The Navajo Tribal Council further confirms the Standing Committee Chairpersons and Vice Chairpersons listed on attached Exhibit "B" and directs the Chairpersons and Vice Chairpersons to recommend committee membership and two (2) candidates for the position of the Speaker of the Navajo Nation Council for final confirmation by the Navajo Tribal Council.

6. The Navajo Tribal Council further authorizes and directs that any amendment to the adopted Title Two (2) amendments and the 1985 Judicial Reform Act, 7 N.T.C., Section 101 et. seq., shall require two-thirds (2/3) vote of the full membership of the Navajo Tribal Council. The two-thirds (2/3) vote requirement shall not apply to technical amendments to Title Two (2); these amendments shall be presented at the regular session of the Navajo Tribal Council.

7. The Navajo Tribal Council further authorizes, declares and directs that Sections 101(b), 102(a), 1008 and 106(a) of the Title Two (2) amendments, shall not apply to amendments duly proposed by the Navajo Nation Commission on Navajo Government Development.

8. The Navajo Tribal Council further designates the Interim Chairman and Interim Vice Chairman of the Navajo Tribal Council to serve as the Interim President and Interim Vice President of the Navajo Nation until the Navajo Tribal Council directs otherwise or until the term of the current administration expires.

9. Present references in the Navajo Tribal Code to the "Chairman of the Navajo Tribal Council" or "Vice Chairman of the Navajo Tribal Council" are hereby declared to refer to the President or the Vice President of the Navajo Nation.

10. Present references in the Navajo Tribal Code to the "Advisory Committee of the Navajo Tribal Council" are hereby declared to refer to the Government Services Committee of the Navajo Nation Council.

11. The Navajo Tribal Council further directs that the Commission members for the Navajo Government Development Project shall be presented for confirmation by the Navajo Tribal Council at the next Navajo Tribal Council session.

12. The Navajo Tribal Council further directs the Ethics and Rules Committee of the Navajo Tribal Council to prepare and present Rules of Order for Navajo Tribal Council Sessions for approval by the Navajo Tribal Council at the next Council session.

13. The Navajo Tribal Council further authorizes and directs the Budget and Finance Committee of the Navajo Tribal Council to declare and reallocate budget savings to fund the Office of the Speaker and salary of the Speaker and other budgetary matters as necessitated by the amendments herein; and that such reallocation shall be completed by January 1, 1990.

14. The Navajo Tribal Council further authorizes and directs the Budget and Finance Committee of the Navajo Tribal Council to resolve the potential personnel layoffs and other potential and unanticipated urgent matters, such as the Capital Improvement Projects, which will require some budget savings declarations and allocations of the same. This is a one time

exemption from Budget Directives contained in Navajo Tribal Council Resolution CS-57-89.

CERTIFICATION

I hereby certify that the foregoing resolution was duly considered by the Navajo Tribal Council at a duly called meeting at Window Rock, Navajo Nation (Arizona), at which a quorum was present and that same was passed by a vote of 44 in favor, 17 opposed and 13 abstained, this 15th day of December 1989.

Interim Chairman
Navajo Tribal Council

Appendix H

Resolution of the Navajo Nation Council

CAP-34-98

Repealing 2 N.N.C. Section 4001 Et. seq., and Enacting of the
"Navajo Nation Local Governance Act" for Navajo Nation
Chapters, Chapter Officials and Chapter Administration

WHEREAS:

1. Pursuant to 2 N.N.C. sec. 102 (A), the Navajo Nation Council is the governing body of the Navajo Nation; and

2. Navajo Nation Chapters are the foundation of the Navajo Nation Government. For the last seventeen (17) years, Chapters have operated under the Plan of Operation for the Navajo Nation Chapters and Chapter Officials exercising authorities conferred by the Navajo Nation Council, 2 N.N.C. sec. 4001 *et. seq.;* and

3. The Commission on Navajo Government Development was created to lead the Nation in the development of the Navajo Government so that self-sufficiency, accountability and government stability can occur; and

4. Pursuant to Resolution CJA-1-96, the Navajo Nation Council directed the standing committees to study and provide recommendations to the Council on ways to provide local governance to the Navajo Nation Chapters; and

5. Subsequently, the Intergovernmental Relations Committee, in Resolution IGRAP-70-96, directed the Commission on Navajo Government Development to assist the standing committees in studying and making recommendations to the Navajo Nation Council concerning the local governance initiative; and

6. The Office of Navajo Government Development staff completed a proposal to provide local governance to the Navajo Nation Chapters. The proposal is referred to as the "Navajo Nation Local Governance Act". The Act is based upon numerous recommendations from the standing committees, as well as the Navajo public, the three Branch Chiefs, the Inter-Branch

Task Force, elected officials, tribal employees and others interested in a more effective Navajo government; and

7.   The "Navajo Nation Local Governance Act" addresses the governmental function of Chapters, improves the Governmental structure and provides the opportunity for local Chapters to make decisions over local matters. This restructuring will in the long run improve community decision making, allow communities to excel and flourish, enable Navajo leaders to lead toward a prosperous future and improve the strength and sovereignty of the Navajo Nation; and

8.   On July 24, 1997, the Commission on Navajo Government Development, by Resolution CNGD-01-97 approved and recommended approval of the "Navajo Nation Local Governance Act" to the Transportation and Community Development Committee and the Navajo Nation Council; and

9.   On January 9, 1998, the Transportation and Community Development Committee, by Resolution TCDCJA-5-98, approved and recommended approval of the "Navajo Nation Local Governance Act" to the Navajo Nation Council; and

10.   Supporting resolutions recommending approval of the "Navajo Nation Local Governance Act" were also adopted by the Agency Executive Council, the five Agency Councils, numerous District Councils and the Navajo Nation Chapters.

NOW THEREFORE BE IT RESOLVED THAT:

1.   The Navajo Nation Council hereby repeals 2 N.N.C. sec. 4001 *et seq.,* and enacts the "Navajo Nation Local Governance Act."

2.   To implement the legislation, the Navajo Nation Council authorizes amendments to the Navajo Nation Code.

3.   The Navajo Nation Council further requires the following:

   a.   All Chapters of the Navajo Nation shall operate under the "Navajo Nation Local Governance Act" upon its enactment by the Navajo Nation Council.

   b.   All Chapters shall establish and operate under a Five Management System.

   c.   By the year 2003, all Chapters shall adopt a land use plan based upon a community assessment.

   d.   The Community Services Coordinators Program and the Commission on Navajo Government Development shall develop a transition plan for the transfer of the Community Services Program to the Chapters and shall present the plan to the Intergovernmental Relations Committee of the Navajo Nation Council for approval.

4. The Navajo Nation Council further recognizes that appropriations are needed to finance the local governance legislation. A permanent local governance trust fund shall be established to assist the Navajo Nation Chapters, subject to the availability of funds.

5. The Navajo Nation Council directs all three branches, entities, enterprises and organizations of the Navajo Nation to assist in implementing the "Navajo Nation Local Governance Act."

6. The Navajo Nation Council further reaffirms all grants of authority to Chapters and Chapter subunits previously authorized not otherwise inconsistent with this Act.

CERTIFICATION

I hereby certify that the foregoing resolution was duly considered by the Navajo Nation Council at a duly called meeting at Window Rock, Navajo Nation (Arizona), at which a quorum was present and that same was passed by a vote of 61 in favor, 10 opposed and 3 abstained, this 20th day of April 1998.

Kelsey A. Begay, Speaker
Navajo Nation Council

4-24-98
Date Signed

Motion: Edward T. Begay
Second: Milton Bluehouse

ACTION BY THE NAVAJO NATION PRESIDENT:

1. I hereby sign into law the foregoing legislation, pursuant to 2 N.N.C. Sec. 1005 (C)(10) on this __27__ day of __April__ 1998.

Thomas E. Atcitty, President
   Navajo Nation

2. I hereby veto the foregoing legislation, pursuant to 2 N.N.C. Sec. 1005 (C)(10), this day of 1998 for the reason(s) expressed in the attached letter to the Speaker.

Thomas E. Atcitty, President
   Navajo Nation

Index

About the Author

David E. Wilkins (Lumbee Nation) is professor of American Indian Studies, Political Science, and Law at the University of Minnesota, Minneapolis. In 1990 he received his Ph.D. in political science from the University of North Carolina at Chapel Hill. He is married to Evelyn Donald (Navajo Nation). They have three children. He has published several books, including *American Indian Politics and the American Political System; The Navajo Political Experience; Uneven Ground: American Indian Sovereignty and Federal Law* (with Tsianina Lomawaima); and *Tribes, Treaties, and Constitutional Tribulations* (with Vine Deloria, Jr.). His articles have appeared in a range of social science, law, historical, and ethnic studies journals.